Portugal

a Lonely Planet travel atlas

Portugal – travel atlas

1st edition

Published by
Lonely Planet Publications
Head Office: PO Box 617, Hawthorn, Vic 3122, Australia
Branches: 155 Filbert St, Suite 251, Oakland, CA 94607, USA
            10 Barley Mow Passage, Chiswick, London W4 4PH, UK
            71 bis rue du Cardinal Lemoine, 75005 Paris, France

Cartography
Steinhart Katzir Publishers Ltd
Fax: 972-3-699-7562
email: 100264.721@compuserve.com

Printed by
Colorcraft Ltd, Hong Kong

Photographs
Bethune Carmichael, John King, Damien Simonis, Tony Wheeler, Julia Wilkinson

Front Cover: A traditionally embellished doorway in Obidos (Damien Simonis)
Back Cover: Barcelos is noted for its regional handicraft exhibits (Julia Wilkinson)
Title Page: The Palacia de Pena, Sintra (Bethune Carmichael)
Contents Page: Espigueiros, Lindoso, Viana do Castelo (John King)
Page 38: A local couple at Seara Velha (Julia Wilkinson)

First Published
July 1997

Although the authors and publisher have tried to make the information as accurate as possible, they accept no responsibility for any loss, injury or inconvenience sustained by any person using this book.

National Library of Australia Cataloguing in Publication Data

King, John (John S).
    Portugal.

    1st ed.
    Includes index.
    ISBN 0 86442 480 9.

    1. Portugal - Maps, Tourist. 2. Portugal - Road maps
    I. Wilkinson, Julia. II. Title. (Series : Lonely Planet travel atlas)

914.690444

Contents

Acknowledgements 4

Locator Maps 5-7
Map Legend 8-9
Main Maps 10-36
Island Maps – The Azores and Madeira 38-40

Getting Around Portugal 42-43
Comment Circuler au Portugal 44-45
Reisen in Portugal 46-47
Cómo Movilizarse dentro de Portugal 48-49
ポルトガルの旅 50-51

Index 52-76

Julia Wilkinson & John King

Julia Wilkinson set out with her first backpack at the age of four in a moment of tempestuous independence and has been hooked on travel ever since. After finishing university in England in 1978 she headed for Australia but got sidetracked in Hong Kong, working in publishing and radio until going freelance as a writer and photographer. Since then she has travelled throughout Asia, writing for various international magazines. She has contributed to guidebooks on Hong Kong, Tibet and Laos, and authored others on Portugal and Thailand. When she wants to get away from it all she takes to the skies, flying hot-air balloons.

John King grew up in the USA, destined for the academic life (in past incarnations he was a university physics teacher and an environmental consultant), but in a rash moment in 1984 he headed off to China for a look around, and ended up living there for half a year. During that time he and Julia crossed paths in Lhasa, the Tibetan capi-

tal. After a three-month journey across China and Pakistan they decided they could manage joint housekeeping, and have since split their time between south-west England and remoter parts of Hong Kong.

In 1988 John wrote Lonely Planet's *The Karakoram Highway*, and with Julia took up full-time travel writing. John is also co-author of LP's *Central Asia, Russia, Ukraine & Belarus* (formerly *USSR*), *Pakistan* and *Czech & Slovak Republics* guidebooks

and of the *Prague city guide*. In 1994 Julia updated the Portugal chapters for LP's *Western Europe on a Shoestring* and *Mediterranean Europe on a Shoestring*.

Since 1995 they have been assisted and entertained by their son Kit, with whom they travelled around Portugal to research this atlas, as well as LP's upcoming *Portugal* guidebook, and the Portugal chapters for the current editions of *Western Europe on a Shoestring* and *Mediterranean Europe on a Shoestring*.

About this Atlas

This book is another addition to the Lonely Planet travel atlas series. Designed to tie in with the equivalent Lonely Planet guidebook, we hope the *Portugal travel atlas* helps travellers enjoy their trip even more. As well as detailed, accurate maps, this atlas also contains a multilingual map legend, useful travel information in five languages and a comprehensive index to ensure easy location-finding.

The maps were checked on the road by Julia Wilkinson and John King as part of their research for the first edition of the *Portugal* guidebook.

From the Publishers

Thanks to Danny Schapiro, chief cartographer at Steinhart Katzir Publishers, who researched and drew the maps with the assistance of Michal Pait-Benny and Iris Sardes; Iris also prepared the index. At Lonely Planet, the maps and index were checked and edited by Lou Byrnes. Louise Keppie-Klep was responsible for all cartographic checking, design, layout, and cover design. The back cover map was drawn by Paul Clifton.

Lou Byrnes coordinated the translations. Thanks to translators Yoshi Abe, Lou Callan, Ade Costanzo, Pedro Diaz, Megan

Fraser, Christine Gruettke, Elisabeth Kern and Nick Tapp.

Request

This atlas is designed to be clear, comprehensive and reliable. We hope you'll find it a worthy addition to your Lonely Planet travel library. Even if you don't, please let us know! We'd appreciate any suggestions you may have to make this product even better. Please complete and send us the feedback page at the back of this atlas to let us know exactly what you think.

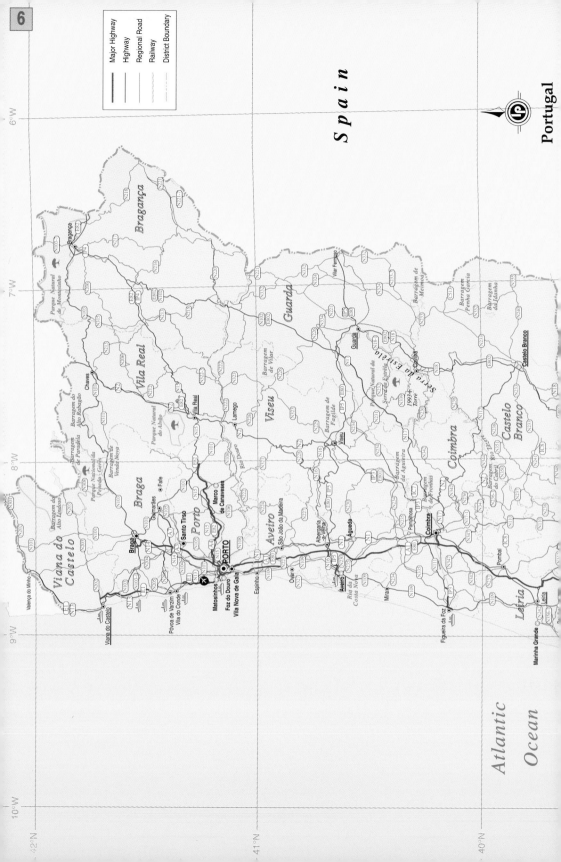

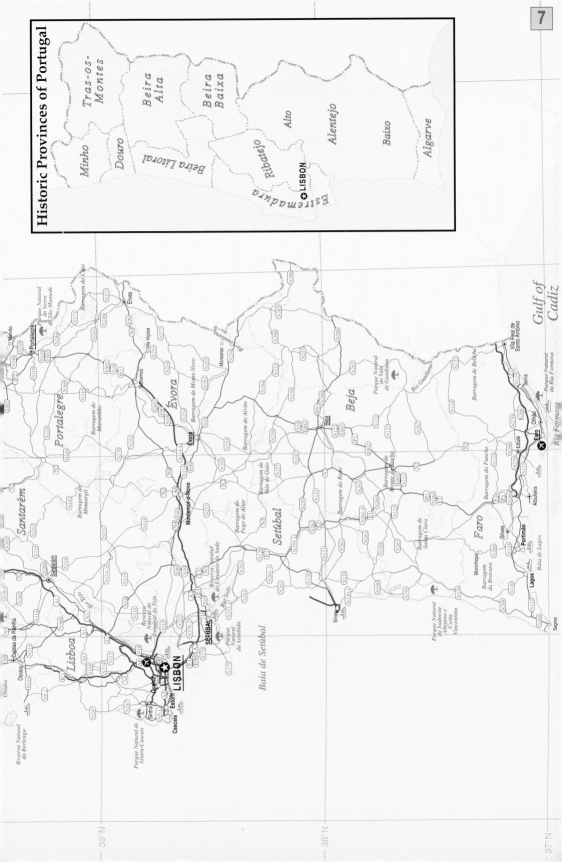

Historic Provinces of Portugal

MAP LEGEND

Number of Inhabitants:

LISBON 500,000 - 1,000,000

PORTO ⊙ 250,000 - 500,000

SETÚBAL ◎ 100,000 - 250,000

Coimbra ⊙ 50,000 - 100,000

Aveiro ◎ 25,000 - 50,000

Ovar ⊙ 10,000 - 25,000

Mangualde ○ <10,000

Brinço ○ Village

LISBON Capital City
Capitale
Hauptstadt
Capital
首都

★ Capital City (Locator map)
Capitale (Carte de situation)
Hauptstadt (Orientierungskarte)
Capital (Mapa Localizador)
首都（地図上の位置）

Vila Real District Capital
Capitale du District
Bezirkshauptstadt
Capital de Distrito
地区の本部

International Boundary
Limites Internationales
Staatsgrenze
Frontera Internacional
国境

District Boundary
Limites du District
Bezirksgrenze
Frontera del Distrito
地区の境界

Major Highway
Route Nationale
Fernstraße
Carretera Principal
主要な国道

Highway
Route Principale
Landstraße
Carretera
国道

Regional Road
Route Régionale
Regionale Fernstraße
Carretera Regional
地方道

Secondary Road
Route Secondaire
Nebenstraße
Carretera Secundaria
二級道路

Unsealed Road
Route non bitumée/piste
Unbefestigte Straße
Carretera sin Asfaltar
未舗装の道

Buro
Railway station
Gare Ferroviaire
Bahnhof
Estación de Ferrocarril
駅

Railway
Voie de chemin de fer
Eisenbahn
Ferrocarril
小道

N218 E82 IP4 Route Number
Numérotation Routière
Routenummer
Ruta Número
道路の番号

99
Distance in Kilometres
Distance en Kilomètres
Entfernung in Kilometern
Distancia en Kilómetros
距離（km）

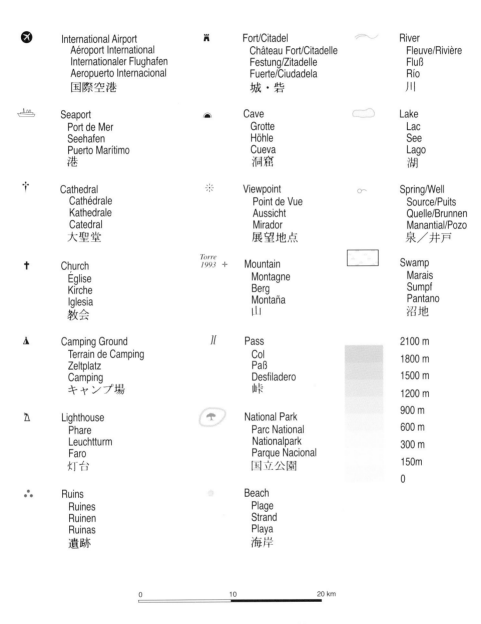

International Airport
  Aéroport International
  Internationaler Flughafen
  Aeropuerto Internacional
  国際空港

Seaport
  Port de Mer
  Seehafen
  Puerto Marítimo
  港

Cathedral
  Cathédrale
  Kathedrale
  Catedral
  大聖堂

Church
  Église
  Kirche
  Iglesia
  教会

Camping Ground
  Terrain de Camping
  Zeltplatz
  Camping
  キャンプ場

Lighthouse
  Phare
  Leuchtturm
  Faro
  灯台

Ruins
  Ruines
  Ruinen
  Ruinas
  遺跡

Fort/Citadel
  Château Fort/Citadelle
  Festung/Zitadelle
  Fuerte/Ciudadela
  城・砦

Cave
  Grotte
  Höhle
  Cueva
  洞窟

Viewpoint
  Point de Vue
  Aussicht
  Mirador
  展望地点

Torre 1993 + Mountain
  Montagne
  Berg
  Montaña
  山

Pass
  Col
  Paß
  Desfiladero
  峠

National Park
  Parc National
  Nationalpark
  Parque Nacional
  国立公園

Beach
  Plage
  Strand
  Playa
  海岸

River
  Fleuve/Rivière
  Fluß
  Río
  川

Lake
  Lac
  See
  Lago
  湖

Spring/Well
  Source/Puits
  Quelle/Brunnen
  Manantial/Pozo
  泉／井戸

Swamp
  Marais
  Sumpf
  Pantano
  沼地

2100 m
1800 m
1500 m
1200 m
900 m
600 m
300 m
150m
0

0   10   20 km

Projection: Universal Transverse Mercator

1 : 400 000

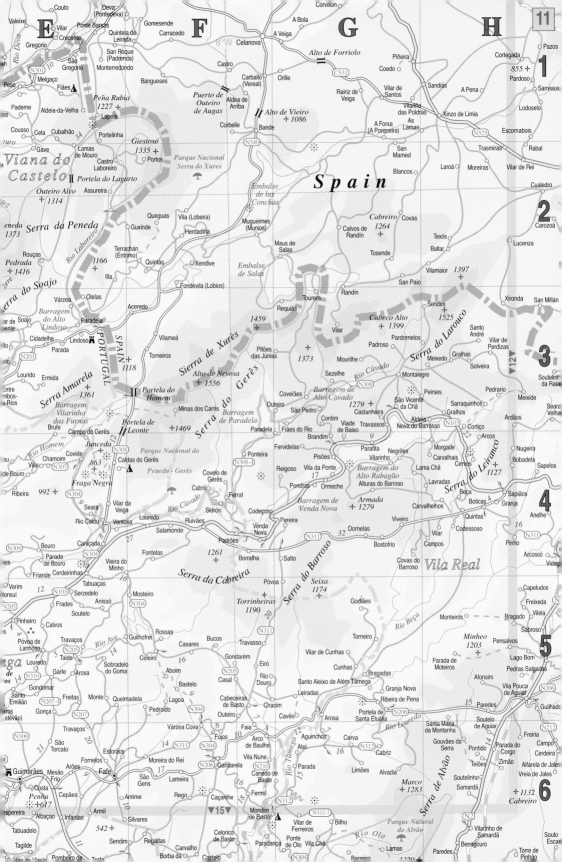

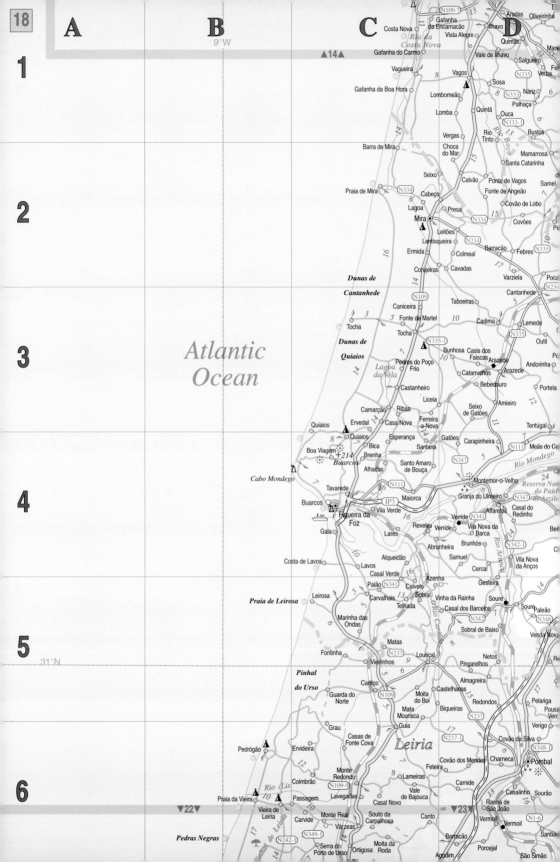

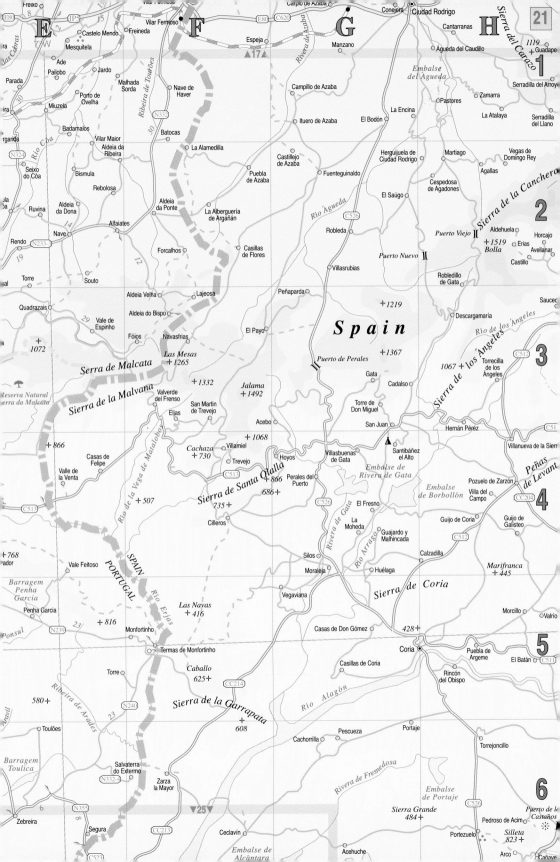

E F G H

1 2 3 4 5 6

Freixo
E80 IP5 Vilar Fermoso
Vilar Fermoso
Castelo Mendo
Freineda
Espeja
Manzano
Conejera Ciudad Rodrigo
Cantarranas
Águeda del Caudillo
Serradilla del Arroyo
Sierra del Carazo
1119 Guadape
Serradilla del Arroyo

Las Cabras
Mesquitela
Ade
Pailobo
Jardo
Nave de Haver

Campillo de Azaba
La Encina
Zamarra
Embalse del Águeda
Pastores
La Atalaya
Serradilla del Llano

Parada
Miuzela
Porto de Ovelha
Badamalos
Vilar Maior
Aldeia da Ribeira
Batocas
La Alamedilla

Ituero de Azaba
El Bodón
Herguijuela de Ciudad Rodrigo
Martiago
Vegas de Domingo Rey
Agallas
N324
Seixo do Côa
Rio Côa
Bismula
Rebolosa

Castillejo de Azaba
Fuenteguinaldo
El Saúgo
Cespedosa de Agadones

Sierra de la Canchera

argarida
Aldeia da Dona
Ruvina
Aldeia da Ponte
Rio Côa
Rendo N233
Nave
Alfaiates
Puebla de Azaba
La Albergueria de Argañán
Rio Águeda
C526
Robleda
El Saúgo
Puerto Viejo
Bolla
+1519
Aldehuela
Horcajo
Erias
Avellanar
Castillo

Torre
Souto
Forcalhos
Casillas de Flores
Villasrubias
Puerto Nuevo
Robledillo de Gata

Quadrazais
Aldeia Velha
Lajeosa
Peñaparda
Descargamaría
Sauce

Vale de Espinho
Aldeia do Bispo
+1219

Rio de los Ángeles
Fóios
1072
Navasfrias
El Payo
Spain
+1367
1067 Torrecilla de los Ángeles
C512

Serra de Malcata
Las Mesas
+1265
Puerto de Perales
Gata
Cadalso
Sierra de los Ángeles

+1332
Jalama
+1492
Torre de Don Miguel
Hernán Pérez
C51

Reserva Natural erra da Malcata
Sierra de la Malvana
Valverde del Fresno
San Martín de Trevejo
Acebo
San Juan
Villanueva de la Sierra

+866
Eljas
+1068
Villamiel
+730
Cachaza
Hoyos
Villasbuenas de Gata
Santibáñez el Alto
Peñas de Levant

Casas de Felipe
Trevejo
+866
Perales del Puerto
Embalse de Rivera de Gata
Pozuelo de Zarzón
Villa del Campo
CC204

Valle de la Venta
735+
686+
C526
Embalse de Borbollón
Villa del Campo

Rio de la Vega de Matalobos
+507
Cilleros
El Fresno
La Moheda
Guijo de Coria
Guijo de Galisteo
C512

+768
Vale Feitoso
Silos
Moraleja
Guajardo y Malhincada
Calzadilla
Marifranca
+445

Barragem Penha Garcia
SPAIN
Las Navas
+416
Vegaviana
Huélaga
Sierra de Coria

Penha Garcia
PORTUGAL
Rio Erjas
Monfortinho
+816
Casas de Don Gómez
428+
Coria
Morcillo
Valrio

Ponsul
N239
Termas de Monfortinho
Caballo
625+
Casillas de Coria
Puebla de Argeme
El Batán
C511

Torre
CC214
Rincón del Obispo
Rio Alagón

580+
Ribeira de Arades
N240
Sierra de la Garrapata
608
Cachorrilla
Pescueza
Portaje
Torrejoncillo

aravil
Toulões
Salvaterra do Extremo
Zarza la Mayor
Acehuche
Embalse de Portaje
C526

Barragem Toulica
N332
Sierra Grande
484+
Puerto de lo Castaños

Zebreira
N355
Segura
CC213
Ceclavín
Pedroso de Acim
Silleta
823+
Portezuelo
Arco

C523
Embalse de Alcántara
Cañave

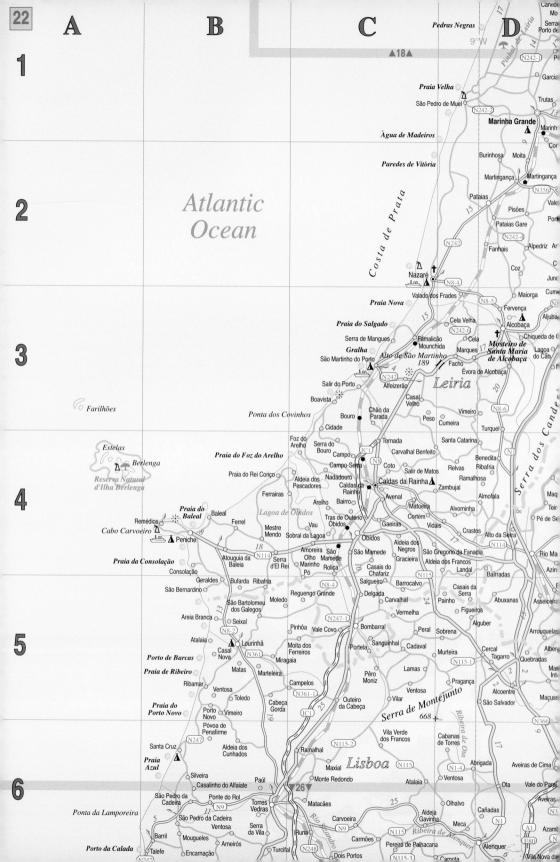

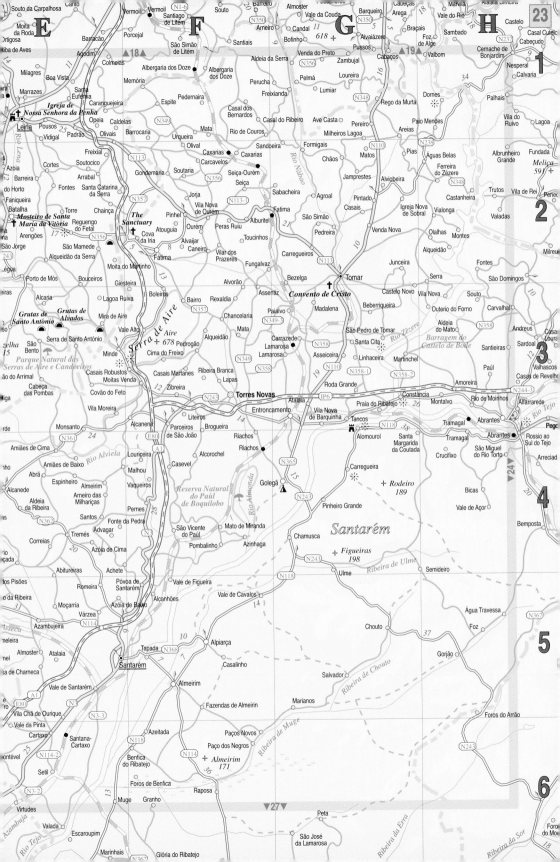

E F G H

1
2
3
4
5
6

Ladoeiro
N240
N353
Zebreira
7°W
CC213
Ceclavin

▲20▲
Peireial
Cabeço Alto
403 +
Rio Erges
C522
Piedras Albas
▲21▲

+380
Cegonhas
Novas
Estorninos
Embalse de Alcántara

Monforte
da Beira
Rosmaninhal
Alcántara
Mata de Alcántara

Farropa
+ 457

Soalheiras
Villa del Rey

Malpica do Tejo
C223
369 +
Los Perales
CC220
C523

Herrera de Alcántara
Brozas

Santiago
de
Alcántara
Carbajo

Rivera Aurela
CC221
+ 621
Santiago
Clavería
Arroyo de Jumadiel
C522

Río Alburrel
Embalse de Zamores
Membrio
Rio Salor

PORTUGAL
SPAIN
+ 613
Lapones
Salorino
Herreruela
N521

lagosa
N359
El Moillarón
Torrico de San Pedro
+ 703
Herreruela

Marvão
Beirã
Barretos
Barrio de la Estación
S p a i n
Chorlo
624 +

Seiçal
Santo António das Areias
Valencia de Alcántara

Portagem
Marvão
La Fontañera
San Vicente de Alcántara
Torrejón
+ 498
Covacha
Tejarejo

scusa
São Salvador
Galegos
San Pedro
+ 662
C530
El Tarro
Golilla
458 +

Porto da Espada
Alvarrões
Las Casiñas
Las Huertas
Rivera del Fraile
Rivera de Albarragena
Rio Zapatón
Puerto de los Brisos
C521

al
gem
Alagoinha
Pino de Valencia
Alcorneo
BA500
Sierra de Santiago
+ 454
BA502

Monte Carvalho
Reguengo
1025 +
Pico São
Mamede
Montinho
São Julião
Jola
Rabaça
Sierra del Narangal
Rivera del Alcorneo
Mayorga

Serra de São Mamede
777 +
Parque Natural
da Serra de
São Mamede
Montinho
La Vega
Sierra del Puerto
Alburquerque
Sierra del Centinela
Embalse de
Villar del Rey

Carvalhal
Caia
Alegrete
Bacoco
Río Gévora
Benavente

Santiago
Urra
Vale de
Cavalos
+ 594
Lamparona
La Codosera
Puerto
de los
Conejeros

N246
Barulho
Parra
El Marco
445 +
Dos Hermanas
Jabarrieja
+ 419

Mosteiros
Nave
Marco
Villar
del Rey

Assumar
N371
Figueira
Esperança
C530
BA501

Senhora do
Rosário
Arronches
N371
Ouguela
Rio Xévora
BA502
N523

Monforte
N243
Casa Branca
+ 270
Contenda
Degolados
▼29▼
Barragem do Caia
Atalaia da Contenda
+ 337
Campo Maior
Serrinha
Bótoa
N243

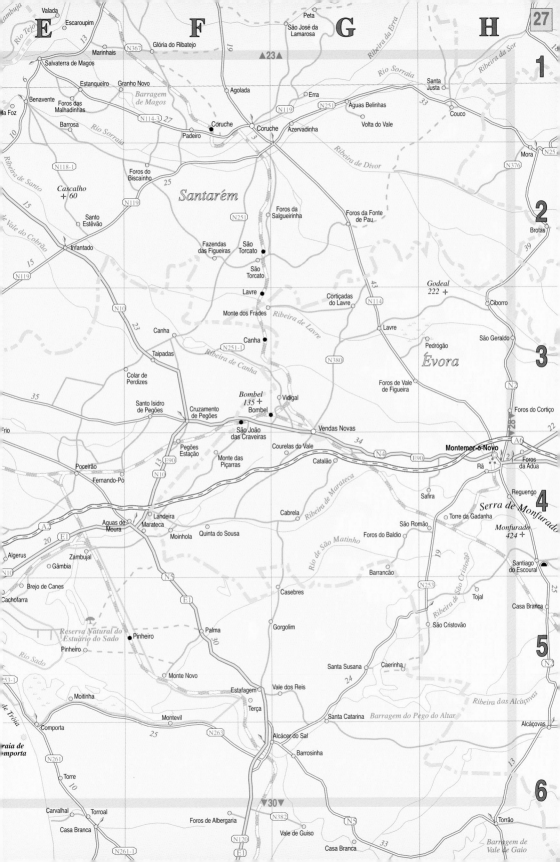

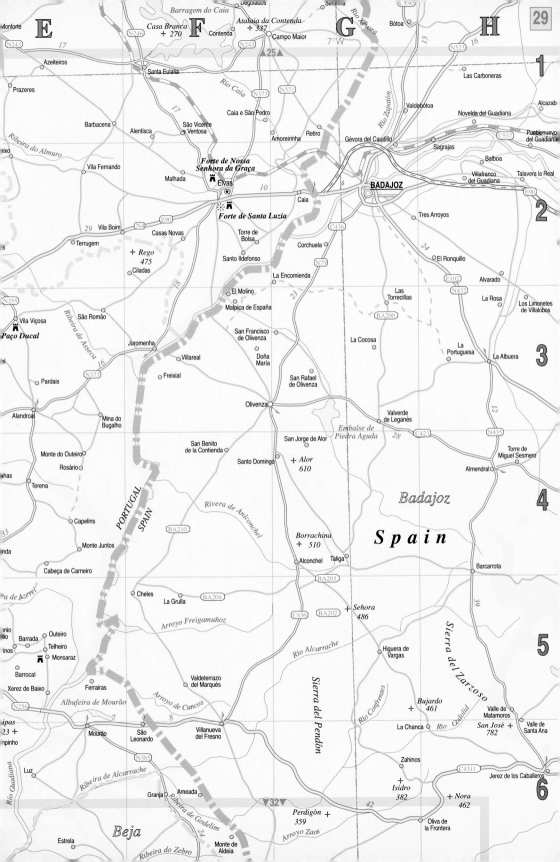

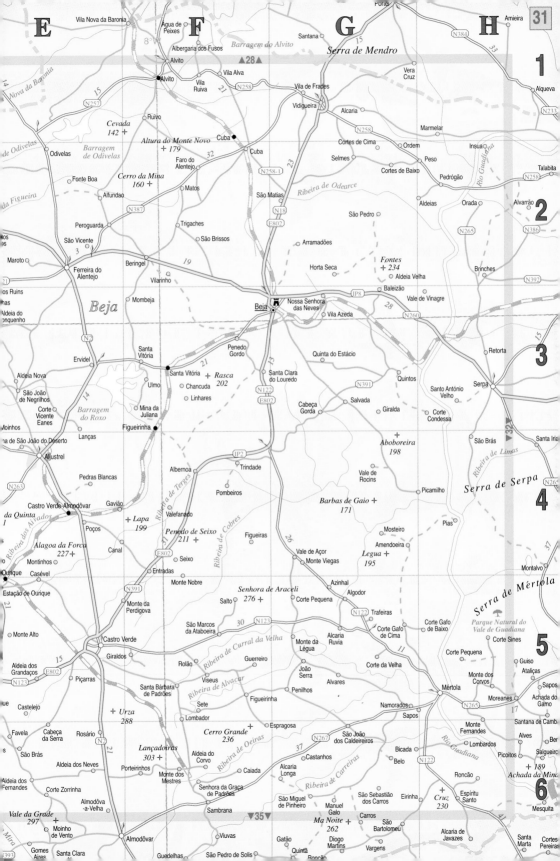

BETHUNE CARMICHAEL

BETHUNE CARMICHAEL

JULIA WILKINSON

Top: House painting, Monsaraz
Bottom left: Waiting for a bus, Monsaraz
Bottom right: Azulego at Pinhão

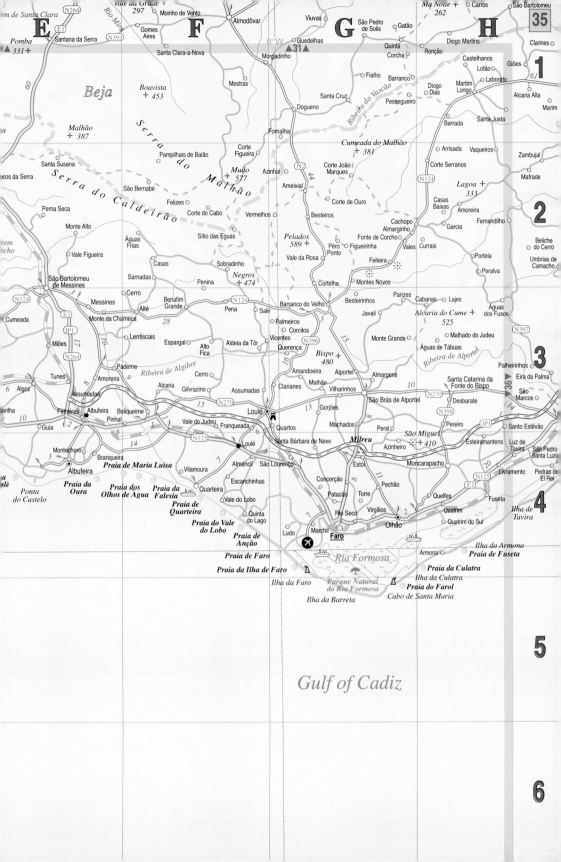

36

São Bartolomeu
Alcaria de Javazes
Clarines

A

Santa Marta
Cortes Pereiras

Alcoutim
Sanlúcar de Guadiana

B

El Granado
El Almendro
Villanueva de los Castillejos
▲32▲

C

Embalse de Tres Picos

H131

D

Embalse de Sanc

Giões
Farelos
61
N124
Coito
Pereiro
Alcaria Alta
Marim
Alcaria
Tacões
N122-1

1

PORTUGAL
SPAIN

Azud de Matacavas
Los Millares
14

El Campillo

San Bartolomé de la Torre
C443

Fornalha + 273
Fonte Zambujo
Balurcos
Palmeira

Corte Tabelião
Balurcos + 226

Zambujal
Mafrade
Soudes
Furnazinhas
Corte de São Tomé
Vale de Pinheiro
Fortes
Monte de Baixo Grande

Ribeira da Foupan

El Romerano
Guerreiros do Rio

Tenencia
Corte das Donas
Foz de Odeleite

S p a i n

Embalse de Piedras

San Silvestre de Guzmán

H122

Huelva

Tariquejo

+ Cebollar 180

Rio Piedras
Canal del Piedras

2

Estrada
Cintados
Beliche do Cerro

Corujos
Corte do Gago
Alcarias
Cortelha

Ribeira de Odeleite
Choça Queimada
Odeleite
Alcaria
Almada de Ouro
Sentinela
N122
Beliche
Azinhal

Monte Gordo + 156

Villablanca

Embalse de los Machos

17

N431
E1

Barragem de Beliche

36

Rio Guadiana

22

H414

Cartaya

Umbrias de Camacho
Cerro do Anho

Junqueira

7

2
El Empalme

Lepe

Vale de Ebros
Miguel Anes + 229
Estorninhos

Rio Seco
Castro Marim
Ayamonte

5

Pozo del Camino
Las Palmeritas
El Terrón

El Rompido

El Portil

3

N397
Zimbral
Eira da Palma
IP1
Vila Nova de Cacela
N125
E1

Vila Nova
Pocinho
São Bartolomeu
19
Aldeia Nova
Altura

Reserva Natural do Sapal de Castro Marim e Vila Real de Santo António
Vila Real de Santo António
Monte Gordo

Isla Cristina
Isla Canela
Playa de Isla Cristina

La Redondela
La Antilla

Playa de la Antilla

Barra de El Rompido

São Marcos
Conceição
Cacela Velha
N270

Manta Rota
Praia da Alagõa
Praia Verde
Praia de Monte Gordo

Playa Canela

Cabanas
Praia da Manta Rota
Tavira
Praia das Cabanas

35
uz de avira
São Pedro
Santa Luzia
Praia das Cascas

Pedras de El Rei
Praia da Ilha de Tavira
Praia do Barril

4

Ilha de Tavira

Gulf of Cadiz

37°N

5

6

BETHUNE CARMICHAEL

JULIA WILKINSON

BETHUNE CARMICHAEL

Left: The unfinished chapel of Batalha Monastery
Top right: Water fountain, Telheiro
Bottom right: Lisbon's fabulous architectural facades are fast disappearing in a frenzy of redevelopment

Locator Map: Azores and Madeira

32°W 28°W 24°W 20°W 16°W 12°W 8°W

40°N

LA CORUÑA

Spa

Braga ⊙
PORTO ⊙

Coimbra ⊙

36°N *Azores*

Portugal

LISBON ★

SETÚBAL

Corvo ○
Flores

São
Jorge *Graciosa*
Faial ○
Pico *Terceira*

São
Miguel

*Atlantic
Ocean*

Fa

Santa
Maria

32°N

CASABLANC

SAFI ○

Marrak

0   200   400 km

Porto Santo

28°N *Madeira* ⌒ Desertas

Moroc

Canary Islands (Sp)

24°N

20°N

16°N

Mauritania

★ NOUAKCHOTT

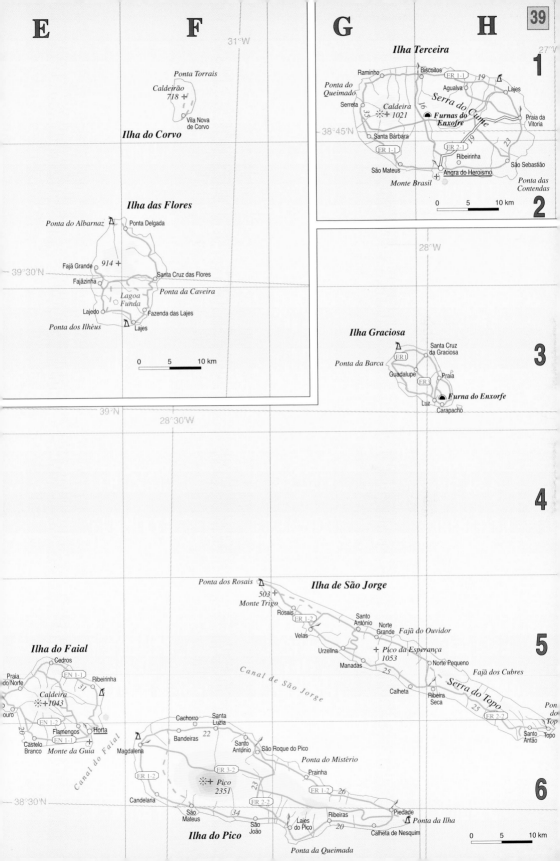

E **F** **G** **H**

31°W

27°V

1

Ilha Terceira

Ponta Torrais

Caldeirão
718 +

Vila Nova
de Corvo

Ilha do Corvo

Raminho
Biscoitos
ER 1-1
19
Lajes

Ponta do
Queimado
Agualva

Serreta
Caldeira
35 + 1021
Furnas do
Enxofre

Serra do Cume

Praia da
Vitória

38°45'N

Santa Bárbara

16

São Sebastião
ER 2-1
Ribeirinha
19
23

ER 1-1

São Mateus
Angra do Heroismo

Monte Brasil
Ponta das
Contendas

2

0   5   10 km

Ilha das Flores

Ponta do Albarnaz
Ponta Delgada

28°W

Fajã Grande
914 +

Fajãzinha

Santa Cruz das Flores

Ponta da Caveira

Lagoa
Funda

Lajedo
Fazenda das Lajes

Ponta dos Ilhéus
Lajes

0   5   10 km

Ilha Graciosa

ER 1

Santa Cruz
da Graciosa

Ponta da Barca

Guadalupe
Praia

ER 3

Furna do Enxorfe

Luz
Carapachõ

3

39°30'N

39°N

28°30'W

4

Ponta dos Rosais
503 +
Monte Trigo

Ilha de São Jorge

Rosais
ER 1-2

Santo
António
Norte
Grande
Fajã do Ouvidor

Velas

Urzelina
Pico da Esperança
1053

Norte Pequeno

Manadas
25
Fajã dos Cubres

Calheta
Serra do Topo

Ilha do Faial

Cedros

EN 1-1
Ribeirinha

Praia
do Norte

Caldeira
+1043

Ribeira
Seca
25

Pon
do
Top

ouro
EN 1-2
Flamengos
EN 1-1
Horta

Castelo
Branco
Monte da Guia

Cachorro
Santa
Luzia
22

Santo
Antão
Topo

Canal de São Jorge

5

Canal do Faial

Bandeiras

Magdalena

Santo
António
São Roque do Pico

Ponta do Mistério

Prainha

ER 3-2

ER 1-2
26

6

ER 1-2
Pico
2351

ER 2-2

23

Candelaria

São
Mateus

São
João

Lajes
do Pico
20

Ribeiras

Piedade
Ponta da Ilha

Calheta de Nesquim

Ilha do Pico

Ponta da Queimada

0   5   10 km

38°30'N

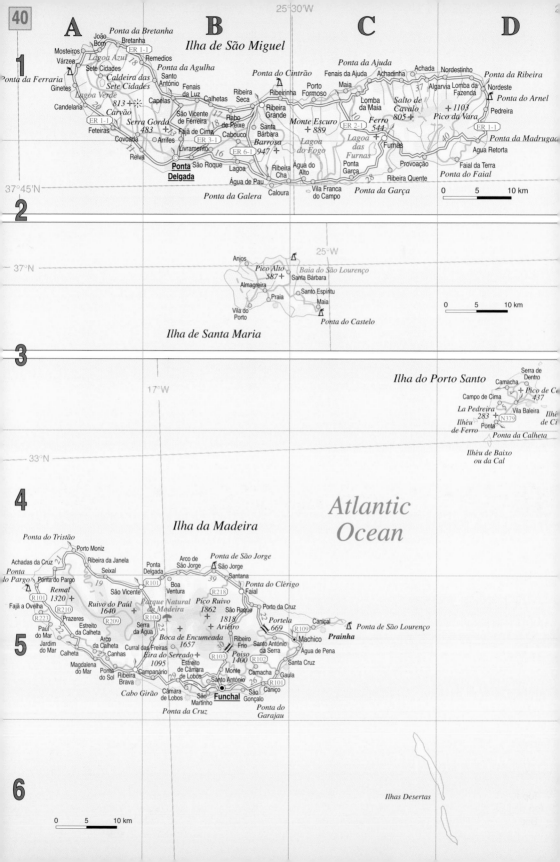

JULIA WILKINSON

BETHUNE CARMICHAEL

JULIA WILKINSON

Top left: Village laneway, Monsanto
Top right: Ornate window in Guarda
Bottom: Barcelos is an ancient, picturesque town built on the banks of the Rio Cávado

Getting Around Portugal

Bus

The demise of the state-run Rodoviária Nacional (RN) bus company spawned a host of private local firms, most of them amalgamated into regional companies which together operate a dense network of bus services. Services are of three general types: *expressos*, comfortable, fast, direct coaches between major cities; *rápidas*, fast regional buses; and *carreiras*, which seem to stop at every crossroad.

Expressos are generally a good cheap way to get around Portugal, and even in summer you'll have little problem booking a ticket for the next or even the same day. By contrast the local services, especially up north, can thin out to almost nothing on weekends, especially in summer when school is out.

Train

Travel with Caminhos de Ferro Portugueses (CP), the state railway company, is cheaper than by long-distance bus, though generally slower. CP operates three main levels of service: *regional* (marked R on timetables),

which stops everywhere; fairly fast *interregional* (marked IR); and express trains, called *rápido* or *intercidade* (marked IC). *Alfa* is a special, marginally faster IC service running between selected northern cities (eg Lisbon and Porto). Most trains have both 1st and 2nd-class carriages.

In most cases you'll have little problem booking a ticket the day before you intend to travel or even the same day, even in summer. Seat reservations are usually mandatory on IC and Alfa trains. Children under age four travel free; those from four to 12 years old travel at half-price.

Road

Thanks to EU subsidies, Portugal's road system is being steadily upgraded; there are now numerous long stretches of highway, including toll-roads. Main roads are sealed and in generally good condition. Minor rural roads have surprisingly little traffic, allowing you some space to watch for the occasional potholes.

The real downside of driving here is Portuguese drivers. Many of them, men and women

alike, drive like maniacs and have never heard of courtesy. Portugal's annual per capita death rate from road accidents is Europe's highest. The coastal roads of the Algarve and the Lisbon to Cascais axis are especially dangerous. City driving tends to be hectic, not least in Portugal's many old walled towns, where roads can taper down to donkey-cart size before you know it. Fiendish one-way systems (usually the only way for towns to cope with cars in their narrow lanes) can trap you or force you far out of your way. Municipal parking is usually very limited.

Portugal's modest network of highways *(estradas)* is gradually spreading across the country. Top of the line are *autoestradas* or motorways, all of them toll-roads *(portagens)*. The longest of these is the 304km Lisbon to Porto road. Other stretches include Porto to Braga, Porto to Amarante and Lisbon to Cascais. The present 575km of toll-roads charges cars and motorcycles about 9$00 per km. Highway nomenclature can be baffling. Motorway numbers prefixed with an E are

Stained-glass window in the Café Santa Cruz, Coimbra

Europe-wide designations. Portugal's toll-roads are prefixed A. Highways in its main network *(rede fundamental)* are prefixed IP, and subsidiary ones *(rede complementare)* are IC. Some highways have several designations, and numbers that change in mid-flow; eg the Lisbon to Porto road is variously called E80, E01, A1 and IP1.

As with the rest of continental Europe, driving is on the right. Most signs use international symbols, and lanes are marked with solid and dashed lines according to international convention. Except when marked otherwise, speed limits for cars (without a trailer) and motorcycles are 60 km/h in built-up areas, 90 km/h outside towns and villages, and 120 km/h on motorways.

Safety belts must be worn in front and back seats, and children under 12 years old may not travel in the front seat. You're not allowed to use your horn in built-up areas after dark except in an emergency. Motorcyclists and their passengers must wear helmets. The legal limit for alcohol in the blood is a minuscule 0.05%, so don't even think about drinking and driving.

Unleaded petrol *(sem chumbo)* and diesel *(gasóleo)* are readily available, along with leaded fuel, in most parts of the country. There are plenty of self-service stations, and major credit cards are readily accepted at many, but not all, stations.

If you are in need of assistance, Automóvel Club de Portugal (ACP), Portugal's national auto club, provides medical, legal and car-breakdown assistance for its members. If you can prove that you belong to an affiliated national auto club, you can also use these services. Their emergency help numbers are tel 01-942 50 95 (Lisbon) for southern Portugal, and tel 02-830 11 27 (Porto) for northern Portugal.

JULIA WILKINSON

Estói Palace Gardens, Faro

Bicycle

Cycling is a cheap, healthy, environmentally sound and, above all, enjoyable way to get around Portugal. With a mountain bike (BTT or *bicyclete tudo terrano*) you can probably see more (and especially more remote) places than most visitors would dream of. Although Portugal has no dedicated bicycle lanes or paths, mountain bikes seem to have the same rights of access to rural trails and tracks as do walkers.

Most Portuguese appear to think that visitors cycle around the country because they can't afford to do it any other way, so cyclists are frequently offered the cheapest accommodation or invited in to dinner with the family. On back roads you may be a source of wonderment: drivers often toot their horns, more from courtesy than anger, and delighted passengers often wave and shout. You may be put off by this the first few times, but on those long and lonely stretches you may find yourself looking forward to the next passing car!

Of course there's a downside. Especially in the north, you may encounter rain for days on end. And while there are bike shops in most larger cities, you probably won't be able to find that spare widget you need. The two biggest problems are Portuguese drivers and Portuguese back roads, a few of which are still paved with little stone blocks that can shake your teeth loose, and some have potholes that can swallow you whole (this is another good reason to bring a mountain bike).

Boat

Other than river cruises along the Rio Douro from Porto and along the Rio Tejo from Lisbon, the only important surviving waterborne transport in Portugal is the cross-river ferry. The longest journeys are the Transtejo commuter ferries across the Rio Tejo between Lisbon and Cacilhas, Montijo and Seixal; and the transado ferries that make the half-hour trip across the mouth of the Rio Sado between Setúbal and Tróia.

Comment Circuler au Portugal

Bus

La disparition de la société nationale routière Rodoviária Nacional (RN) a permis à de nombreuses entreprises locales privées de se développer, souvent en se regroupant au sein de compagnies régionales qui couvrent un vaste réseau. Trois types de bus s'offrent à vous : les expressos, confor-tables, rapides, directs et reliant les grandes villes ; les *rápidas*, régionaux ; et les *carreiras*, qui s'arrêtent pratiquement à chaque intersection.

Les expressos permettent de voyager à peu de frais. Il est possible d'ailleurs de réserver pour le jour même ou le lendemain, même en été. S'agissant des liaisons locales, surtout au nord, elles s'interrompent souvent le weekend, en particulier pendant les vacances d'été.

Train

Voyager avec la société de chemins de fer nationale, les Caminhos de Ferro Portugueses (CP), est moins onéreux que de se déplacer en bus, mais prend plus de temps. Il existe trois types de trains : les regional (signalés par un R sur les horaires) qui s'arrêtent partout ; les interregional (IR) relativement rapides ; et les express, appelés *rápido* ou *intercidade* (IC). L'alfa, service spécial IC plus rapide, relie certaines villes du nord (par exemple Lisbonne et Porto). La plupart des trains comportent des voitures de 1e et 2e classe.

Vous pouvez effectuer vos réservations le jour même ou la veille, même en été. Elles sont généralement obligatoires pour les IC et les Alfa. Jusqu'à 4 ans, les enfants voyagent gratuitement et de 4 à 12 ans, ils bénéficient de billets demi-tarif.

Route

Grâce aux subventions européennes, le réseau routier du Portugal a pu s'améliorer considérablement. Les longues nationales très nombreuses et

A trip to Portugal wouldn't be complete without a ride on one of Lisbon's antique trams

parfois payantes sont bitumées et généralement en bon état. Les départementales sont peu fréquentées, ce qui permet à l'automobiliste de repérer plus facilement d'éventuels nids de poule.

L'inconvénient majeur tient aux fait que nombre d'automobilistes, hommes et femmes, conduisent à toute allure. Le Portugal connaît d'ailleurs le taux annuel de décès dus à des accidents de la route le plus élevé d'Europe. Les routes côtières en Algarve et l'axe Lisbonne-Cascais sont particulièrement dangereuses. La conduite en ville présente autant de risques, en particulier dans les vieilles cités où les rues se rétrécissent subitement à la largeur d'une charrette. En outre, les tortueux systèmes de sens unique, seul moyen d'organiser le trafic dans les ruelles, peuvent vous entraîner loin de votre destination initiale. Les parkings municipaux se font très rares.

Le réseau modeste des nationales (*estradas*) s'étend progressivement à tout le pays. Les meilleures sont les *auto-estradas* ou autoroutes, toutes à péage (*portagens*). La plus longue relie Lisbonne à Porto sur 304 km, mais il existe d'autres tronçons entre Porto et Braga, Porto et Amarante, ou Lisbonne et Cascais. Sur ce réseau de 575 km, le péage coûte 9 $ le km pour les voitures et les motos. Les numéros d'identification des autoroutes commençant par un E indiquent des axes européens. Les autoroutes avec péage sont précédées d'un A, les nationales du réseau principal (*rede fundamental*) de IP, et celles du réseau secondaire (*rede complementare*) de IC. Certaines nationales couvrant plusieurs destinations, leur numérotation change à mi-parcours. Par exemple, l'axe Lisbonne-Porto porte successivement les numéros E80, E01, A1 et IP1.

Comme partout sur le continent européen, on roule à droite. Les panneaux routiers respectent la signalisation internationale et des lignes continues ou en pointillés séparent les voies. Sauf mention contraire, la limite pour les voitures (sans caravane) et les motos est de 60 km/h en agglomération, 90 km/h sur route et 120 km/h sur autoroute.

La ceinture de sécurité est obligatoire à l'avant et à l'arrière des véhicules, et les enfants de moins de 12 ans ne doivent pas voyager à l'avant. Il est interdit de klaxonner en ville après le coucher du soleil, sauf en cas d'urgence. Les motocyclistes et leurs passagers doivent porter un casque. Le taux d'alcoolémie autorisé au volant ne devant pas dépasser 0,05%, il est vivement déconseillé de boire avant de conduire.

On trouve de l'essence sans plomb (*sem chumbo*), du diesel (*gasóleo*) et de l'essence ordinaire dans les nombreuses stations-service du pays qui, à quelques exceptions près, acceptent la plupart des cartes de crédit.

Si vous avez besoin d'aide, l'Automóvel Club de Portugal (ACP), le club automobile national, offre une assistance médicale, légale et mécanique à ses membres. Si vous appartenez à un club national affilié, vous pouvez bénéficier de ses services. En cas de besoin, appelez le 01-942 50 95 (Lisbonne) pour le sud du pays et le tel 02-830 11 27 (Porto) pour le nord.

Bicyclette

Le cyclotourisme est un moyen économique, écologique et agréable de visiter le Portugal. Avec un VTT (BTT ou bicyclete tudo terrano), vous admirerez sans doute plus de sites (le plus souvent hors des sentiers battus) que la plupart des visiteurs rêvent d'en voir. Bien que les pistes cyclables fassent défaut au Portugal, les VTT ont

les mêmes droits d'accès aux chemins et sentiers ruraux que les randonneurs.

Les Portugais pensent souvent que les visiteurs qui voyagent à vélo manquent de moyens, raison pour laquelle ces derniers se voient fréquemment offrir les hébergements les moins onéreux et inviter à dîner chez l'habitant. Sur les petites routes, les cyclistes créent l'événement : les conducteurs les klaxonnent souvent en manière d'avertissement amical, et les passagers émerveillés leur font des signes de la main en les interpellant. Cela surprend certainement les premières fois mais, sur les longues routes isolées, on en vient rapidement à espérer le passage de la prochaine voiture !

Bien sûr, il y a un revers de la médaille. Au nord du pays en particulier, il peut pleuvoir sans arrêt pendant des jours entiers. Malgré l'existence de boutiques spécialisées dans les grandes villes, il est parfois difficile de trouver la pièce de rechange indispensable. Mais les deux problèmes majeurs sont les conducteurs portugais, les plus dangereux d'Europe, et les routes secondaires : certaines encore pavées de blocs de pierre sont cahoteuses et d'autres sont parsemées d'énormes nids de poule (autre bonne raison d'avoir un VTT).

Bateau

Outre les croisières sur le Douro depuis Porto et sur le Tage depuis Lisbonne, les ferries trans-fluviaux sont les seuls moyens de transport fluviaux qui subsistent. La traversée la plus longue s'effectue sur le Tage avec la compagnie Transtejo entre Lisbonne et Cacilhas, Montijo et Seixal. A l'embouchure du Sado, les ferries Transado relient, quant à eux, Setúbal à Tróia en une demi-heure.

Reisen in Portugal

Bus

Nach dem Hinscheiden der staatlichen Busgesellschaft Rodoviária Nacional (RN) sind unzählige örtliche Privatunternehmen auf der Bildfläche erschienen, von denen die meisten in ein dichtes Busdienstnetz unterhaltende regionale Gesellschaften zusammengeschlossen sind. Im allgemeinen kann sich der Reisende von drei verschiedenen Busarten befördern lassen: Von *expressos* (komfortablen, größere Städte direkt verbindenden Schnellbussen), *rápidas* (schnelle Regionalbussen) und an jeder Straßenecke haltenden *carreiras*.

Mit expressos läßt sich Portugal im allgemeinen gut und preisgünstig erkunden, und auch im Sommer hat man kaum Probleme beim Lösen einer Fahrkarte für den gleichen oder nächsten Tag. Im Gegensatz dazu können die örtlichen Dienste besonders im Norden an Wochenenden, und besonders während der Sommerferien, auf ein bares Minimum zusammenschrumpfen.

Zug

Das Reisen mit Caminhos de Ferro Portugueses (CP), der staatlichen Eisenbahngesellschaft, ist billiger als mit dem Langstreckenbus, wenn auch im allgemeinen langsamer. CP unterhält drei Hauptdienstklassen: den überall haltenden *regional*-Service (in den Fahrplänen mit R gekennzeichnet); die relativ schnellen *interregionales* (IR) und die *rápido* oder *intercidade* genannten Expreßzüge (IC im Fahrplan). Der kaum schnellere Sonder-IC-Service Alfa verbindet bestimmte Städte im Norden (z. B. Lissabon und Porto). Die meisten Züge führen Wagons erster und zweiter Klasse.

In den meisten Fällen hat man auch im Sommer kaum Schwierigkeiten beim Lösen einer Fahrkarte für eine Reise am gleichen oder nächsten Tag. Platzreservierungen sind normalerweise bei IC- und Alfa-Zügen obligatorisch. Kleinkinder unter vier Jahren reisen kostenlos, größere von 4 bis 12 Jahren zum halben Preis.

Straße

Dank Subventionen der EU wird Portugals Straßensystem jetzt immer weiter verbessert und verfügt nun über zahlreiche Fernstraßen einschließlich mautpflichtiger Abschnitte. Die Hauptstraßen sind befestigt und in allgemein gutem Zustand. Nebenstraßen auf dem Land weisen so überraschend wenig Verkehr auf, so daß man nach dem gelegentlichen Schlagloch Ausschau halten kann.

Was einem die Freude am Fahren hier allerdings wirklich trüben kann, sind die portugiesischen Autofahrer, von denen viele, Männer wie auch Frauen, wie Verrückte fahren und noch nie etwas von Höflichkeit gehört zu haben scheinen. Portugal hat die höchste Jahresrate an Straßenunfällen mit tödlichem Ausgang pro Kopf in Europa. Die Küstenstraßen der Algarve und die Achse Lissabon-Cascais sind besonders berüchtigt. In den Städten ist der Fahrstil im allgemeinen hektisch. Das gilt auch nicht zuletzt für Portugals viele alten von Wällen umgebenen Ortschaften, in denen Straßen nach einer Schlankheitskur unvorhergesehen zu am besten für Eselskarren geeigneten Spuren werden können. Verzwickte Einbahnstraßensysteme (üblicherweise die einzige Möglichkeit für Gemeinden, mit den Autos auf ihren schmalen Verkehrswegen fertig zu werden) können zur Falle werden oder einen auf weite Umwege zwingen. Parkmöglichkeiten im Ortsbereich sind gewöhnlich sehr beschränkt.

Portugals bescheidenes Landstraßensystem (*estradas*) erschließt langsam das gesamte Land. Im besten Zustand sind die *auto-estradas* oder Autobahnen, die alle mautpflichtig (*portagens*) sind. Die längste Strecke verbindet Lissabon mit Porto über 304 km. Andere Abschnitte sind zum Beispiel Porto-Braga, Porto-Amarante und Lissabon-Cascais. Das gegenwärtig 575 km umspannende Mautstraßennetz verlangt Auto- und Motorradfahrern etwa 9$00 pro km ab. Die Beschilderung kann im wahrsten Sinne des Wortes rätselhaft sein. Straßennummern mit vorangestelltem E kennzeichnen Europastraßen. Portugals mautpflichtige Straßenabschnitte sind mit einem A ausgewiesen. Straßen im Hauptnetz (*rede fundamental*) werden mit IP und Nebenstraßen im *rede complementare* mit IC identifiziert. Manche Fernstraßen führen zu mehreren Zielorten, und Nummern können sich mitten auf der Strecke ändern: Beispielsweise wird die Lissabon mit Porto verbindende Straße stellenweise E80, E01, A1 und IP1 genannt.

Wie im restlichen Kontinentaleuropa fährt man in Portugal rechts. Die meisten Schilder verwenden internationale Symbole, und Spuren sind mit durchgehenden bzw. unterbrochenen Linien gemäß internationaler Konvention gekennzeichnet. Außer wo spezifisch festgelegt, liegen die Geschwindigkeitsbegrenzungen für Autos (ohne Anhänger) und Motorräder bei 60 km/h in geschlossenen Ortschaften, 90 km/h außerhalb von Orten und Dörfern und 120 km/h auf der Autobahn.

Sicherheitsgurte sind in Vorder- und Rücksitzen zu

tragen, und Kinder unter 12 Jahren dürfen überhaupt nicht im Vordersitz sitzen. Nach Einbruch der Dunkelheit darf in geschlossenen Ortschaften die Hupe nur in Notfällen benutzt werden. Motorradfahrer und ihre Beifahrer müssen Helme tragen. Die gesetzliche Blutalkoholgehaltsgrenze liegt bei 0.05% – man denkt also am besten gar nicht an Alkoholkonsum, wenn man noch fahren muß.

Bleifreies (*sem chumbo*) und verbleites Benzin wie auch Diesel (*gasóleo*) sind in den meisten Teilen des Landes problemlos erhältlich. Es gibt viele SelfServe-Tankstellen, von denen viele, jedoch nicht alle, die weitverbreitetsten Kreditkarten annehmen.

Zusätzlich zur Pannenhilfe geht Portugals nationaler Automobilklub, der Automóvel Club de Portugal (ACP) seinen Mitgliedern auch mit ärztlicher und juristischer Hilfestellung zur Hand. Kann man die Mitgliedschaft bei einem angeschlossenen nationalen Autoklub nachweisen, stehen einem diese Leistungen ebenfalls zur Verfügung. Die Notrufnummern lauten 01-942 50 95 (Lissabon) für Südportugal und 02-830 11 27 (Porto) für Nordportugal.

Fahrrad

Radfahren ist billig, gesund, umweltfreundlich und obendrein eine angenehme Art und Weise, Portugal zu entdecken. Mit einem Mountain Bike (BTT oder *bicyclete tudo terrano*) sieht man wahrscheinlich mehr (und besonders abgelegenere) Orte als die meisten Besucher sich auch nur in ihren Träumen vorstellen können. Obgleich Portugal keine spezifisch ausgewiesenen Fahrradwege oder -spuren aufweist, scheinen Mountain Bikes die gleichen Rechte auf Benutzung ländlicher Wege und Pfade wie Wanderer zu haben.

Walls of Castelo dos Mouros, Sintra

BETHUNE CARMICHAEL

Die meisten Portugiesen scheinen zu glauben, daß die Besucher ihr Land mit dem Fahrrad erkunden, weil sie sich das auf andere Weise nicht leisten können, und somit werden Fahrradfahrer oft zum Abendessen mit der Familie eingeladen bzw. bekommen die billigste Unterkunft angeboten. Auf weniger befahrenen Landstraßen kann man viele Blicke auf sich ziehen: Autofahrer hupen oft, meist aufgrund reiner Höflichkeit denn aus Ungehaltenheit, und die Beifahrer winken oft und haben ein gutes Wort für den Radler übrig. Das mag die ersten paar Male abschreckend wirken, doch kann man sich auf diesen langen einsamen Strecken wirklich auf das nächste Auto freuen!

Natürlich gibt es hier auch eine Kehrseite. Besonders im Norden kann es tagelang ununterbrochen regnen. Obwohl es in den meisten größeren Städten Fachgeschäfte gibt, wird man wahrscheinlich das gerade dringendst benötigte Fahrradersatzteil nicht bekommen. Die zwei größten

Probleme sind portugiesische Autofahrer (die zu den unhöflichsten und draufgängerischsten in Europa gehören) und portugiesische Landstraßen, von denen manche nicht nur noch mit Kopfsteinen gepflastert sind, die einem die Zähne im Munde wackeln lassen, sondern obendrein noch Schlaglöcher haben können, in denen man sich voll und ganz verlieren kann (ein weiterer guter Grund für ein Mountain Bike).

Boot

Außer Flußkreuzfahrten auf dem Douro von Porto und dem Tejo von Lissabon sind die einzigen noch existierenden Wassertransportmittel von Bedeutung in Portugal flußüberquerende Fähren. Die längsten Reisen darauf legt man auf den Transtejo Pendelfähren über den Tejo zwischen Lissabon und Cacilhas, Montijo und Seixal und auf den Transado-Fähren zurück, die das andere Ufer an der Mündung des Sado zwischen Setúbal und Tróia in halbstündiger Fahrt erreichen.

Cómo Movilizarse dentro de Portugal

En Autobús

El desmantelamiento de la compañía de autobuses del gobierno Rodoviária Nacional (RN) generó una cantidad de firmas privadas locales, la mayoría de ellas amalgamadas en compañías regionales, que unidas ofrecen una densa red de servicios de autobuses. Los servicios son de tres tipos generales: los *expressos* que son autocares cómodos, rápidos y directos entre las ciudades principales; las *rápidas* que son autobuses regionales rápidos; y las *carreiras* que parecen detenerse en todos los cruces de carretera.

Los expressos, por lo general, son una forma buena y barata de movilizarse en Portugal y, aun en el verano, no es difícil reservar una plaza para el siguiente día, o incluso para el mismo día. En contraste, los servicios locales, especialmente hacia el norte, pueden reducirse a casi nada durante los fines de semana, sobre todo durante el verano cuando las escuelas están de vacaciones.

En Tren

El viajar con la compañía ferroviaria del gobierno Caminhos de Ferro Portugueses (CP) es más barato que viajar en los autobuses de larga distancia, aunque es generalmente más lento. CP ofrece tres niveles principales de servicio: el *regional* (marcado con la letra R en los horarios), que se detiene en todas partes; el *interregional* (marcado con las letras IR), que es bastante rápido; y los trenes expresos llamados *rápido* o *intercidade* (marcados con las letras IC). *Alfa* es un servicio IC especial, marginalmente más rápido, que va entre ciertas ciudades seleccionadas del norte (por ejemplo, desde Lisboa a Oporto). La mayoría de los trenes ofrecen las categorías de primera y de segunda clases.

En la mayoría de los casos es fácil reservar plazas el día antes de viajar y aún el mismo día, inclusive en verano. Las reservaciones son generalmente obligatorias en los trenes IC y en los Alfa. Los niños menores de 4 años viajan gratis y los que estén entre los 4 y los 12 años de edad viajan a mitad de precio.

Por Carretera

Gracias a los subsidios estadounidenses, el sistema de carreteras de Portugal está siendo mejorado constantemente. Ahora existen numerosos tramos largos de autopistas, que incluyen las de peaje. Las carreteras principales son asfaltadas y están en buenas condiciones generales. Las carreteras secundarias rurales son sorprendentemente descongestionadas lo que le permite a uno alertarse a los baches ocasionales.

El principal aspecto negativo de manejar en Portugal son los conductores. Muchos de ellos, tanto hombres como mujeres, conducen como maníacos y no saben nada de cortesía. El porcentaje de muertes por accidentes de carretera en Portugal es el más alto de Europa. Las carreteras costeras de Algarve y el eje entre Lisboa y Cascais son especialmente peligrosas. El tráfico en la ciudad tiende a ser turbulento, y no es mejor en muchas ciudades viejas amuralladas de Portugal, donde las carreteras pueden ir estrechándose hasta llegar a la anchura de camino para carro tirado por burro antes de que uno se haya dado cuenta. Sistemas diabólicos de una sola vía (generalmente la única manera en que los pueblos pueden soportar los automóviles en sus calles estrechas) pueden atraparlo a uno o forzarlo a desviarse mucho de su

ruta. El aparcamiento municipal es por lo general muy limitado.

La modesta red de autopistas de Portugal (*estradas*) gradualmente se está extendiendo a lo largo y ancho del país. Las mejores son las *auto-estradas*, todas ellas con cobro de peaje (*portagens*). La más larga de ellas es la que va de Lisboa a Oporto de 304 km. Otros trechos incluyen los que van de Oporto a Braga, de Oporto a Amarante y de Lisboa a Cascais. En los 575km actuales de carreteras con cobro de peaje, se cobra más o menos 9$00 por kilómetro a los autos y motocicletas. La nomenclatura de las carreteras puede ser confusa. Los números de las autopistas con el prefijo E son rutas con destino a toda Europa. Las carreteras de Portugal con cobro de peaje tienen el prefijo A. Las carreteras de la red principal (*rede fundamental*) tienen el prefijo IP, y las subsidiarias (*rede complementare*) IC. Algunas carreteras tienen varias designaciones y números que cambian a mitad de ruta, por ejemplo, la carretera de Lisboa a Oporto es variablemente llamada E80, EO1, A1 y IPI.

Como en el resto de la Europa continental, se conduce por la derecha. La mayoría de los avisos utilizan símbolos internacionales y los carriles están marcados con líneas sólidas y fragmentadas, según las convenciones internacionales. Excepto cuando se indique de otra manera, el límite de velocidad para los automóviles (que no lleven remolque) y para las motocicletas es de 60 km/h en las áreas edificadas y de 90 km/h fuera de los pueblos y villas, y de 120 km/h en las autopistas.

Es obligatorio utilizar los cinturones de seguridad en los asientos delanteros y traseros, y los niños menores de 12 años

no pueden viajar en el asiento delantero. No se puede utilizar la bocina en las zonas pobladas después de oscurecerse, excepto en emergencias. Los motociclistas y sus pasajeros tienen que utilizar cascos protectores. El límite legal de alcohol en la sangre es sólo 0,05%, así que ni se piense en tomar bebidas alcohólicas y conducir.

En la mayor parte del país la gasolina sin plomo (*sem chumbo*) y el diesel (*gasóleo*) son fácil de obtenerse, de la misma manera que la gasolina con plomo. Hay muchas estaciones de gasolina de autoservicio y las tarjetas de crédito principales son aceptadas en muchas, pero no en todas las estaciones.

Si se requiere asistencia el Automóvil Club de Portugal (ACP), que es el club nacional de Portugal, ofrece a sus miembros asistencia médica, legal y cuando se averíe el auto. Si se puede comprobar ser miembro de un club nacional afiliado también se pueden utilizar los servicios. Los números de emergencia del club son 01-942 50 95 (en Lisboa) para el sur de Portugal y 02-830 11 27 (en Oporto) para el norte de Portugal.

En Bicicleta

La bicicleta es una manera barata, saludable, buena para el entorno y sobre todo agradable para movilizarse dentro de Portugal. Con una bicicleta de montaña (BTT o *bicyclete tudo terrano*) se pueden ver probablemente más (y especialmente más remotos) lugares de los que la mayoría de los visitantes soñarían ver. Aunque Portugal no tiene vías ni sendas dedicadas especialmente para las bicicletas, las bicicletas de montaña parecen tener el mismo derecho de acceso que tienen los caminantes a las vías y a las sendas rurales.

La mayoría de los portugueses parecen pensar que los visitantes recorren el país en bicicleta por carecer de los medios económicos de hacerlo de otra manera y por eso frecuentemente los ciclistas reciben ofertas de alojamiento más barato o son invitados a comer con la familia. En las carreteras secundarias el ciclista puede ser una fuente de admiración: los conductores tocan la bocina, más en señal de cortesía que de enojo, y los deleitados pasajeros a menudo agitan las manos y gritan. Uno puede sentirse desanimado por esto las primeras veces, pero una vez se está en los trechos largos y solitarios, puede que se espere con anticipación la aparición del próximo automóvil.

Naturalmente que hay un lado negativo. Especialmente en el norte, puede uno enfrentarse a lluvias que no tienen fin. Y, aunque existen tiendas de bicicletas en la mayoría de las ciudades grandes, es probable que no se pueda obtener la parte mecánica que se necesita. Los dos mayores problemas son los conductores portugueses, que están entre los más groseros y alocados de Europa, y las carreteras secundarias de Portugal, algunas de las cuales todavía están pavimentadas con adoquines pequeños y la vibración le puede hacer chocar los dientes a uno hasta casi aflojárselos, y algunas carreteras tienen baches que se lo pueden tragar a uno entero (esta es otra buena razón para traer una bicicleta de montaña).

En Bote

Aparte de los cruceros a lo largo del Río Duero desde Oporto y a lo largo del Río Tajo desde Lisboa, el único transporte acuático que sobrevive en Portugal es el de los pontones para cruzar los ríos. Los viajes más largos son los de los barcos de pasajeros de Transtejo a través del Río Tajo entre Lisboa y Cacilhas, Montillo y Seixal; y los barcos transado que hacen el viaje de media hora a través de la desembocadura del Río Sado entre Setúbal y Tróia.

One of the beautiful 'moliceiros' boats that sail the canals of Aveiro

ポルトガルの旅

バス

国営のロドヴィアリア・ナシオナル・バス会社（Rodoviaria Nacional、略してRN）がその終わりを迎えたあと、地元の私営会社が多数でき、その後そのほとんどが地域毎に合併した。そして現在密集したバス運輸網が運営されている。バスの便にはおもに次の3タイプがある。エスプレソス（expressos）は乗り心地がよく、高速の直行便で主要都市を結ぶ。ラーピダス（rapidas）は高速地方バス。それに対してカレイラス（carreiras）は十字路のたびに停車するほどだ。

一般的に言うと、ポルトガルを旅するにはエスプレソスが安くて良い方法だ。また、夏でも1日前か当日に予約できるほど席がすいている。その逆に、ローカルバス（とくに北部）は、週末になると便数がほとんどなくなる。学校が夏休みの期間はさらにひどい。

電車

国営鉄道会社のカミニョス・ド・フェロ・ポルトゲーゼス（Caminhos de Ferro Portugueses、略してCP）を使った旅は長距離バスより安いが全体的に遅い。CPにはおもに3種類のクラスがある。各駅停車のレジョナール（regional、時刻表にRと記載）、快速のインテレジョナール（inter-regional、IRと記載）、ラーピド（rapido）、またはインテシダード（intercidade）と呼ばれる急行（ICと記載）だ。アルファ（Alfa）は特急で北部の一部の都市間（たとえばリスボン：Lisbon－ポルト：Porto 間）を結び、IC便よりわずかに速い。列車のほとんどに一等、二等客車がある。

夏期でも前日かまたは当日にチケットが予約切れになる心配はまずない。ICとアルファ便は通常予約が義務づけられている。4歳未満の子供は無料、4歳から12歳までは半額料金だ。

道路

ECの助成金のおかげで、ポルトガルの道路は順調に改良されている。現在は有料道を含む数多くの長距離幹線道路がある。主要な道路は舗装してあり、全体的にコンディションが良い。地方の道路は驚くほどすいているので、たまに穴があいていても目につきやすい。

車を利用する時の問題点はこの国の運転手にある。男女を問わず、多くの人がまるで交通道徳などどこ吹く風といったほとんどスピード狂的運転をする。人口比でみると、ポルトガルの交通事故による年間死亡率はヨーロッパで最も高い。

海岸道路のアルガルヴェ（Algarve）－カーシカイス（Cascais）間、リスボン－カーシカイス間は特に危険だ。市内の道路、とりわけ壁に囲まれたポルトガルの古い町はひどい状態で、気付くとロバの荷車がやっと通れるほどのサイズに先細りしていることがよくある。たいへん面倒な一方通行制度（車が通るのがやっとの市街地にとってはおそらく唯一の対処方法）のせいで道に閉じ込められたり、目的地から大変遠いところまで押し出されたりする。私営の駐車場も限られた数しかないことが多い。

ポルトガルの幹線道路網であるエストラーダス（estradas）は現在さほど延長距離が大きくはないが、次第に拡大しつつある。エストラーダスの最上ランクは高速道路であるアウト・エストラーダス（auto-estradas）で、すべて有料（ポルタージェンス：portagens）だ。リスボンからポルトまでのものが最長で、全長304kmだ。そのほかにもポルト－ブラーガ（Braga）間、ポルト－アマランテ（Amarante）間、リスボン－カーシカイス間などがある。全長575kmの有料道路の現在の料金は、車、オートバイとも1キロメートル当たり9$00だ。幹線道路の名称は紛らわしいことがある。Eという文字が頭につく高速道路はヨーロッパ全域で通じる名称だ。ポルトガルの有料道路はAで始まる。主要幹線道路網であるレド・フンダメンタール（rede fundamental）はIP、補助の道路であるレド・コンプレメンター rede complementare）はICという記号で始まる。幹線道路のいくつかには名称が数種類あり、途中で番号が変わることがある。たとえばリスボンからポルトまでの道路はE80、E01、A1、IP1と名称がいくつもある。

他のヨーロッパ大陸の国と同様に、ポルトガルは右側運転だ。交通標識はほとんど国際記号で、車線は国際協定により連続線と破線で区切られている。特別に指示されていなければ自動車（トレーラーなし）とオートバイの制限速度は市街地で時速60km、市街

地をはずれた場所や村では時速90km、高速道路では時速120kmだ。

　シートベルトは前・後部座席とも着用が義務づけられている。また、12歳未満の子供は前部座席に座ってはいけない。市街地では日没後緊急時以外に警笛を鳴らすことは禁止。オートバイは運転手、後部の相乗りともヘルメットの着用が必要だ。飲酒運転に関する法的制限は血液中のアルコールがたったの0.05パーセントなので、酒気帯び運転は禁物だ。

　有鉛ガソリンに加えて、無鉛ガソリン(セン・シュンブ：*sem chumbo*)とディーゼル(ガソリオ：*gasoleo*)は国内どこでもたやすく入手できる。セルフサービスのガソリンスタンドが多く、ほとんどのガソリンスタンドで主要クレジットカードが使える。

　運転中に救援が必要な時のためにポルトガルの自動車協会、アウトモヴェール・クルブ・デ・ポルトガール(*Automovel Club de Port-ugal*、略してACP)が会員に対して医療、法律、自動車故障の援助を行なっている。もし、自分の自動車協会がこの協会に加盟しているときは、その会員証明があれば、同様のサービスを受けることができる。ポルトガル南部の協会の緊急連絡先は電話番号01-942 50 95(リスボン)、北部は02-830 11 27(ポルト)だ。

ボート
ポルトのリオ・ドール川(Rio Douro)とリスボンのリオ・テージョ川(Rio Tejo)のクルージングを除くと、ポルトガルで残存する重要な水上運輸は川越え用のフェリーだけ

BETHUNE CARMICHAEL

Looking west into Spain from Marvão

だ。最長の航程のものには、リオ・テージョ川をリスボン、カシリャース(Cacilhas)、モンティージョ(Montijo)、セシャル(Seixal)で渡るトランステージョ社 *(Transtejo)* の通勤フェリー、そしてリオ・サード川の河口のセトゥバル(Setubal)とトロイア(Troia)を30分で結ぶトランザド社 *(Transado)* のフェリーの旅がある。

自転車
サイクリングでのポルトガルの旅は、安く健康的で環境にもやさしい。また、大変楽しい旅の方法だ。マウンテンバイク(ビシクレット・トゥド・テラーノ：*bicyclete tudo terrano*、略してBTT)を使うと、普通の旅行者が見られない(とくに人里離れた)ところなどを見ることができる。ポルトガルには自転車専用道はないが、マウンテンバイクはトレッキングと同様、田舎道に入る権利があるようだ。

　ポルトガル人のほとんどは、旅行者が自転車で旅している理由を資金不足だと考えてい

るので、サイクリストは最も安い宿泊施設を紹介してもらったり、家族の夕食に誘われることがある。田舎道では地元の人の驚きの的になることが多い。しばしば運転手が警笛を鳴らし、乗客が手を振って、大声で声をかけることがあるが、これは怒りよりは挨拶の意味がある。最初の2、3回は腹が立つかもしれないが、道程が長いと次の車が待ち遠しくなること請け合いだ。

　サイクリングにはもちろん短所もある。とくに北部は連日雨に降られることがある。自転車屋は大都市のほとんどにあるが、必要な部品が手に入らないことが多い。さらに大問題が二つある。一つはポルトガルの自動車運転手で、ヨーロッパでもっとも無礼でむちゃくちゃだということ。もう一つは田舎道で、いくつかはまだじゃり道のため、あまりの振動で歯が抜け落ちるほど。さらに人を呑み込むくらい大きな穴があいていることがある(だからマウンテンバイクを持って行くほうが良い)。

Index

Note: Geographical and cultural features are listed separately at the end of the general index in their appropriate categories.

GENERAL INDEX
All places are in Portugal except:
Sp - Spain

For duplicate names in Portugal, the district abbreviations are:

A - Aveiro
B - Braga
Be - Beja
Br - Bragança
C - Castelo Branco
Co - Coimbra
É - Évora
F - Faro
Fa - Ilha do Faial
Fl - Ilha das Flores
G - Guarda
Gr - Ilha Graciosa
L - Lisboa
Le - Leira
M - Madeira
P - Porto
Pc - Ilha do Pico
Po - Portalegre
S - Santarém
Sa - Ilha de Santa Maria
Se - Setúbal
Sj - Ilha de São Jorge
Sm - Ilha de São Miguel
T - Ilha Terceira
V - Vila Real
Vc - Viana do Castelo
Vi - Viseu

Abaças 16 A2
Abade de Neiva 10 C5
Abambres 12 C5
A Barxa (Sp) 12 C2
Abedes (Sp) 12 B2
Abela 30 C3
Abitureiras 23 E4
Abiúl 19 E6
Aboadela 15 G1
Aboboreira (S) 24 A3
Aboboreira (Be) 31 G4
Aboim 11 F5
Aboim da Nóbrega 10 D4
Aboim das Choças 10 D2
A Bola (Sp) 11 G1
Aborim 10 C5
Abra 23 E4
Abragao 15 F2
Abrantes 23 H3
Abreiro 12 B6
Abrigada 22 D6
Abrunheira 18 C4
Abrunhosa a-Velha 16 A6
Abuxanas 22 D5
Acebo (Sp) 21 G3
Acehuche (Sp) 21 G6
Aceredo (Sp) 11 F3
Achada (L) 26 B1
Achada (Sm) 40 C1
Achada da Mina 31 H6
Achada do Gamo 31 H5
Achadas da Cruz 40 A4
Achadinha 40 C1
Achete 23 E4

Aciberos (Sp) 12 D1
Açoreira 16 D2
Açores 16 C6
Adaes 10 C5
Adao 20 D2
Adaúfe 10 D5
Ade 21 E1
A de Barros 16 A4
Adenodeiro 15 G5
A-do-Pinto 32 A3
Adorigo 16 A2
A Dos Ferreiros (Av) 15 E6
A-dos-Ferreiros (G) 16 C5
Adoufe 15 H1
Adraga 26 A3
Advagar 23 E4
Afife 10 B3
Afonsim 11 H5
A Forxa (A Porqueira) (Sp) 11 G1
Agadao 19 F1
Agallas (Sp) 21 H2
A Garda (Sp) 10 B3
Agilde 15 F1
Agodim 18 D6
Agolada 27 F1
Agrela 14 D2
Agroal 23 G2
Agrobom 12 D6
Agrochao 12 D4
Agua Branca 30 C4
Aguada de Baixo 19 E1
Aguada de Cima 19 E1
Agua de Alte 15 H5
Agua de Madeiros 22 D1
Agua de Pau 40 B2
Agua de Peixes 28 B6
Agua de Pena 40 C5
Agua do Alto 40 C2
Agualonga 10 C3
Agua Longa 14 D2
Agualva 39 G6
Agualva Cacém 26 B3
Agua Negra 32 A4
Agua Retorta 40 D2
Aguas 20 D4
Aguas Belas (G) 20 D2
Aguas Belas (S) 23 H2
Aguas Belinhas 27 G1
Aguas Boas 16 A4
Aguas de Moura 27 F4
Aguas de Tábuas 35 H3
Aguas dos Fusos 35 H3
Aguas Frias (V) 12 B3
Aguas Frias (F) 35 F2
Aguas Réves-e-Castro 12 B5
Aguas Santas (B) 11 E5
Aguas Santas (P) 14 D2
Agua Travessa 23 H5
Aguçadoura 10 B6
A Gudiña (Sp) 12 C1
Agueda 19 E1
Agueda del Caudillo (Sp) 17 G6
Aguia 10 D3
Aguiar 28 B6
Aguiar da Beira 16 B5
Aguiar de Sousa 14 D3
Aguinchos 11 G6
Ahigal de Los Aceiteros (Sp) 17 F4
Ahigal de Villarino (Sp) 17 H2
Airaes 15 F1
Aire 23 F3
Alagoa 24 D4
Alagoa da Forca 31 E4
Alagoinha 25 E4

Alamo 32 B3
Alandroal 29 E3
Albaçao 11 E6
Alba de Yeltes (Sp) 17 H6
Albarellos (Sp) 12 A2
Albergaria (Le) 22 D1
Albergaria (S) 22 D5
Albergaria-a-Nova 14 D5
Albergaria-a-Velha 14 D6
Albergaria dos Doze 23 F1
Albergaria dos Fusos 28 B6
Alberguería (Sp) 12 A1
Albernoa 31 F4
Albrunheiro Grande 23 H2
Albufeira 35 E4
Albufeira de Mourao 29 E5
Alburitel 23 F2
Alburquerqe (Sp) 25 G5
Alcabideche 26 B3
Alcácer do Sal 27 F6
Alcáçovas 27 H6
Alcafozes 20 D5
Alcaide 20 C4
Alcainao Grande 26 B2
Alcains 20 C6
Alcanede 23 E4
Alcanena 23 F3
Alcanhoes 23 F5
Alcántara (Sp) 25 H1
Alcantarilha 35 E3
Alcañices (Sp) 13 G4
Alcaravela 24 A3
Alcaravica 29 E2
Alcaria (C) 20 B4
Alcaria (Le) 23 E3
Alcaria (Be) 31 G1
Alcaria (F) 35 F3
Alcaria (F) 36 A1
Alcaria (F) 36 B2
Alcaria Alta 35 H1
Alcaria de Javazes 31 H6
Alcaria do Cume 35 H3
Alcaria Longa 31 G2
Alcaria Ruiva 31 G5
Alcarias (Be) 31 E4
Alcarias (F) 36 B2
Alcazaba (Sp) 29 H1
Alcobaça 22 D3
Alcobertas 22 D4
Alcochete 26 D3
Alcoentre 22 D5
Alcofra 15 F6
Alconchel (Sp) 29 G4
Alcongosta 20 B4
Alcorcillo (Sp) 13 G4
Alcomeo (Sp) 25 F4
Alcorochel 23 F4
Alcoutim 36 B1
Aldeadávila de la Ribera (Sp) 17 F2
Aldea de Arriba (Sp) 11 F1
Aldea del Obispo (Sp) 17 F5
Aldeanueva de Portanobis (Sp) 17 F5
Aldehuela (Sp) 21 H2
Aldehuela de Yeltes (Sp) 17 H6
Aldeia 15 G4
Aldeia da Cruz 19 F6
Aldeia da Dona 21 E2
Aldeia da Mata 24 C4
Aldeia da Ponte 21 F2
Aldeia da Ribeira (G) 21 E2
Aldeia da Ribeira (S) 23 E4
Aldeia das Amoreiras 30 D5
Aldeia das Dez 19 H3

Aldeia da Serra (Le) 23 G1
Aldeia da Serra (E) 28 B3
Aldeia da Serra (E) 28 D3
Aldeia da Tôr 35 F3
Aldeia-da-Velha 11 E1
Aldeia de Ana de Avis 19 F6
Aldeia de Eiras 24 A2
Aldeia de Irmaos 26 D5
Aldeia de Joanes 20 B4
Aldeia de João Pires 20 D4
Aldeia de Nacomba 16 A4
Aldeia de Santa Margarida 20 D5
Aldeia de Santo Antùnio 20 D3
Aldeia de São Francisco de Assis 20 A4
Aldeia do Bispo (C) 20 D4
Aldeia do Bispo (G) 21 F3
Aldeia do Carvalho 20 B3
Aldeia do Corvo 31 F6
Aldeia do Mato 23 H3
Aldeia do Ronquenho 31 E3
Aldeia dos Cunhados 22 B6
Aldeia dos Delbas 30 D4
Aldeia dos Femandes 31 E6
Aldeia dos Francos 22 D4
Aldeia dos Grandaços 31 E5
Aldeia dos Negros 22 C4
Aldeia dos Neves 31 E6
Aldeia dos Palheiros 31 E6
Aldeia dos Pescadores 22 C4
Aldeia dos Ruins 31 E3
Aldeia Formosa 19 H2
Aldeia Nova (Br) 13 H5
Aldeia Nova (Vi) 16 A5
Aldeia Nova (G) 16 B6
Aldeia Nova (G) 17 E6
Aldeia Nova (Be) 31 E3
Aldeia Nova (F) 36 B3
Aldeia Nova do Barroso 11 H3
Aldeia Rica 16 C6
Aldeias (Vi) 15 H3
Aldeias (G) 20 B2
Aldeias (Be) 31 G2
Aldeias de Montoito 28 D5
Aldeia Velha (G) 21 F3
Aldeia Velha (Po) 24 A6
Aldeia Velha (Be) 31 G2
Aldeia Viçosa 16 C6
Aldeja Gavinha 22 C6
Aldreu 10 C5
Alegrete 25 E5
Além de Agua 19 E5
Alenquer 22 D6
Alentisca 29 F1
Alfafar 19 E5
Alfaiao 13 E3
Alfaiates 21 E2
Alfambra 34 B3
Alfandega da Fé 12 D6
Alfanzina 34 D4
Alfarela de Jales 12 A6
Alfarelos 18 D4
Alfarim 26 C5
Alfarrarede 23 H3
Alfeizerao 22 C3
Alfena 14 D2
Alferce 34 D2
Alforgemel 23 E5
Alfrivida 24 D1
Alfundao 31 E2
Algaça 19 F4
Algar Seco 34 D4
Algarvia 40 C1
Algeriz 12 B5

Algerus 27 E4
Algoceira 30 B6
Algodor 31 G5
Algodres 16 D4
Algosinho 17 G1
Algoso 13 F5
Algoz 35 E3
Alguber 22 D5
Algueirao-Mem Martins 26 B3
Alhadas 18 C4
Alhais 15 H4
Alhandra 26 D2
Alheira 10 C5
Alhoes 15 G4
Alhos Vedros 26 D4
Alijó 16 B1
Alimonte 12 D3
Aljezur 34 B2
Aljubarrota 22 D3
Aljustrel 31 E4
Almaça 19 F3
Almaceda 20 B5
Almacinha 19 F2
Almada 26 C3
Almada de Ouro 36 B2
Almadena 34 B4
Almagreira (Sa) 40 B3
Almalaguês 19 E4
Almancil 35 F4
Almargem 15 G5
Almargem do Bispo 26 B2
Almargens 35 G3
Almarginho 35 G2
Almarjao 34 D3
Almeida 17 E5
Almeidinha 16 D6
Almeirim (S) 23 E4
Almeirim (S) 23 F5
Almeirim (S) 23 F6
Almeirim (E) 28 B4
Almendra 16 D3
Almendra (Sp) 17 H2
Almendral (Sp) 29 H4
Almodôvar 31 E6
Almodôvar-a-Velha 31 E6
Almofala (Vi) 15 H4
Almofala (G) 17 E4
Almofala (Le) 22 D4
Almograve 30 A5
Almoster (Le) 19 E6
Almoster (S) 23 E5
Alomourol 23 G3
Alor (Sp) 29 G4
Alosno (Sp) 32 C6
Alpalhao 24 D4
Alpedrinha 20 C4
Alpedriz 22 D2
Alpendres de Lagares 32 A3
Alpiarça 23 F5
Alportel 35 G3
Alqueidao (Co) 18 C4
Alqueidao (S) 23 F3
Alqueidao (S) 23 H2
Alqueidao da Serra 23 E2
Alqueidao do Arrimal 23 E3
Alqueva 31 H1
Alté 35 F3
Alter do Chao 24 C5
Alter Pedroso 24 D5
Alto das Cabeças 28 D3
Alto da Serra 22 D4
Alto de Estivadas (Sp) 12 A2
Alto de Forriolo (Sp) 11 G1
Alto de Fumaces (Sp) 12 B2
Alto de Nevosa 11 F3
Alto de São Martinho 22 D3
Alto de Velao 15 G1
Alto de Vieiro (Sp) 11 F1

Alto do Canizo (Sp) 12 C1
Alto do Espinho 15 G1
Alto do Trevim 19 F4
Alto Fica 35 F3
Altura 36 B3
Altura do Monte Novo 31 F2
Alturas do Barroso 11 G4
Alva 15 G5
Alvaçoes do Corgo 15 H2
Alvadia 11 G6
Alvaiade 24 C2
Alvaiázere 19 E6
Alvaijar 23 F2
Alvalade 30 D3
Alvarado (Sp) 29 H2
Alvaraes 10 B4
Alvarelhos 12 B4
Alvareng 15 F4
Alvares (Co) 19 G5
Alvares (Be) 31 G5
Alvaro 19 H5
Alvarrao 31 H2
Alvarroes 25 E4
Alvega 24 A3
Alveite Grande 19 F4
Alveite Pequeno 19 F4
Alvelos 10 C5
Alvendre 16 C6
Alverca de Beira 16 C6
Alverca do Ribatejo 26 D2
Alves 31 H6
Alviobeira 23 G2
Alvite 15 H4
Alvito 31 F1
Alvito da Beira 19 H6
Alvoco da Serra 20 A3
Alvoco das Várzeas 19 H3
Alvor 34 C3
Alvorao 23 F3
Alvorge 19 E5
Alvominha 22 D4
Alvre 15 E3
Amadora 26 C3
Amandoeira 35 G3
Amaraleja 32 B1
Amarante 15 F2
Amares 10 D5
Ameada 29 F6
Amedo 16 C2
Ameiras de Baixo 30 C1
Ameixial 35 G2
Améndoa 24 A2
Amendoeira 31 G4
A Mezquita (Sp) 12 C2
Amiaes de Baixo 23 E4
Amiaes de Cima 23 E4
Amieira (C) 19 H5
Amieira (E) 28 B4
Amieira Cova 24 B4
Amieira do Tejo 24 C3
Amieiro (V) 16 B1
Amieiro (Co) 18 D3
Amonde 10 B3
Amor 23 E1
Amora 26 C4
Amoreira (G) 16 D6
Amoreira (Le) 22 C4
Amoreira (S) 23 H3
Amoreira (L) 26 C3
Amoreira (F) 35 E3
Amoreira (F) 35 H2
Amoreira da Gandara 18 D2
Amoreiras 30 D3
Amoreirinha 29 G1
Amorim 10 B6
Amorosa 10 B4
Anadia 19 E2
Anais 10 C4

Ança 19 E3
Ancas 19 E2
Ancora 10 B3
Andam 22 D2
Andorinha 18 D3
Andraes 15 H2
Andreus 23 H3
Anelhe 11 H4
Angeja 14 D6
Angra do Heroismo 39 H2
Angueira 13 G4
Anha 10 B4
Anhoes 10 D2
Anissó 11 E5
Anjos 39 C1
Anobra 19 E4
Anreade 15 G3
Ansiaes 16 C2
Ansiao 19 E6
Anta 14 D3
Antanhol 19 E4
Antas (B) 10 B5
Antas (V) 16 A2
Antas (Vi) 16 A6
Antas (Vi) 16 B4
Antigo Convento de Santa Maria de
   Aguiar 17 E4
Antime 11 E6
A Pena (Sp) 11 H1
Apostiça 26 C4
Apúlia 10 B6
Aquda 19 F6
Arada 14 D4
Aradas 14 C6
A Ramallosa (Sp) 10 B1
Aranhas 20 D4
Arao 34 C3
Arazede 18 D3
Arbo (Sp) 11 E1
Arca 15 F6
Arcas (Vi) 15 G5
Arcas (Vi) 15 H4
Arcas Espadanedo 12 D4
Arcillera (Sp) 13 H4
Arco 16 C1
Arco (Sp) 21 H6
Arco da Calheta 40 A5
Arco de Baulhe 11 F6
Arco de São Jorge 40 B4
Arcos (Vc) 10 C4
Arcos (V) 11 H4
Arcos (Vi) 16 A3
Arcos (E) 28 D2
Arcos de Valdevez 10 D3
Arcossó 11 H4
Arcozelo (Vc) 10 C3
Arcozelo (B) 10 C5
Arcozelo (G) 20 B1
Arcozelo das Maias 15 E5
Arcozelos 16 A4
Arcucelos (Sp) 12 A2
Ardaos 11 H3
Area (Sp) 10 B1
Areas (Sp) 10 C1
Areas (Sp) 10 C2
Arega 19 F6
Areia (B) 10 B6
Areia (L) 26 A3
Areias 23 G1
Areias de Vilar 10 C5
Areja 24 B3
Arelho 22 C4
Arengoes 23 E2
Areosa 10 B4
Arez 24 C3
Arga de Baixo 10 B3
Arga de Cima 10 C3
Arga de São João 10 B3

Arganil (Co) 19 G3
Arganil (S) 24 B2
Argañín (Sp) 13 H6
Argela 10 B3
Argemil 12 B5
Argomil 16 D6
Argozelo 13 F4
Aricera 16 A3
Arieiro 26 C4
Arieiro 40 B5
Ariz 16 A4
Armação de Péra 35 E4
Armada 11 G4
Armadouro 19 H5
Armamar 15 H3
Armil 11 E6
Armona 35 H4
Arnas 16 B4
Arneiro (C) 19 E6
Arneiro (Po) 24 C2
Arneiro das Milhariças 23 E4
Arneirós 22 B6
Arnoia 11 F6
Aroche (Sp) 32 D2
Aroche (Sp) 32 D3
Arões (B) 11 E6
Arões (A) 15 E5
Arosa (B) 11 E5
Arosa (V) 11 G5
Arouca 15 F4
Arrabal (Oia) (Sp) 10 B2
Arrabal 23 E2
Arraiolos 28 B3
Arramadoes 31 G2
Arrancada (A) 15 E6
Arrancada (Le) 18 D5
Arranhó 26 C2
Arreciadas 23 H4
Arreia de Baixo 24 B3
Arrentela 26 C4
Arrifana (Br) 12 D5
Arrifana (A) 14 D4
Arrifana (Co) 19 E4
Arrifana (Co) 19 F3
Arrifana (G) 20 D1
Arrifana (F) 34 B2
Arrifana 34 B2
Arrifes 40 B1
Arrisada 35 H2
Arronches 25 F6
Arrouquelas 22 D5
Arroyo de Albanacar (Sp) 32 B4
Arroyo de Cuncos (Sp) 29 F5
Arroyo de Jumadiel (Sp) 25 G-H2
Arroyo Freigamuñoz (Sp) 29 F5
Arroyo Zaos (Sp) 29 G6
Arruda dos Pisoes 23 E4
Arruda dos Vinhos 26 C1
Arvore 14 C1
Arzádigos (Sp) 12 B3
Arzila 19 E4
As Lamas (Sp) 11 H1
As Neves (Sp) 10 D1
Assafarge 19 E4
Assafora 26 B2
Assares 16 D1
Asseiceira (S) 22 D5
Asseiceira (S) 23 G3
Asseiceira (Be) 30 D3
Assentiz (S) 22 D5
Assentiz (S) 23 F3
Assumadas (F) 35 E3
Assumadas (F) 35 F3
Assumar 25 E6
Assureira 11 E2
Assureiras de Baixo 12 B4
Asturianos (Sp) 13 F1
Ataes 10 D4

Atalaia (G) 16 D6
Atalaia (L) 22 B5
Atalaia (L) 22 C6
Atalaia (S) 23 E5
Atalaia (S) 23 G3
Atalaia (Po) 24 B3
Atalaia (C) 24 C2
Atalaia (Se) 26 D3
Atalaia (E) 28 C6
Atalaia (Se) 30 B2
Atalaia (F) 34 C4
Atalaia Cimeira 19 F6
Atalaia da Contenda 25 F6
Atalaia do Campo 20 C5
Ataliças 31 H5
Atei 11 G6
Atenor 13 G6
Atouguia (Co) 19 G3
Atouguia (S) 23 F2
Atouguia da Baleia 22 B4
Atrave (Sp) 12 C2
Avanca 14 D5
Avantos 12 C5
Avedillo de Sanabria (Sp) 13 E1
A Veiga (Sp) 11 G1
Aveira 19 G3
Aveiras de Baixo 22 D6
Aveiras de Cima 22 D6
Aveiro 14 C6
Avelada 10 D5
Avelanoso 13 G4
Avelar 19 E6
Avelas de Caminho 19 E2
Avelas de Cima 19 E2
Avelas de Ribeira 16 C6
Aveleda 13 E3
Aveledas 12 B4
Avellanar (Sp) 21 H2
Aveloso (Vi) 15 G5
Aveloso (G) 16 C4
Avenal 22 C4
A Ver-o-Mar 10 B6
Aves 10 D6
Avessada 15 F2
Avezedo 10 B3
Avidagos 12 B6
Avidos 10 D6
Avinhó 13 F5
Avintes 14 D3
Avioso 14 D2
Avis 24 B6
Avô 19 H3
Ayamonte (Sp) 36 B3
Azagala (Sp) 25 H5
Azambuja 22 D6
Azambujeira 23 E5
Azaruja 28 C3
Azeitada 23 F6
Azeiteiros 29 E1
Azelha 23 E3
Azenha 18 C5
Azenhas do Mar 26 A2
Azere 19 G3
Azervadinha 27 G1
Azevo 16 D4
Azias 10 D3
Azinhaga 23 F4
Azinhal (Be) 31 G5
Azinhal (F) 35 G2
Azinhal (F) 36 B2
Azinheira (S) 22 D4
Azinheira (C) 24 A1
Azinheira dos Barros 30 C2
Azinheiro 35 G4
Azoia 23 E2
Azóia de Baixo 23 E5
Azóia de Cima 23 E4
Azóla 26 C5

Azud de Matacavas (Sp) 36 B-C1
Azurara 14 C1

Babe 13 F3
Baçal 13 E3
Bacoco (Sp) 25 F5
Badajoz (Sp) 29 G2
Badamalos 21 E1
Bade 10 C2
Badilla (Sp) 13 H6
Bagueixe 13 E5
Baía de Lagos 34 C4
Baía de Setúbal 26 D6, 30 A1
Baia do São Lourenço 40 C2
Baião 15 G2
Baiona (Sp) 10 B1
Bairrada 24 B2
Bairradas 22 D4
Bairro (B) 11 F5
Bairro (Le) 22 C4
Bairro (S) 23 F3
Bairro do Degebe 28 B4
Baixa de Banheira 26 D4
Balancho 28 D5
Balazar 10 C6
Balboa (Sp) 29 H2
Baldio 24 D4
Baldos 16 A4
Baldriz (Sp) 12 A2
Baleal 22 B4
Baleizao 31 G3
Balsa 16 A1
Baltar (Sp) 11 H2
Balugaes 10 C4
Balurcos 36 B1
Bande (Sp) 11 F1
Bandeiras 39 F6
Bando dos Santos 24 B2
Bangueses (Sp) 11 F1
Banhos da Ariola 16 C4
Banquerença 20 D3
Bañóbárez (Sp) 17 F4
Baraçal (G) 16 C6
Baraçal (G) 20 D2
Barao de São João 34 B3
Barao de São Miguel 34 B4
Barbacena 27 G4
Barbadaes 12 A5
Barbaído 20 B6
Barbas de Gaio 31 G4
Barbudo 10 D4
Barca de Alva 17 E3
Barcarrota (Sp) 29 H4
Barceino (Sp) 17 G3
Barcel 12 C6
Barcelinhos 10 C5
Barcelos 10 C5
Barco 20 B4
Barcos 16 A3
Barcouço 19 E3
Baredo (Sp) 10 B1
Barjacoba (Sp) 12 D1
Barosa 23 E1
Barqueiro 19 F6
Barqueiros 10 C6
Barquilla (Sp) 17 F6
Barracao (Co) 18 D2
Barracao (Le) 18 D6
Barrada (Sp) 25 A4
Barrada (E) 29 E5
Barrada (F) 35 H1
Barra de El Rompido (Sp) 36 D3
Barra de Mira 18 C2
Barragem da Aguieira 19 F2
Barragem da Bravura 34 C3
Barragem da Idanha 20 D5
Barragem da Penida 10 C5
Barragem das Mercês 32 C-D2

Barragem da Vigia 28 D4
Barragem de Alto Cávado 11 G3
Barragem de Arade 34 D3
Barragem de Beliche 36 A-B2
Barragem de Belver 24 B3
Barragem de Campilhas 30 B4
Barragem de Fagilde 15 H6
Barragem de Fronhas 19 G3
Barragem de Magos 27 E-F1
Barragem de Maranhao 24 B6
Barragem de Meimoa 20 D3
Barragem de Montargil 24 A6
Barragem de Monte da Rocha
    30 D5
Barragem de Monte Novo 28 C4-5
Barragem de Morgavel 30 B3-4
Barragem de Odivelas 31 E1
Barragem de Paradela 11 F3
Barragem de Peramanca 28 A5
Barragem de Póvoa 24 D3
Barragem de Pracana 24 C3
Barragem de Santa Clara 30 D6
Barragem de Santa Luzia 19 H4
Barragem de Santa Maria 17 E4
Barragem de Tapada Grande 32 A5
Barragem de Vale de Gaio 27 H6,
    30 D1
Barragem de Venda Nova 11 G4
Barragem de Vilar 16 B4
Barragem do Alto Lindoso 11 E3
Barragem do Alto Rabagao 11 G4
Barragem do Alvito 28 B6
Barragem do Cabril 19 G6
Barragem do Caia 25 F6
Barragem do Castelo de Bode
    23 H3
Barragem do Divor 28 B3
Barragem do Funcho 35 E2
Barragem do Pego do Altar 27 G-H5
Barragem do Poio 24 D3
Barragem do Roxo 31 E-F3
Barragem Fonte Serne 30 C4
Barragem Penha Garcia 21 E5
Barragem Toulica 21 E6
Barragem Vilarinho das Furnas
    11 E3
Barrancao 27 G4
Barranco 35 G1
Barranco da Vaca 34 B2
Barranco do Bebedouro 30 C4
Barranco do Cailogo 30 C5
Barranco do Milho 34 C3
Barranco do Velho 35 G3
Barrancos 32 D2
Barranquinho 30 B5
Barreira (G) 16 C4
Barreira (Le) 23 E2
Barreiras 24 A5
Barreiro (V) 11 G6
Barreiro (Le) 19 E6
Barreiro (Se) 26 C4
Barreiro de Besteiros 19 F1
Barreiros (Vi) 15 H5
Barreiros (Le) 23 E1
Barreosa 20 A3
Barreras (Sp) 17 G3
Barretos 25 E4
Barril 22 B6
Barril de Alva 19 H3
Bárrio 10 C3
Barrio de la Estación (Sp) 25 F4
Barrio de Lomba (Sp) 13 E1
Barrio de Rábano (Sp) 13 F1
Barrô (Vi) 15 G3
Barrô (A) 19 E1
Barro Branco 28 D3
Barroca 20 A4
Barroca Grande 20 A4

Barrocal 29 E5
Barrocal do Douro 13 G6
Barrocalvo 22 C5
Barrocaria 23 F1
Barroças e Taias 10 D2
Barrosa 27 E1
Barrosa 40 B2
Barrosas 15 E1
Barrosellos 10 C4
Barrosinha 27 G6
Barruecopardo (Sp) 17 F3
Barulho 25 E5
Basteiros 30 D5
Bastelo 11 F5
Batalha 23 E2
Batocas 21 F1
Bebedouro 18 D3
Beberriqueira 23 G3
Beça 11 H4
Beco 15 E6
Beduído 14 D5
Beijós 19 G1
Beiriz 10 C6
Beja 31 G3
Belas 26 B3
Belazaima 19 E1
Belesar (Sp) 10 B1
Beliche 36 B2
Beliche do Cerro 35 H2
Belide 18 D4
Belinho 10 B5
Belmequel 32 A3
Belmonte 20 C2
Belo 31 G6
Belver (Br) 16 C2
Belver (Po) 24 B3
Bemposta (Sp) 12 B2
Bemposta (Br) 17 G1
Bemposta (C) 20 D5
Bemposta (S) 23 H4
Bemposta (L) 26 C2
Benafim Grande 35 F3
Benagouro 11 H6
Benavente (Sp) 25 F5
Benavente 27 E1
Benavila 24 B6
Bencatel 28 E3
Bendada 20 D2
Benedita 22 D4
Benespera 20 D2
Benfeita 19 H3
Benfica 26 C3
Benfica do Ribatejo 23 E6
Benquerenças 24 D1
Bens 31 H6
Bensafrim 34 C3
Benvende 16 B5
Bercianos de Aliste (Sp) 13 H3
Berganciano (Sp) 17 H2
Beringel 31 F2
Berlenga 22 A4
Bermellar (Sp) 17 F3
Bermillo de Sayago (Sp) 13 H6
Bernardia 24 A1
Bertelhe 15 H5
Besteirinhos 35 G3
Besteiros (Br) 16 C2
Besteiros (F) 35 G2
Béstida 14 C5
Bezelga 23 G2
Bica 18 C4
Bicada 31 G6
Bicas 23 H4
Bico (Vc) 10 D3
Bico (A) 14 C5
Bicos 30 C4
Bigas (Lordosa) 15 G5
Bigorne 15 G3

Bilho 11 G6
Biqueiras 18 C5
Biscoitos 39 H1
Bismula 21 E2
Bispo 35 G3
Bitaraes 15 E2
Bizarril 16 D5
Blancos (Sp) 11 G2
Boa Aldeia 15 F6
Boada (Sp) 17 H5
Boa Farinha 24 A2
Boalhosa 10 D4
Boa Ventura 40 B5
Boa Viagem 18 C4
Boavista (Le) 22 C3
Boa Vista 23 E1
Boavista (Po) 24 D4
Boavista (Be) 35 F1
Boavista do Paiol 30 B3
Boavista dos Pinheiros 30 B6
Bobadela (V) 11 H4
Bobadela (V) 12 B3
Bobadela (Co) 19 H2
Bocacara (Sp) 17 H6
Boca Chanza (Sp) 32 A6
Boca de Encumeada 40 B5
Boca do Inferno 26 A3
Bodiosa 15 G5
Boelhe 15 F3
Bofinho 19 E6
Bogajo (Sp) 17 G4
Bogalhal 16 D5
Bogas de Baixo 20 A5
Bogas de Cima 20 A4
Boialvo 19 E1
Boiças (S) 22 D5
Boiças (Se) 30 B1
Boidobra 20 B3
Boivaes 10 D4
Boivao 10 C2
Boleiros 23 F3
Bolembre 26 B2
Bolfiar 19 E1
Bolho 19 E2
Boliqueime 35 F3
Bolla (Sp) 21 H2
Bombarral 22 C5
Bombel 27 F3
Bom Jesus do Monte 10 D5
Borba 29 E2
Borba da Montanha 11 F6
Borba de Godim 15 F1
Borbela 15 H1
Bordeira 34 B3
Bornes 12 D6
Borrachina (Sp) 29 G4
Borralha (V) 11 F4
Borralha (A) 19 E1
Borralhal (Vi) 19 G2
Bostofrio 11 G4
Botao 19 E3
Botica Sete 26 C2
Boticas 11 H4
Bótoa (Sp) 25 G6
Bouça 12 C4
Bouceguedim 15 F4
Bouceiros 23 E2
Bouçoaes 12 C4
Bouro 11 E4
Bousés (Sp) 12 A3
Bouzas (Sp) 13 E1
Boxinos 20 A4
Boya (Sp) 13 G2
Braçais 19 F6
Bracial 30 B4
Braga 10 D5
Bragada 12 D4
Bragadas 11 G5

Bragado 11 H5
Bragança 13 E3
Bramadero (Sp) 32 B5
Branca 14 D5
Brandara 10 C3
Brandilanes (Sp) 13 H4
Brandim 11 G4
Branqueira 35 E4
Brasfemes 19 E3
Bravaes 10 D3
Bravo 19 G6
Brejao 34 B1
Brejo 30 C1
Brejo de Canes 27 E5
Brejos do Fetal 30 B1
Brenha 18 C4
Brenha 35 E1
Bretanha 40 A1
Brinches 31 H2
Brinço 12 C5
Brincones (Sp) 17 H2
Briteiros (Santo Estêvao) 11 E5
Britelo 11 E3
Britiande 15 H3
Brito 10 D6
Brogueira 23 F3
Brotas 27 H2
Brozas (Sp) 25 H2
Bruçó 17 F2
Brufe 11 E3
Brunheda 16 C1
Brunheira (Se) 30 C2
Brunheiras 30 B5
Brunhós 18 D4
Brunhosinho 13 F6
Brunhoso 13 E6
Buarcos 18 C4
Buçaco 19 F2
Bucelas 26 C2
Bucos 11 F5
Budens 34 B4
Budiño (Sp) 10 C1
Buenamadre (Sp) 17 H4
Bufarda 22 B5
Bugio 26 B4
Bugios 24 C1
Bujardo (Sp) 29 G5
Bunheira 34 B2
Bunheiro 14 C5
Bunhosa 18 D3
Burga 12 D6
Burgau 34 B4
Burgo 15 E4
Burgueira (Sp) 10 B2
Burinhosa 22 D2
Bustelo (V) 12 A3
Bustelo (P) 15 E2
Bustelo (P) 15 G4
Bustelo (Vi) 15 G4
Bustelo (A) 19 E1
Bustos 18 D1

Cabaços (Vc) 10 C4
Cabaços (Vi) 16 A3
Cabaços (Le) 19 F6
Caballo (Sp) 21 F5
Cabana Maior 10 D3
Cabanas (Vi) 19 G2
Cabanas (Se) 26 D4
Cabanas (F) 35 H3
Cabanas (F) 36 A3
Cabanas de Torres 22 D6
Cabanelas (B) 10 D5
Cabanelas (Br) 12 C5
Cabanelas (P) 14 C2
Cabeça 20 A3
Cabeça Alta 20 C1
Cabeça Boa 16 D2

Cabeça da Serra 31 E6
Cabeça das Pombas 23 E3
Cabeça da Velha 20 A2
Cabeça de Carneiro 29 E4
Cabeça do Velho 20 B2
Cabeça Gorda (L) 22 B5
Cabeça Gorda 30 B6
Cabeça Gorda (Be) 31 G3
Cabeço 28 A1
Cabeças 19 F6
Cabeça Santa 15 E3
Cabeceiras de Basto 11 F5
Cabeço 18 D2
Cabeço Alto (V) 11 G3
Cabeço Alto (C) 25 G1
Cabeço da Neve 19 F1
Cabeço de Vide 24 D6
Cabeço Monteiro 20 D5
Cabeço Rainha 19 H6
Cabeçudo 19 G6
Cabeza de Framontanos (Sp) 17 G2
Cabeza del Caballo (Sp) 17 G2
Cabezas del Pasto (Sp) 32 B5
Cabezas Rubias (Sp) 32 C5
Cabezo Gordo (Sp) 32 C4
Cabo Carvoeiro (Le) 22 B4
Cabo Carvoeiro (F) 34 D4
Cabo da Roca 26 A3
Cabo de Santa Maria 35 G5
Cabo de São Vicente 34 A4
Cabo de Sines 30 A3
Cabo Espichel 26 C5
Cabo Girao 40 B5
Cabo Mondego 18 C4
Cabo Raso 26 A3
Cabo Sardao 30 A6
Cabo Silleiro (Sp) 10 B1
Cabouco 40 B1
Cabração 10 C3
Cabreira 19 G4
Cabreiro (Vc) 10 D2
Cabreiro (Sp) 11 G2
Cabreiro (V) 11 H6
Cabreiroá (Sp) 12 B2
Cabrela 27 G4
Cabril (V) 11 F4
Cabril (Vi) 15 F4
Cabril (Co) 19 H4
Cabriz 11 G6
Cabrum 15 E5
Caçarelhos 13 G5
Caçarilhe 11 F6
Cacela Velha 36 A3
Cachao 12 C6
Cachaza (Sp) 21 F4
Cachofarra 27 E5
Cachopo 35 G2
Cachorrilla (Sp) 21 G6
Cachorro 39 F6
Cacia 14 D6
Cacilhas 26 C3
Cadafais 26 D1
Cadafaz (G) 16 C6
Cadafaz (Co) 19 G4
Cadafaz (Po) 24 B3
Cadalso (Sp) 21 G3
Cadaval 22 C5
Cadavos (Sp) 12 D2
Cadima 18 D3
Cadraço 19 F1
Caeiro 34 C1
Caeiros 30 C4
Caerinha 27 G5
Cafede 20 B6
Caia (Po) 25 E5
Caia (Po) 29 G2
Caiada 31 F6
Caia e São Pedro 29 F1

Caíde de Rei 15 F2
Caixeiro 28 D2
Calabor (Sp) 13 E2
Calañas (Sp) 32 D5
Caldas da Cavaca 16 A5
Caldas da Felgueira 19 H2
Caldas da Rainha 22 C4
Caldas de Aregas 15 G3
Caldas de Manteigas 20 B2
Caldas de Monchique 34 D2
Caldas de Vizela 11 E6
Caldas do Gerês 11 E4
Calde 15 G5
Cal de Bois 12 A6
Caldeira (Fa) 39 E5
Caldeira (T) 39 G1
Caldeira das Sete Cidades 40 A1
Caldeirao 39 F1
Caldelas (Sp) 10 C1
Caldelas (B) 10 D4
Caldelas (Le) 23 E1
Caldelas (Taipas) 10 D6
Calendario 10 D6
Calhariz 26 C5
Calheiros 10 C3
Calheta (M) 40 A5
Calheta (Sj) 39 G5
Calheta de Nesquim 39 G6
Calhetas 40 B1
Caloura 40 B2
Calvao (V) 12 A3
Calvao (A) 18 D2
Calvaria 23 H1
Calvaria de Cima 23 E2
Calvelhe 13 E5
Calvete 18 C5
Calvos 11 E5
Calvos de Randín (Sp) 11 G2
Calzadilla (Sp) 21 H4
Camacha (M) 40 B5
Camacha (M) 40 D3
Camachos 30 B6
Câmara de Lobos 40 B5
Camarção 18 C3
Camaroes 26 C2
Cambas 19 H5
Cambeses 10 D6
Cambra 15 F6
Cambres 15 H3
Camelo 19 G5
Caminha 10 B3
Campa de Arca 15 E5
Campanário 40 B5
Campea 15 G1
Campelo 19 F5
Campelos (Br) 16 C2
Campelos (L) 22 C5
Campia 15 F6
Campillo de Azaba (Sp) 21 G1
Campinho 29 E6
Campizes 18 D4
Campo (V) 11 H6
Campo (P) 14 D2
Campo (P) 15 E1
Campo (Vi) 15 G6
Campo (Le) 22 C4
Campobecerros (Sp) 12 B1
Campocerrado (Sp) 17 H5
Campo de Besteiros 19 G1
Campo de Cima 40 D3
Campo de Viboras 13 F5
Campo do Gerés 11 E4
Campogrande de Aliste (Sp) 13 H3
Campo Maior 25 F6
Campo Redondo 30 C4
Campos (Vc) 10 C2
Campos (V) 11 H4
Camposa 14 D2

Camposancos 10 B3
Canada 16 C4
Cañadas 22 D6
Canadelo 15 G1
Canal 31 E4
Canal de El Granado (Sp) 32 A6
Canal del Piedras (Sp) 36 C2
Canal de Ovar 14 C6
Canal de São Jorge 39 B-C5
Canal do Faial 39 E6
Canal do Sado Morgavel 30 C-D3
Canas de Santa Maria 19 G1
Canas de Senhorim 19 H1
Cañaveral (Sp) 21 H6
Canaveses 12 B5
Canaviais 28 B4
Candal (Le) 19 E6
Candal (Co) 19 F5
Candedo 12 B6
Candeeira 19 E1
Candelaria (Pc) 39 F6
Candelaria (Sm) 40 A1
Candemil (Vc) 10 C2
Candemil (P) 15 G2
Candosa 19 H3
Candoso 16 C1
Caneças 26 C2
Canedo 14 D3
Canedo de Basto 11 G6
Caneiro 23 F2
Canelas (A) 14 D5
Canelas (P) 15 E3
Canelas (A) 15 F4
Canha 27 F3
Canhas 40 A5
Canhestros 30 D3
Caniçada 11 E4
Caniçal 40 C5
Caniceira 18 C3
Caniço 40 B5
Canidelo 14 C3
Cano 28 C1
Cansado 24 A5
Cantanhede 18 D3
Cantarranas (Sp) 17 G6
Canto 18 C6
Caparica 26 C4
Caparrosa 15 F6
Capela (P) 15 E3
Capela (S) 24 B2
Capela (Po) 24 D6
Capelas 40 B1
Capelins 29 E4
Capelo 39 E5
Capeludos 11 H5
Capinha 20 C4
Caramulinho 19 F1
Caramulo 19 F1
Caranguejeira 23 E1
Carapacho 39 H3
Carapeços 10 C5
Carapetosa 24 D1
Carapinheira 18 D4
Carapito 16 B5
Caratao 19 G4
Caravelas 12 C6
Carbajalinos (Sp) 13 F1
Carbajo (Sp) 25 F2
Carballo (Vereal) (Sp) 11 F1
Carcalhinho 19 F5
Carção 13 F5
Carcavelos (S) 23 F2
Carcavelos (L) 26 B3
Cardanha 16 D2
Cárdigos 24 A2
Cardosa 20 A6
Caria (Vi) 16 A4
Caria (C) 20 C3

Caridade 28 D5
Carlao 16 B1
Carmoes 22 C6
Carnaxide 26 B3
Carneiro 15 G2
Carnicaes 16 C5
Carnide 18 D6
Carnota 22 D6
Carozoá (Sp) 11 H2
Carpio de Azaba (Sp) 17 F6
Cárquere 15 G3
Carracedo (Sp) 11 F1
Carracolva 10 D3
Carragosa 13 E3
Carrapatas 12 D5
Carrapateira 34 B3
Carrapatelo 28 D5
Carrapichana 20 B1
Carrascais 30 D1
Carrascal (S) 24 B1
Carrascal (Po) 24 B3
Carrascalinho 34 B2
Carrazeda de Ansiaes 16 C2
Carrazede 23 G3
Carrazedo (Br) 12 D3
Carrazedo (Vi) 16 A3
Carrazedo de Motenegro 12 B5
Carreço 10 B4
Carregado 26 D1
Carregal 16 A4
Carregal do Sal 19 G2
Carregosa 15 E4
Carregueira 23 G4
Carregueiros 23 G2
Carreira (B) 10 C6
Carreira (B) 10 D6
Carreiras 25 E4
Carriço 18 C5
Carril 15 F3
Carroqueiro 20 D5
Carros 31 G6
Cartaxo 23 E6
Cartaya (Sp) 36 D2
Caruncho 18 D5
Carva 12 A6
Carvalha 15 H4
Carvalhais (V) 11 H4
Carvalhais (Br) 12 C5
Carvalhais (Vi) 15 F5
Carvalhais (Co) 18 C5
Carvalhal (B) 10 C5
Carvalhal (Vi) 15 G5
Carvalhal (Vi) 15 G6
Carvalhal (G) 16 C4
Carvalhal (G) 16 C6
Carvalhal (Co) 19 G4
Carvalhal (C) 19 G6
Carvalhal (C) 20 C3
Carvalhal (Le) 22 C5
Carvalhal (S) 23 H3
Carvalhal (Po) 25 E5
Carvalhal (Se) 27 E6
Carvalhal (Be) 30 A6
Carvalhal Benfeito 22 C4
Carvalhal das Vinhas 25 E4
Carvalhal de Estanho 15 G6
Carvalhal de Vermilhas 15 F6
Carvalhal Redondo 19 H1
Carvalheira 15 E1
Carvalhelhos 11 H4
Carvalho (B) 11 F6
Carvalho (Co) 19 F3
Carvalho de Egas 16 C1
Carvalhos 14 D3
Carvalhosa (P) 15 E1
Carvalhosa (Vi) 15 G4
Carvalhoso 17 E2
Carvao 40 A1

Carvas 12 A6
Carvela 12 A4
Carviçais 17 E2
Carvide 18 C6
Carvoeira (L) 22 C6
Carvoeira (L) 26 B2
Carvoeiro (S) 24 B2
Carvoeiro (F) 34 D4
Casa Branca (Po) 25 F6
Casa Branca (Se) 27 E6
Casa Branca (Se) 27 G6
Casa Branca (E) 27 H5
Casa Branca (Po) 28 C2
Casa de Charneca 23 E5
Casais (S) 23 G2
Casais (F) 34 C2
Casais da Serra 22 D5
Casais de Granja 19 E5
Casais do Chafariz 22 C4
Casais Martanes 23 F3
Casais Robustos 23 F3
Casal 11 F5
Casal Comba 19 E2
Casal Cutelo 19 G6
Casal de Cinza 20 D1
Casal de Ermio 19 F4
Casal de São Jose 19 G4
Casal do Redinho 18 D4
Casal do Ribeiro 23 F1
Casal dos Barcelos 18 D5
Casal dos Bernardos 23 F1
Casalinho (Le) 18 D6
Casalinho (S) 23 F5
Casalinho (Po) 24 B5
Casalinho do Alfaiate 22 B6
Casal Nova (L) 22 B5
Casal Nova (C) 24 A2
Casal Novo (Le) 18 C6
Casal Novo (Co) 19 F4
Casal Vasco 16 A6
Casal Velho 22 C3
Casal Verde 18 C5
Casa Nova (Co) 18 C3
Casa Nova (Be) 30 B5
Casares 11 F5
Casas (L) 26 A3
Casas (F) 35 F2
Casas Baixas 35 H2
Casas de Don Gómez (Sp) 21 G5
Casas de Felipe (Sp) 21 E4
Casas de Fonte Cova 18 C6
Casas de Revelhos 23 H3
Casas de Zebreira 20 A5
Casas Louras 23 H3
Casas Novas 29 F2
Cascais 26 A3
Cascalho 27 E2
Casebres 27 G5
Casegas 20 A4
Casevel (S)23 F4
Casével (Be) 31 E5
Casillas de Coria (Sp) 21 G5
Casillas de Flores (Sp) 21 F2
Casis dos Faiscas 18 D3
Castaiço 16 B3
Castanheira (Vc) 10 C3
Castanheira (V) 11 G3
Castanheira (Br) 13 F6
Castanheira (G) 16 C5
Castanheira (G) 16 D6
Castanheira (Co) 19 H4
Castanheira (S) 23 H2
Castanheira de Pêra 19 F5
Castanheira do Ribatejo 26 D1
Castanheira do Vouga 19 E1
Castanheiro 18 C3
Castanheiro do Sul 16 B3
Castanhos 31 G6

Castedo (V) 16 B2
Castedo (Br) 16 D2
Casteiçao 16 C4
Castelaos 12 D5
Casteleiro 20 D3
Castelejo (C) 20 B4
Castelejo (Be) 31 E5
Castelhanas 18 C5
Castelhanos 35 H1
Castelo (B) 11 F6
Castelo (Vi) 15 G5
Castelo (Vi) 16 A3
Castelo (Vi) 19 F1
Castelo (Le) 19 F6
Castelo (S) 24 B2
Castelo Bom 17 E6
Castelo Branco (Br) 17 F1
Castelo Branco (C) 20 C6
Castelo Branco (Fa) 39 E6
Castelo de Maia 14 D2
Castelo de Paiva 15 E3
Castelo de Penalva 16 A6
Castelo de Vide 25 E4
Castelo do Neiva 10 B5
Casteloes 15 E5
Castelo Melhor 16 D3
Castelo Mendo 17 E6
Castelo Novo (C) 20 B4
Castelo Novo (S) 23 G3
Castelo Rodrigo 17 E4
Castillejo de Azaba (Sp) 21 G2
Castillejo de dos Casas (Sp) 17 F5
Castillejo de Martín Viejo (Sp) 17 F5
Castillo (Sp) 21 H2
Castiñeira (Sp) 12 C1
Castraz (Sp) 17 H5
Castrelo de Cima (Sp) 12 C2
Castrelo do Val (Sp) 12 B2
Castrelos (Sp) 12 D2
Castrelos 12 D3
Castro (Sp) 11 F1
Castro Daire 15 G4
Castro de Alcañices (Sp) 13 H5
Castro de Avelas 13 E3
Castro Laboreiro 11 E2
Castro Marim 36 B3
Castromil (Sp) 12 D2
Castro Roupal 13 E5
Castro Verde 31 E5
Castro Vicente 13 E6
Catalao 27 G4
Catarruchos 18 D3
Catifarras 30 B5
Cativelos 20 A1
Catrao 20 C4
Cava 19 G6
Cavadas 18 D2
Cavadoude 16 C6
Cavaleiro 30 A6
Cavalinhos 23 E2
Caveira 30 B2
Cavernaes 15 H6
Cavês 11 G5
Caxarias 23 F2
Caxias 26 B3
Caxinas 10 B6
Ceadea (Sp) 13 H4
Cebolais de Baixo 24 D1
Cebolais de Cima 24 D1
Cebollar (Sp) 36 D2
Ceclavín (Sp) 21 F6
Cedaes 12 C6
Cedainhos 12 C6
Cedillo (Sp) 24 D2
Cedovim 16 C3
Cedrim 18 E6
Cedros 39 E5
Cegonhas Novas 25 F1

Ceira 19 E4
Ceiroquinho 19 H4
Ceivaes 10 D1
Cela (Vc) 11 E1
Cela (Le) 22 D3
Celanova (Sp) 11 F1
Celas 12 D4
Cela Velha 22 D3
Celavisa 19 G4
Celeiro 11 F5
Celeirós (B) 10 D5
Celeiros (V) 12 B4
Celeirós (V) 16 A2
Celorico da Beira 16 B6
Celorico de Basto 11 F6
Centum Cellas 20 C2
Cepaes 11 E6
Cepedelo (Sp) 12 D1
Cepelos 15 E5
Cepoes (Vi) 15 H3
Cepoes (Vi) 15 H5
Cepos 19 H4
Cercal (Co) 18 D4
Cercal (L) 22 D5
Cercal (Se) 30 B4
Cercio 13 G5
Cerda 10 C2
Cerdedelo (Sp) 12 B1
Cerdeira (V) 11 H6
Cerdeira (Vi) 15 H4
Cerdeira (Co) 19 G4
Cerdeira (Co) 19 H3
Cerdeira (G) 21 E1
Cerdeirinhas 11 E4
Cerejais 17 E1
Cerejeira 20 A6
Cerezal de Peñahorcada (Sp) 17 F2
Cernache 19 E4
Cernache de Bonjardim 23 H1
Cernadilla (Sp) 13 G1
Cerralbo (Sp) 17 G4
Cerro (F) 35 F3
Cerro da Mina 31 F2
Cerro das Pedras 30 C6
Cerro do Anho 36 B2
Cerro Grande 31 F6
Cerros 28 D6
Cerva 11 G6
Cervaes 10 D5
Cervos 11 H4
Cesar 15 E4
Cespedosa de Agadones (Sp) 21 H2
Cete 15 E2
Cevada 31 F1
Cha 16 B1
Chacim (B) 11 F5
Chacim (Br) 12 D5
Chainça 23 E2
Chairos Carriça 12 C4
Chaissa Madriz 30 C5
Chamadouro 19 F3
Chamoim 11 E4
Chamusca 23 G4
Chança 24 C5
Chancelaria (S) 23 F3
Chancelaria (Po) 24 B5
Chancuda 31 F3
Chao da Parada 22 C3
Chao das Servas 24 C1
Chao da Va 20 B6
Chao da Velha 24 C3
Chao de Codes 24 A2
Chao de Couce 19 E6
Chao de Lopes 24 A2
Chao do Galego 24 C1
Chao Pardo 22 D2
Chaos 23 G2

Charneca (Le) 18 D6
Charneca (L) 26 C4
Charneca (Be) 32 A3
Charnequinha Silveiras 30 B4
Chas (Av) 15 F5
Chas (G) 16 D3
Chas de Tavares 16 A6
Chavaes 16 A3
Chaves 12 A4
Cheires 16 A1
Cheleiros 26 B2
Cheles (Sp) 29 F5
Chelo 19 F3
Chenlo (Sp) 10 C1
Chiqueda de Cima 22 D3
Choca do Mar 18 D2
Choça Queimada 36 B2
Chorente 10 C6
Chorlo (Sp) 25 H4
Chosendo 16 B4
Chouto 23 G5
Ciborro 27 H3
Cicouro 13 G4
Cidade 22 C3
Cidadelhe (Vc) 11 E3
Cidadelhe (G) 16 D4
Cidade Nova de Santo André 30 A2
Cid Almeida 32 A1
Cidral 21 E5
Cidreira 19 E3
Cilados 29 F2
Cilleros (Sp) 21 F4
Cimadas Cimeiras 24 B1
Cimadas Fundeiras 24 B1
Cima do Freixo 23 F3
Cimbres 15 H3
Cinco Vilas 17 E5
Cinfaes 15 F3
Cintados 36 A2
Cional (Sp) 13 G2
Cipérez (Sp) 17 H3
Cisterna 12 C2
Citania de Briteiros 11 E5
Ciudad Rodrigo (Sp) 17 G6
Clarianes 35 G3
Clarines 35 H1
Clavería (Sp) 25 F3
Cobreros (Sp) 13 E1
Codaval 12 A6
Codeçais (Vi) 15 G4
Codeçais (Br) 16 C1
Codeçoso (V) 11 F4
Codeçoso (B) 15 G1
Codesal (Sp) 13 G2
Codesseiro 16 C6
Codessoso 11 H4
Coedo (Sp) 11 G1
Coelheira 15 F5
Coelhoso 13 F4
Coentral 19 F5
Cogula 16 C5
Coimbra 19 E4
Coimbrao 18 C6
Coina 26 D4
Coito 36 A1
Coja 19 G3
Colar de Perdizes 27 F3
Colares 26 A3
Colaria 26 B1
Colmeal (Co) 18 D2
Colmeal (Co) 19 G4
Colmeal (C) 20 C2
Colmeias 23 E1
Colonia de la Estación (Sp) 17 E6
Colos (S) 24 A4
Colos (Be) 30 C5
Comeira 22 D1
Comenda 24 C4

Comporta 27 E6
Concavada 24 A3
Conceiçao (Be) 31 E4
Conceiçao (F) 36 A3
Concerçao 35 G4
Condeixa-a-Nova 19 E4
Condeixa-a-Velha 19 E4
Conehada 10 B4
Conejera (Sp) 17 G6
Conimbriga 19 E4
Conlelas 12 D3
Consolaçao 22 B4
Constance 15 F2
Constância 23 G3
Constantim 15 H1
Constatim 15 H1
Contenças 19 F3
Contenda 25 F6
Contensas de Baixo 20 A1
Contim (V) 11 G3
Contim (Br) 12 C2
Contim (Vi) 16 A3
Convento de Cristo 23 G3
Convento de Tomina 32 C2
Corbelle (Sp) 11 F1
Corcha 35 G1
Corchuela (Sp) 29 G2
Corcitos 35 G3
Cordinha 19 E3
Corga (B) 10 C6
Corga (A) 14 D4
Corga (G) 20 A3
Corgas 24 B1
Coria (Sp) 21 H5
Coriscada 16 C4
Cornes 10 C2
Corona 12 D2
Coronado 14 D1
Correias 23 E4
Correlha 10 C4
Corroios 26 C4
Corte 19 F1
Corte Azinha 32 A5
Corte Brique 30 C6
Corte Condessa 31 H3
Corte das Donas 36 B2
Corte da Velha 31 G5
Corte de Ouro 35 G2
Corte de São Tomé 36 A2
Corte do Cabo 35 F2
Corte do Gago 36 A2
Corte Figueira 35 F2
Cortegaça (A) 14 D4
Cortegaça (Vi) 19 F2
Cortegada (Sp) 11 H1
Corte Gafo de Baixo 31 H5
Corte Gafo de Cima 31 G5
Corte João Marques 35 G2
Cortelha (F) 35 G2
Cortelha (F) 36 A2
Cortém 22 C4
Corte Pequena (Be) 31 G5
Corte Pequena (Be) 31 H5
Corte Pinto 32 A5
Cortes (Vc) 10 D1
Cortes (C) 20 B3
Cortes (Le) 23 E2
Cortes (Be) 32 C2
Cortes de Baixo 31 G2
Cortes de Cima 31 G2
Corte Serranos 35 H2
Corte Sines 31 H5
Cortes Pereiras (Be) 30 D6
Cortes Pereiras (F) 31 H6
Corte Tabeliao 36 B1
Corte Vicente Eanes 31 E3
Corte Zorrinha 31 E6
Cortiçada (G) 16 B5

Cortiçada (Vi) 19 G1
Cortiçadas do Lavre 27 G3
Cortiço (V) 11 H3
Cortiço (G) 16 B6
Cortiço da Serra 16 B6
Cortiços 12 D5
Cortinhas 12 A6
Cortins 12 C5
Coruche 27 F1
Corujas 12 D5
Corujeira (Vi) 15 H5
Corujeira (G) 20 C1
Corujeiras 18 C2
Corujos 36 A2
Corva 26 C5
Corval 28 D5
Corveira 19 F1
Corvelo do Monte 15 G1
Corvillón (Sp) 11 G1
Cossourado 10 C5
Costa (Vc) 10 B4
Costa (Vc) 10 C2
Costa (B) 11 E6
Costa de Caparica 26 B4
Costa de Lavos 18 C4
Costa de Prata 22 C2
Costa de Santo André 30 A2
Costa do Estoril 26 A-B4
Costa do Sol 26 B4
Costa Nova 14 C6
Cota 15 H5
Cotas 16 B2
Cotelo 15 G3
Cótimos 16 C5
Coto 22 C4
Coucieiro 10 D4
Couco 27 H1
Coudelaria de Alter 24 C5
Coura 10 C3
Courelas (G) 16 C5
Courelas (É)28 D6
Courelas do Vale 27 G4
Cousso 11 E1
Coutada 20 B4
Couto (Vc) 10 D3
Couto (Sp) 11 E1
Couto (P) 14 D1
Couto de Esteves 15 E5
Couto de Mosteiro 19 G2
Covacha (Sp) 25 G4
Cova da Iria 23 F2
Cova da Lua 13 E2
Cova da Piedade 26 C4
Cova da Zorra 30 B5
Covao da Silva 18 D6
Covao de Lobo 18 D2
Covao do Feto 23 E3
Covao dos Mendes 18 D6
Covas (Vc) 10 C3
Covas (Sp) 11 G2
Covas (P) 15 E1
Covas (Co) 19 H3
Covas do Barroso 11 G4
Covas do Douro 16 A2
Covas do Monte 15 F4
Covas do Rio 15 F4
Covelaes 11 G3
Covelas 10 D5
Covelo (P) 14 D3
Covelo (Vi) 15 F5
Covelo (Co) 19 G3
Covelo de Gerés 11 F4
Covide 11 E4
Covilha 20 B3
Covoada 40 A1
Covoes 18 D2
Coz 22 D2
Cozcurrita (Sp) 13 H6

Crasto 10 D4
Crastos 22 D4
Crato 24 C5
Crecente (Sp) 11 E1
Crestuma 14 D3
Crias 10 B6
Cristelo (Vc) 10 C3
Cristelo (B) 10 C6
Cristiñade (Sp) 10 C1
Cristo de la Laguna (Sp) 17 H6
Croca 15 E2
Crucifixo 23 H4
Cruz (B) 10 D6
Cruz (Be) 31 H6
Cruzamento de Pegoes 27 F3
Cruz da Légua 23 E2
Cruz de João Mendes 30 B2
Cruzes 15 E6
Cualedro (Sp) 11 H2
Cuba 31 F2
Cubalhao 11 E1
Cubo da Benavente (Sp) 13 H1
Cujó 15 H4
Cumeada (C) 24 A1
Cumeada (F) 35 E3
Cumeada do Malhao 35 G2
Cumeira (Le) 22 D3
Cumiada 28 D6
Cumieira (V) 15 H2
Cumieira (Co) 19 E6
Cunha (Vc) 10 C3
Cunha (G) 16 B5
Cunha Alta 15 H6
Cunha Baixa 20 A1
Cunhas 11 G5
Cunheira 24 C4
Curalha 12 A4
Curia 19 E2
Curobos 12 C3
Currais 35 H2
Curral das Freiras 40 B5
Curros 12 A5
Curvos 10 B5
Custóias 16 C3

Dadim 12 B3
Dalvares 15 H3
Dardavaz 19 G2
Darque 10 B4
Dáspera 20 A6
Decermilo 16 A5
Degolados 25 F6
Degrácia Cimeira 24 B3
Degracias 19 E5
Deilao 13 F3
Delaes 10 D6
Delgada 22 C5
Deocriste 10 C4
Derreada Cimeira 19 G5
Desbarate 35 H3
Descargamaría (Sp) 21 H3
Desejosa 16 B3
Destriz 15 E6
Deva (Pontedeva) (Sp) 11 F1
Devesa (Sp) 12 B2
Dine 12 D2
Diogo Dias 35 H1
Diogo Martins 31 G6
Dios le Guarde (Sp) 17 H6
Dogueno 35 G1
Dois Portos 22 C6
Dómez (Sp) 13 H4
Domingos da Vinha 24 B3
Dominguiso 20 B4
Donai 13 E3
Dona Maria 26 B2
Doña María (Sp) 29 F3
Donas (Sp) 10 B1

Donas 20 B4
Dornelas (V) 11 G4
Dornelas (A) 15 E5
Dornelas (G) 16 B5
Dornelas do Zêzere 20 A4
Dornes 23 H1
Dornilas (Sp) 13 G1
Dos Hermanas (Sp) 25 G6
Dreia 19 H3
Duas Igrejas (B) 10 D4
Duas Igrejas (Br) 13 G5
Duas Igrejas (P) 15 E2
Dume 10 D5
Dunas de Cantanhede 18 C2-3
Dunas de Ovar 14 C4
Dunas de Quiaios 18 C3
Durao 17 E3

Edral 12 C3
Edrosa 12 D3
Edroso 12 D5
Ega 18 D4
Eira da Palma 35 H3
Eira de Calva 19 F4
Eirado 16 B5
Eira do Serrado 40 B5
Eiras 19 E3
Eiras Meiores 12 D4
Eirinha 31 H6
Eirinhas 32 A1
Eiriz 15 E1
Eiró 11 F5
Eirogo 10 C5
Eixes 12 C5
Eixo 14 D6
Eja 15 E3
El Almendro (Sp) 32 B6
El Batán (Sp) 21 H5
El Bodón (Sp) 21 G1
El Buitrón (Sp) 32 B4
El Campillo (Sp) 36 D1
El Carpio (Sp) 32 D4
El Cerro de Andévalo (Sp) 32 D5
El Cobujón (Sp) 32 D6
El Cubo de don Sancho (Sp) 17 H4
El Empalme (Sp) 36 C2
El Fresno (Sp) 21 G4
El Granado (Sp) 32 A6
Eljas (Sp) 21 F3
El Manzano (Sp) 17 H2
El Marco (Sp) 25 F5
El Moillarón (Sp) 25 F3
El Molino (Sp) 29 F3
El Payo (Sp) 21 F3
El Perrunal (Sp) 32 D5
El Portil (Sp) 36 D3
El Poyo (Sp) 13 G3
El Romeran (Sp) 36 B1
El Rompido (Sp) 36 D3
El Ronquillo (Sp) 29 H2
El Saúgo (Sp) 21 G2
El Tarro (Sp) 25 G4
El Terrón (Sp) 36 C3
El Toro (Sp) 32 C5
Elvas 29 F2
Embalse de Alcántara (Sp) 21 F6
Embalse de Alcántara (Sp) 25 H1
Embalse de Almendra (Sp) 17 H1-2
Embalse de Bao (Sp) 12 C1
Embalse de Borbollón (Sp) 21 G4
Embalse de Castro (Sp) 13 H5
Embalse de Cernadilla (Sp) 13 F1-2
Embalse del Agueda (Sp) 21 H1
Embalse de Lagunazo (Sp) 32 C6
Embalse de la Hoja (Sp) 32 D5
Embalse de las Conchas (Sp) 11 F2
Embalse de las Portas (Sp) 12 C1
Embalse del Calabazar (Sp) 32 D5

Embalse del Chanza (Sp) 32 A6
Embalse de los Machos (Sp) 36 C2
Embalse del Risco (Sp) 32 B6
Embalse de Pías (Sp) 12 D1
Embalse de Piedra Aguda (Sp)
    29 G3-4
Embalse de Piedras (Sp) 36 C1
Embalse de Portaje (Sp) 21 H6
Embalse de Puente Porto (Sp) 13 E1
Embalse de Rivera de Gata (Sp)
    21 G4
Embalse de Salas (Sp) 11 F2
Embalse de Sancho (Sp) 32 C6
Embalse de San Sebastián (Sp)
    12 D1
Embalse de Tres Picos (Sp) 32 B6
Embalse de Valparaíso (Sp) 13 G2
Embalse de Villar del Rey (Sp)
    25 H5
Embalse de Zamores (Sp) 25 F3
Embalse Grande (Sp) 32 C-D6
Encamaçao 22 B6
Encinasola (Sp) 32 D2
Encinasola de Los Comendadores
    (Sp) 17 G3
Entradas 31 F4
Entre Ambos-os-Rios 11 E3
Entrecinsa (Sp) 12 C1
Entre-os-Rios 15 E3
Entroncamento 23 G3
Envendos 24 B3
Enxabarda 20 B4
Enxara do Bispo 26 B1
Erada 20 B3
Ereira 22 D5
Erias (Sp) 21 H2
Ericeira 26 B1
Ermelo (Vc) 11 E3
Ermelo (V) 15 G1
Ermesinde 14 D2
Ermida (Vc) 11 E3
Ermida (Br) 12 D3
Ermida (V) 15 G4
Ermida (Co) 18 C2
Ermida (C) 24 B1
Ermidas Aldeia 30 D3
Ermidas Sado 30 C3
Erra 27 G1
Ervas Tenras 16 C5
Ervedal (Co) 18 C3
Ervedal (Co) 19 H2
Ervedal (Po) 24 C6
Ervededo 12 A3
Ervedeira 24 B5
Ervedosa (Br) 12 C4
Ervedosa (G) 16 C4
Ervedosa do Douro 16 B2
Ervideira 18 C6
Ervidel 31 E3
Ervilhal 15 G4
Ervoes 12 B4
Escalhao 17 E4
Escalos de Baixo 20 C6
Escalos de Cima 20 C6
Escalos do Meio 19 G5
Escanchinhas 35 F4
Escapaes 19 E2
Escarige 20 C3
Escarigo 17 E4
Escariz (Vc) 10 C4
Escariz (V) 15 H1
Escariz de Poiares 15 E4
Escaroupim 23 E6
Escornabois (Sp) 11 H1
Escudeiros 10 D6
Escuernavacas (Sp) 17 H4
Esculqueira (Sp) 12 C2
Escurquela 16 B3

Escusa (Po) 24 B4
Escusa (Po) 25 E4
Esfarrapada (Sp) 10 C1
Esfrega 19 H6
Esgueira 14 D6
Esmolfe (Vi) 15 H6
Esmoriz 14 C4
Espadaña (Sp) 17 H3
Espadanal 19 G3
Espadanedo (Br) 12 D4
Espadanedo (Sp) 13 G1
Espadanedo (Vi) 15 F3
Espargal 35 F3
Especiosa 13 G5
Espeja (Sp) 17 F6
Esperança (Co) 18 C4
Esperança (Po) 25 F6
Espiche 34 C4
Espinhal (Co) 19 F5
Espinhal (G) 20 D2
Espinheira 28 C5
Espinheiro 23 E4
Espinho (A) 14 C3
Espinho (Vi) 15 F6
Espinho (Vi) 19 F2
Espinho (Vi) 19 H1
Espinhosa 16 B3
Espinhosela 13 E3
Espinhoso 12 C3
Espírtu Santo 31 H6
Espite 23 F1
Espiuncá 15 F4
Esporoes 10 D5
Esposende 10 B5
Espragosa 31 F6
Estaçao de Ourique 31 E5
Estaçao de Viana 28 A6
Estacas 30 C6
Estafagem 27 F5
Estanqueiro 27 E1
Estarreja 14 D5
Este 10 D5
Esteiramantens 35 H4
Esteiro 19 H4
Estela 10 B6
Estelas 22 A4
Ester 15 G4
Estevais (Br) 16 D2
Estevais (Br) 17 E2
Esteveira 24 A4
Esteves 24 B2
Estibeira 30 B6
Estói 35 G4
Estômbar 34 D3
Estoraos (Vc) 10 C3
Estoraos (B) 11 E6
Estoril 26 B3
Estorninhos 36 A3
Estorninos (Sp) 25 G1
Estrada 35 H2
Estreito 19 H5
Estreito da Calheta 40 A5
Estreito de Câmara de Lobos 40 B5
Estrela 29 E6
Estremoz 28 D2
Esturaos 12 B4
Eucisia 16 D1
Évora 28 B4
Évora de Alcobaça 22 D3
Évoramonte 28 C3
Extremo 10 D2

Fábrica de São Pedro 20 C6
Facha 10 C4
Facho (Le) 22 D3
Facho (Be) 32 A3
Fadagosa (S) 24 B3
Fadagosa (Po) 25 E3

Fafe 11 E6
Faia 11 F6
Faial 40 B5
Faial da Terra 40 D2
Fail 15 G6
Failde 13 E4
Faioes 12 B4
Faja a Ovelha 40 A5
Faja de Cima 40 B1
Faja do Ouvidor 39 G5
Faja dos Cubres 39 H5
Faja Grande 39 E2
Fajao 19 H4
Fajazinha 39 E2
Fajoes 15 E4
Falcoeiras 28 D5
Famalicao (G) 20 C2
Famalicao (Le) 22 C3
Fanhais 22 D2
Fanhoes 26 C2
Faniqueira 23 E2
Fao 10 B5
Farelos 36 A1
Faria 10 C6
Farilhoes 22 A3
Fariza (Sp) 13 H6
Farminhao 15 G6
Faro 35 G4
Faro do Alentejo 31 F2
Farropa 25 E1
Fataca 30 B6
Fatauços 15 F5
Fatela 20 C4
Fátima 23 F2
Favacal 19 F5
Favaios 16 B1
Favela 31 E6
Favoes 15 F3
Fazamoes 15·G3
Fazenda 24 B5
Fazenda das Lajes 39 F3
Fazendas das Figueiras 27 F2
Fazendas de Almeirin 23 F5
Febres 18 D2
Feces de Abaixo 12 B3
Feces de Cima (Sp) 12 B3
Feira (Vc) 10 C4
Feira (Vi) 15 E6
Feirao 15 G3
Feitais 15 H1
Feiteira 35 G2
Feitos 10 C5
Feitosa 10 C4
Felgar 17 E2
Felgueira (A) 15 E5
Felgueira (Vi) 19 F2
Felgueiras (Br) 12 D6
Felgueiras (P) 15 F1
Felgueiras (Vi) 15 G3
Felgueiras (Br) 16 D2
Felizes 35 F2
Fenais da Ajuda 40 C1
Fenais da Luz 40 B1
Fermedo 15 E4
Fermela 14 D6
Fermentelos 18 D1
Fermil 11 F6
Fermoselle (Sp) 17 H1
Fernandilho 35 H2
Fernao Ferro 26 C4
Fernao Joanes 20 C2
Ferradosa (Br) 12 C4
Ferradosa (Br) 17 E1
Ferragudo 34 D4
Ferrairas (Le) 22 B4
Ferrairas (E) 29 E5
Ferral 11 F4
Ferreira (Vc) 10 C2

Ferreira (Br) 12 D4
Ferreira (P) 15 E2
Ferreira-a-Nova 18 C3
Ferreira de Aves 16 A5
Ferreira do Alentejo 31 E2
Ferreira do Zézere 23 H2
Ferreiras 35 E3
Ferreirim (Vi) 15 H3
Ferreirim (Vi) 16 B4
Ferreiros (B) 10 D5
Ferreiros (B) 11 E5
Ferreirós do Dao 19 G2
Ferrel 22 B4
Ferreras Arriba (Sp) 13 H2
Ferreros (Sp) 13 F1
Ferro (C) 20 C3
Ferro (Sm) 40 C1
Ferronha 16 B4
Fervença (V) 11 G6
Fervença (P) 15 F1
Fervença (Le) 22 D3
Fervidelas 11 G4
Feteira 18 D6
Feteiras 40 A1
Fiaes (Vc) 11 E1
Fiaes (V) 12 B4
Fiaes (Br) 14 D4
Fiaes (G) 16 B5
Fiaes do Rio 11 G3
Fiais da Beira 19 H2
Fialho 35 G1
Figueira (Vi) 15 H3
Figueira (Br) 17 E5
Figueira (C) 24 B1
Figueira (P) 25 F6
Figueira (F) 34 B4
Figueira (F) 34 C3
Figueira da Foz 18 C4
Figueira de Castelo Rodrigo 17 E4
Figueira de Lorvao 19 F3
Figueira dos Cavaleiros 31 E2
Figueira e Barros 24 C6
Figueiras (S) 23 G4
Figueiras (Be) 30 D3
Figueiras (Be) 31 F4
Figueiredo (B) 10 D5
Figueiredo (B) 10 D6
Figueiredo (C) 19 G6
Figueiredo de Alva 15 G5
Figueirinha (Be) 31 F5
Figueirinha (F) 35 G2
Figueiró da Granja 16 B6
Figueiró da Serra 20 B1
Figueiró do Campo 18 D4
Figueiró dos Vinhos 19 F6
Figueiros 22 D5
Figueiro (São Cipriano) 15 G6
Figueruela de Arriba (Sp) 13 G3
Fiolhoso 12 A6
Flamengos 39 E6
Flariz (Sp) 12 A2
Flegueiras (Vc) 11 E1
Flegueiras (Br) 12 D4
Flor da Rosa 24 C5
Florderrei (Sp) 12 B3
Fogueteiro 26 C4
Fóia 34 C2
Fóios 21 F3
Fojos 11 F6
Folgado 28 D2
Folgosa 15 H2
Folgosinho 20 B1
Folgoso 15 G4
Folhada 15 F2
Folhadal 19 H1
Folhadela 15 H1
Folques 19 G3
Fondevila (Lobios) (Sp) 11 F2

Fontainhas (P) 10 C6
Fontainhas (Se) 30 B1
Fontao 10 C4
Fontao Fundeiro 19 F5
Fonte Arcada 16 B4
Fonte Boa (B) 10 B5
Fonte Boa (Be) 31 E2
Fonte Boa da Brincosa 26 B1
Fonte da Pedra 23 E4
Fonte de Aldeia 13 G6
Fonte de Angeao 18 D2
Fonte de Corcho 35 G2
Fonte de Martel 18 C3
Fonte de Seixas 16 B2
Fonte de Telha 26 C4
Fontefria (Sp) 12 B2
Fonte Ladrao 13 G5
Fontelas (B) 11 F4
Fontelas (V) 15 H2
Fonte Limpa 19 G5
Fonte Longa (Br) 16 C2
Fonte Longa (G) 16 C3
Fonte Mercê 12 B5
Fontes (V) 15 H2
Fontes (Le) 23 E2
Fontes (S) 23 H2
Fontes 31 G2
Fonte Santa (C) 20 C6
Fonte Santa (F) 34 C2
Fontes da Matosa 34 D3
Fonte Zambujo 36 A1
Fontinha (Le) 18 C5
Fontinha (Be) 30 B6
Forcadela (Sp) 10 C2
Forcalhos 21 F2
Forjaes 10 B5
Forles 16 A4
Formariz (Sp) 13 H6
Formigais 23 G2
Formilo 15 H3
Fornalha (Be) 35 G1
Fornalha (F) 36 A1
Fornalhas Novas 30 C4
Fornalhas Velhas 30 C4
Fornelos (Sp) 10 B2
Fornelos (Vc) 10 C4
Fornelos (Sp) 10 D1
Fornelos (B) 11 E6
Fornelos (Vi) 15 F3
Fornilhos 32 C1
Fornillos de Aliste (Sp) 13 H4
Fornillos de Fermoselle (Sp) 13 G6
Forninhos 16 B6
Fornos 17 F2
Fornos de Algodres 16 B6
Fornos do Pinhal 12 B4
Forno Telheiro 16 B6
Foros da Adúa 27 H4
Foros da Caiada 30 C4
Foros da Fonte de Pau 27 G2
Foros da Fonte Seca 28 D4
Foros da Salgueirinha 27 F2
Foros das Malhadinhas 27 E1
Foros das Pombas 28 C4
Foros de Albergaria 27 F6
Foros de Benfica 23 F6
Foros de Casa Nova 30 C4
Foros de Vale de Figueira 27 G3
Foros do Arrao 23 H5
Foros do Baldio 27 G4
Foros do Biscainho 27 F2
Foros do Cortiço 27 H3
Foros do Freixo 28 D3
Foros do Mocho 23 H6
Foros do Pereira 30 B5
Foros do Queimado 28 C4
Fortaleza da Santa Catarina (F)
  34 D4

Forte de Nossa Senhora da Graça
  29 F2
Forte de Santa Luzia 29 F2
Fortes 36 A2
Fortios 24 D4
Fotoura 10 C2
Foz 23 H5
Foz de Alge 19 F6
Foz de Arouce 19 F4
Foz de Odeleite 36 B2
Foz de Sousa 14 D3
Foz do Arelho 22 C4
Foz do Arroio 34 C2
Foz do Douro 14 C2
Foz do Farelo 34 C2
Foz do Lisandro 26 A2
Foz do Sabor 16 D2
Foz Giraldo 20 A5
Fradellos (Sp) 13 H3
Fradelos 10 C6
Frades (B) 11 E5
Frades (Be) 12 C3
Fradizela 12 C4
Fraga Negra 11 E4
Fragosela 15 H6
Fragoso 10 C5
Fráguas (Vi) 15 H5
Fráguas (S) 23 E4
Fraiao 10 D5
França 13 E2
France (Vc) 10 B3
France (V) 12 A4
Francelos 16 B1
Franco 12 B6
Franqueada 35 F3
Franqueira (Sp) 10 D1
Franzilhal 16 B1
Fratel 24 C2
Frazao 15 E2
Freamunde 15 E1
Frechas 12 C6
Freches 16 C5
Freineda 17 E6
Freiria (V) 11 H6
Freiria (L) 26 B1
Freitas 11 E5
Freixeda (V) 11 H5
Freixeda (Br) 12 C6
Freixeda do Torrao 16 D4
Freixedas 16 D6
Freixedelo 13 E4
Freixial (Le) 23 E2
Freixial (E) 28 D2
Freixial (Sp) 29 F3
Freixial do Campo 20 B6
Freixianda 23 G1
Freixieiro 10 B3
Freixiel 16 C1
Freixiosa (Br) 13 G6
Freixiosa (Vi) 15 H6
Freixo (Vc) 10 C4
Freixo (P) 15 F2
Freixo (G) 16 D6
Freixo (Vi) 19 F2
Freixo (Co) 19 F4
Freixo da Serra 20 B1
Freixo de Baixo 15 F1
Freixo de Cima 15 F1
Freixo de Espada á Cinta 17 E3
Freixo de Numao 16 C3
Freixoeiro 24 B2
Freixofeira 26 B1
Frende 15 G3
Fresulfe 12 D2
Friande 11 E4
Friastelas 10 C4
Frido 15 G1
Frieiras 13 E5

Friestas 10 C2
Frioes 12 B4
Friúmes 19 F3
Fronfría (Sp) 13 H4
Fronteira 24 C6
Frossos 14 D6
Fuenteguinaldo (Sp) 21 G2
Fuenteliante (Sp) 17 G4
Fuentes de Oñoro (Sp) 17 F6
Funchal 40 B5
Funcheira 30 D5
Fundada 23 H2
Fundao 20 B4
Fungalvaz 23 F2
Furadouro (Av) 14 C4
Furadouro (Co) 19 E5
Furna do Enxorfe 39 H3
Furnas 40 C1
Furnas do Enxofre 39 H1
Furnazinhas 36 A2
Furtado 24 B3
Fuseta 35 H4

Gaeiras 22 C4
Gafanha da Boa Hora 18 C1
Gafanha da Encarnacao 14 C6
Gafanha da Nazaré 14 C6
Gafanha do Carmo 14 C6
Gafanhao 15 G4
Gafanhoeira 28 A3
Gafanhoeiras 28 D5
Gáfete 24 C4
Gagos 16 D6
Gaia 20 C2
Gaiate 19 F4
Gala 18 C4
Galafura 15 H2
Galegos 25 E4
Galende (Sp) 13 E1
Galifonge 15 G5
Galiñeiro (Sp) 10 C1
Galizes 19 H3
Gallegos de Argañan (Sp) 17 F6
Gallegos del Campo (Sp) 13 G3
Gallegos del Río (Sp) 13 H4
Galva 15 H3
Galveias 24 B6
Gâmbia 27 E4
Gamelas 16 D5
Gamil 10 C5
Gamones (Sp) 13 H6
Gándara 23 E1
Gandara de Espariz 19 G3
Gandarela 11 F6
Gandra (Vc) 10 C2
Gandra (Vc) 10 D3
Gandra (P) 14 D2
Garcaosinho 14 E0
Garcia (Le) 22 D1
Garcia (F) 35 H2
Gardete 24 C3
Garfe 11 E5
Garrochais 32 B2
Garvao 30 D5
Gata (Sp) 21 G3
Gatao (P) 15 F1
Gatao (Be) 31 G6
Gateira 16 D4
Gatoes 18 D4
Gaula 40 B5
Gave 11 E2
Gávea 10 B3
Gaviao (B) 10 D6
Gaviao (Po) 24 B3
Gaviao (C) 24 C2
Gaviao (Be) 30 C5
Gaviao (Be) 31 E4
Gaviaozinho 24 C1

Gebelim 12 D6
Genísio 13 G5
Gens 14 D3
Geraldes 22 B5
Geraz do Lima 10 C4
Gercal 19 F6
Gestaçõ 15 G2
Gesteira 18 D5
Gestosa (Br) 12 C3
Gestosa (Vi) 19 G2
Gestoso 15 E5
Gévora del Caudillo (Sp) 29 G2
Gia 15 F3
Giao 14 C1
Gibraltar (Sp) 32 B5
Giela 10 D3
Giesteira (A) 19 E1
Giesteira (S) 23 F3
Giesteiras 24 B1
Giestoso 11 F2
Gilmonde 10 C5
Gilvrazino 35 F3
Gimonde 13 E3
Ginetes 40 A1
Gioes 35 H1
Giralda 31 G3
Giraldos 31 F5
Glória 28 D3
Glória do Ribatejo 23 F6
Goaes (B) 10 D4
Goaes (B) 11 E4
Godeal 27 H3
Godiaes 11 G5
Godinhanços 10 D4
Goián (Sp) 10 B2
Góis 19 G4
Golega 23 G4
Golfeiras 12 C5
Golilla (Sp) 25 H4
Gomeciego (Sp) 17 H3
Gomes Aires 31 E6
Gomesende (Sp) 11 F1
Gonça 11 E5
Gonçalo 20 C2
Gonçalo Bocas 16 D6
Gondar (Vc) 10 C2
Gondar (B) 10 D6
Gondar (P) 15 G2
Gondarém (Vc) 10 B2
Gondarém (B) 11 F5
Gondelim 10 C2
Gondelim de Reiva 19 F3
Gondemaria 23 F2
Gondesende 12 D3
Gondifelos 10 C6
Gondomar (Sp) 10 B1
Gondomar (B) 11 E5
Gondomar (P) 14 D2
Gondomil 10 C2
Gondoriz 10 D3
Gondulfes (Sp) 12 B2
Gorgolim 27 F5
Gorjao 23 H5
Gorjoes 35 G3
Gosende 15 G3
Gostei 13 E3
Gouvaes da Serra 11 H6
Gouveia (Br) 16 D1
Gouveia (G) 16 D6
Gouveia (G) 20 B1
Gouveia (L) 26 A2
Gouvinhas 16 A2
Gove 15 G3
Graça 19 F6
Gracieira 22 C4
Gradil 26 B1
Gradiz 16 B4
Gralha 22 C3

Gralhas 11 H3
Gralhos (V) 11 H3
Gralhos (B) 13 E5
Gramaça 19 H3
Granado (Sp) 32 A6
Grandais 13 E3
Grande 19 G2
Grândola 30 C1
Granho 23 F6
Granho Novo 27 E1
Granja (Vc) 10 D2
Granja (V) 11 H4
Granja (Br) 13 G5
Granja (P) 14 C3
Granja (V) 16 B2
Granja (Vi) 16 B3
Granja (Co) 19 F3
Granja (Be) 29 F6
Granja do Ulmeiro 18 D4
Granjal 16 B4
Granja Nova (V) 11 G5
Granja Nova (Vi) 15 H3
Granjinha 16 B3
Grau 18 C6
Gravaz 15 H4
Gravelos 15 H1
Gregorio (Sp) 11 E1
Grijó (Br) 12 D5
Grijó (P) 14 D3
Grijó de Parada 13 E4
Grisuela (Sp) 13 G3
Groba (Sp) 10 B1
Grocinas 19 E5
Grovelas 10 D4
Grutas de Alvados 23 E3
Guadalupe (E) 28 B4
Guadalupe (Gr) 39 G3
Guadapero (Sp) 17 H6
Guadramil 13 F2
Guadramiro (Sp) 17 G3
Guajardo y Malhincada (Sp) 21 G4
Gualtar 10 D5
Guarda 20 D1
Guarda do Norte 18 C5
Guardao 15 F6
Guardeiras 14 C2
Guedelhas 31 F6
Guedieiros 16 B3
Guerreiro 31 F5
Guerreiros do Rio 36 B1
Guia (Le) 18 C6
Guia (F) 35 E3
Guijo de Coria (Sp) 21 H4
Guijo de Galisteo (Sp) 21 H4
Guilhabreu 14 C1
Guilhado 11 H5
Guilheiro 16 B4
Guilheta 10 B5
Guilhofrei 11 E5
Guilhufe 15 E2
Guillade (Sp) 10 D1
Guillarei (Sp) 10 C1
Guimaraes 11 E6
Guimil 10 D2
Guisande 14 D4
Guiso 31 H5
Guláns (Sp) 10 C1
Gulpilhares 14 C3
Gumiei 15 G5
Guxinde 11 F2

Hedroso (Sp) 12 D1
Herdadiña (Sp) 11 F2
Herguijuela de Ciudad Rodrigo (Sp) 21 H2
Hermisende (Sp) 12 D2
Hernán Pérez (Sp) 21 H3
Herrera de Alcántara (Sp) 25 E2

Herreruela (Sp) 25 G3
Higuera de Vargas (Sp) 29 G5
Hinojosa de Duero (Sp) 17 F4
Horcajo (Sp) 21 H2
Horta (G) 16 C3
Horta (Fa) 39 E6
Horta da Vilariça 16 D2
Hortas do Tabual 34 B4
Horta Seca 31 G2
Hortinhas 29 E4
Hoyos (Sp) 21 G4
Huélaga (Sp) 21 G4

Idanha-a-Nova 20 D6
Idanha-a-Velha 20 D5
Ifanes 13 H5
Igreja de Nossa Senhora da Penha 24 D4
Igreja Nova 26 B2
Igreja Nova de Sobral 23 G2
Igrejinha 28 B3
Ilha da Armona 35 H4
Ilha da Barreta 35 G5
Ilha da Culatra 35 H4
Ilha da Faro 35 G5
Ilha das Flores 39 E-F 2-3
Ilha de Santa Maria 40 B-C 2-3
Ilha de São Jorge 39 F5-H6
Ilha de São Miguel 40 A-D 1-2
Ilha de Tavira 35 H4
Ilha do Corvo 39 F1
Ilha do Faial 39 E5-6
Ilha do Pico 39 F-G6
Ilha do Porto Santo 40 D3
Ilha Graciosa 39 G3
Ilhas 28 B3
Ilhas Desertas 40 C-D6
Ilha Terceira 39 F-65
Ilhavo 14 C6
Ilhéu de Baixo ou da Cal 40 D4
Ilhéu de Cima 40 D3
Ilhéu de Ferro 40 D3
Illa (Sp) 11 E2
Infantado 27 E2
Infantas 11 E6
Inguias 20 C3
Insalde 10 C2
Insua 31 H2
Iruelos (Sp) 17 H2
Isidro (Sp) 29 G6
Isla Canela (Sp) 36 C3
Isla Cristina (Sp) 36 C3
Islas As Estelas (Sp) 10 B1
Isna 19 H6
Ituero de Azaba (Sp) 21 G1
Izeda 13 E5

Jabarrieja (Sp) 25 H6
Jalama (Sp) 21 F3
Jamprestes 23 G2
Janas 26 A2
Janeiro de Baixo 19 H5
Janeiro de Cima 19 H5
Jardim do Mar 40 A5
Jardo 21 E1
Jarmelo 16 D6
Javali 35 G3
Jazente 15 G2
Jerez de los Caballeros (Sp) 29 H6
Joane 10 D6
João Antao 20 D2
João Bom 40 A1
João Serra 31 G5
Jola (Sp) 25 F5
Jolda 10 D3
Jorja 23 F2
Jou 12 B6
Jovim 14 D3

Juizo 16 D4
Junça 17 E6
Juncais 16 B6
Juncal (Le) 22 D2
Juncal (C) 24 C2
Juncal do Campo 20 B6
Junceda 11 E4
Junceira 23 G2
Jungeiros 31 E3
Junqueira (P) 10 C6
Junqueira (Br) 13 F5
Junqueira (A) 15 E5
Junqueira (Be) 16 D1
Junqueira (F) 36 B3
Junquera de Tera (Sp) 13 H2
Juromenha 29 F3
Justel (Sp) 13 G1

La Alameda de Gardón (Sp) 17 F6
La Alamedilla (Sp) 21 F2
La Albergueria de Argañán (Sp) 21 F2
La Albuera (Sp) 29 H3
La Antilla (Sp) 36 C3
La Atalaya (Sp) 21 G3
La Atalaya (Sp) 21 H1
Laborato 35 H1
La Bouza (Sp) 17 F5
Labrojo 10 C3
Labruge 14 C1
La Chanca (Sp) 29 H6
La Cocosa (Sp) 29 G3
La Codosera (Sp) 25 F5
La Contienda (Sp) 32 D2
Ladaino 12 D6
Ladário 15 H6
Ladeira (C) 24 A2
Ladeira (S) 24 B2
Ladeira (C) 24 C2
Ladoeiro 20 D6
La Encina (Sp) 21 G1
La Encomienda (Sp) 29 G2
La Fontañera (Sp) 25 E4
La Fregeneda (Sp) 17 E3
La Fuente de San Esteban (Sp) 17 H5
Lagarejos (Sp) 13 G1
Lagarelhos (V) 12 A4
Lagarelhos (Br) 12 D3
Lagares (P) 15 E3
Lagares (P) 15 F1
Lagares (Co) 19 H2
Lagarinhos 20 A2
Lagarteira 19 E5
Lagoa (B) 11 F5
Lagoa (Br) 13 E6
Lagoa (Co) 18 C2
Lagoa (C) 23 H1
Lagoa (L) 26 B1
Lagoa (F) 34 D3
Lagoa (F) 35 H2
Lagoa (Sm) 40 B2
Lagoa Azul 40 A1
Lagoaça 17 F2
Lagoa Comprida 20 B2
Lagoa das Furnas 40 C2
Lagoa da Vela 18 C3
Lagoa de Albufeira 26 C5
Lagoa de Obidos 22 C4
Lagoa do Cao 22 D3
Lagoa do Fogo 40 B-C2
Lagoa Funda 39 E3
Lagoa Parada 19 E6
Lagoa Ruiva 23 E3
Lagoas 12 B4
Lagoa Verde 40 A1
Lago Bom 11 H5
Lago de Sanabria (Sp) 13 E1

Lago de Santo André 30 A2
Lagomar 13 E3
Lagos 34 C4
Lagos da Beira 19 H2
La Grulla (Sp) 29 F5
Lagunazo (Sp) 32 C5
La Isabel (Sp) 32 B6
Laje 10 D5
Lajedo 39 E3
Lajeosa (Vi) 19 G1
Lajeosa (G) 21 F3
Lajeosa do Mondego 16 C6
Lajes (G) 20 A2
Lajes (F) 35 H3
Lajes (Fl) 39 F3
Lajes (T) 39 G6
Lajes do Pico 39 G6
La Joya (Sp) 32 D5
Lalim 15 H3
Lama 10 C5
Lama Cha 11 G4
Lama de Arcos 12 B3
Lamalonga 12 C4
Lamares 16 A1
Lamarosa 23 G3
Lamas (V) 11 G6
Lamas (Sp) 12 A2
Lamas (A) 14 D4
Lamas (Vi) 15 G5
Lamas (Co) 19 E4
Lamas (L) 22 C5
Lamas de Ferreira 15 H5
Lamasdeite (Sp) 12 B2
Lamas de Mouro 11 E2
Lamas de Orelhao 12 B6
Lamas de Podence 12 D5
Lamas do Vouga 14 D6
Lamegal 16 D6
Lamego 15 H3
Lameira 11 F6
Lameira do Martins 24 B2
Lameiras (G) 16 D5
Lameiras (Le) 18 C6
Lameiras (Co) 19 G3
La Moheda (Sp) 21 G4
La Moralita (Sp) 17 H4
Lamosa 16 A4
Lamparona (Sp) 25 F5
Lampreia 24 B4
Lancada 26 D3
Lançadoiras 31 F6
Lanças 31 E3
Landal 22 D4
Landedo 12 D2
Landeira (Vi) 15 F5
Landeira (É) 27 F4
Landim 10 D6
Lanhas 10 D4
Lanhelas 10 B3
Lanheses 10 C4
Lapa (Vc) 10 D2
Lapa (Vi) 16 A4
Lapa (G) 20 A2
Lapa (S) 22 D6
Lapa (Be) 31 F4
Lapa do Lobo 19 H2
Lapa dos Dinheiros 20 A2
Lapas 23 F3
La Pedreira 40 D3
Lapela (Sp) 11 E1
La Peña (Sp) 17 G2
Lapones (Sp) 25 F3
La Portuguesa (Sp) 29 H3
Lara 10 D2
Larça 19 E3
Lardosa 20 C5
La Redona (Sp) 17 F4
La Redondela (Sp) 36 C3

Lares 18 C4
Largo da Coroa 14 C5
Larinho 16 D2
Laroá (Sp) 11 H2
La Rosa (Sp) 29 H3
Las Carboneras (Sp) 29 H1
Las Casiñas (Sp) 25 E4
Las Chilladeras (Sp) 32 D6
Las Hedradas (Sp) 12 D1
Las Herrerías (Sp) 32 B5
Las Huertas (Sp) 25 E4
Las Mesas (Sp) 21 F3
Las Navas (Sp) 21 F5
Las Palmeritas (Sp) 36 C3
Las Torrecillas (Sp) 29 G3
Las Torres de Aliste (Sp) 13 G3
Las Uces (Sp) 17 G3
Latedo (Sp) 13 F4
La Tejera (Sp) 13 E2
La Torerera (Sp) 32 D6
Laundos 10 B6
La Vaca (Sp) 32 A5
Lavacolhos 20 B4
Lavandeira 19 E1
La Vega (Sp) 25 F5
Lavegadas (Le) 18 C6
Lavegadas (Co) 19 F3
La Vídola (Sp) 17 G2
Lavos 18 C4
Lavra 14 C2
Lavradas (V) 11 H4
Lavradio 26 D3
Lavre 27 G3
Laza (Sp) 12 A1
La Zaraz de Pumereda (Sp) 17 F2
Lazarim 15 H3
Lebre 32 A4
Lebuçao 12 B4
Leça 14 C2
Leça da Palmeira 14 C2
Legua 31 G4
Leiradas 11 G5
Leirado (Sp) 10 D1
Leiria 23 E1
Leirosa 18 C5
Leitoes (B) 10 D6
Leitoes (Co) 18 D2
Lemede 18 D3
Lençao 13 E4
Lentiscais (C) 24 D1
Lentiscais (F) 35 F3
Lentisqueira 18 D2
Leomil 16 A4
Lepe (Sp) 36 C2
Lever 14 D3
Levira 18 D2
Liceia 18 C3
Ligares 17 E3
Lijo 10 C5
Lilela 12 B5
Limaos (V) 12 B4
Limaos (Br) 13 E5
Limões 11 G6
Linarejos (Sp) 13 F2
Lindoso 11 E3
Linhaceira 23 G3
Linhares (Br) 16 B2
Linhares (G) 20 C1
Linhares (Be) 31 F3
Lisbon 26 C3
Liteiros 23 F3
Livramento 35 H4
Livramento 40 B2
Lixa 15 F1
Lobao da Beira 19 G1
Lober (Sp) 13 H4
Lodoes 16 D1
Lodoselo (Sp) 11 H1

Loivo 10 B2
Loivos 12 A4
Loivos do Monte 15 G2
Lomar 10 D5
Lomba (P) 15 G2
Lomba (A) 18 D1
Lomba da Fazenda 40 D1
Lomba da Maia 40 C1
Lombador 31 F5
Lombardos 31 H6
Lombo 13 E6
Lombomeao 18 D1
Lomero (Sp) 32 D4
Longomel 24 B4
Longos 10 D5
Longos Vales 10 D2
Longra (P) 15 F1
Longra (Vi) 16 A3
Longroiva 16 C4
Lordelo (B) 10 D6
Lordelo (P) 15 E2
Lordelo (V) 15 H1
Loriga 20 A3
Los Cristales (Sp) 32 D6
Los Limonetes de Villalobos (Sp) 29 H3
Los Millares (Sp) 36 C1
Los Perales (Sp) 25 G2
Los Pérez (Sp) 32 C4
Lotao 35 H1
Loucainha 19 F5
Loulé 35 F3
Loureda 10 D2
Louredo (B) 11 E5
Louredo (B) 11 F4
Louredo (A) 14 D4
Louredo (V) 15 H2
Loureira 23 G1
Loureiro (A) 14 D5
Loureiro (Co) 19 E4
Loureiro de Silgueiros 19 G1
Loures 26 C2
Loureza (Sp) 10 B2
Louriçal 18 C5
Louriçal do Campo 20 B5
Louriceira (S) 23 F4
Louriceira (S) 24 A2
Lourido 11 E3
Lourinha 22 B5
Louro 10 C6
Lourosa (A) 14 D4
Lourosa (Co) 19 H3
Lousa (Be) 16 C2
Lousa (Co) 19 F4
Lousa (C) 20 C6
Lousa (C) 24 A2
Lousa (L) 26 C2
Lousada 15 E2
Lousadela 15 H5
Lousado (Sp) 10 B2
Lousando 14 D1
Lovelhe 10 B2
Lubián (Sp) 12 D1
Lucenza (Sp) 11 H2
Ludares 16 A1
Ludo 35 G4
Luelmo (Sp) 13 H6
Lufrei 15 G1
Lumbrales (Sp) 17 F4
Lumiar 23 G1
Luneda (Sp) 11 E1
Luso 19 E2
Lustosa (P) 15 E1
Lustosa (Vi) 15 G5
Luz (Br) 13 G4
Luz (Be) 29 E6
Luz (Gr) 39 H3

Luz de Tavira 35 H4
Luzianes 30 C6
Luzim 15 E2

Maçãinhas 20 C2
Macainhas de Baixo 20 C1
Maçal do Chao 16 C6
Maçao 24 B3
Maças de Caminho 19 E6
Maças de Dona Maria 19 F6
Maceda 14 D4
Macedo de Cavaleiros 12 D5
Macedo do Mato 13 E5
Macedo do Peso 13 F6
Maceira (Br) 12 C3
Maceira (Le) 22 D2
Machados (Be) 32 A2
Machados (F) 35 G3
Machico 40 C5
Machio 19 G5
Macieira (B) 10 C6
Macieira (A) 15 E5
Macieira (Vi) 15 G4
Macieira da Maia 14 C1
Macieira de Alcoba 15 E6
Macieira de Lixa 15 F1
Maçinhata do Vouga 14 D6
Maçores 16 D2
Maçussa 22 D5
Madalena (P) 14 C3
Madalena (G) 16 D4
Madalena (S) 23 G3
Madeira 19 G6
Madorra 10 B4
Mafra 26 B2
Mafrade 35 H2
Magdalena 39 F6
Magdalena do Mar 40 A5
Magoito 26 A2
Magueija 15 G3
Mahide (Sp) 13 G3
Maia (P) 14 C2
Maia (Sm) 40 C1
Maia (Sa) 40 C3
Maiorca 18 C4
Maiorga 22 D3
Mairos 12 B3
Mairos (Sp) 12 B3
Majuges (Sp) 17 G3
Malarranha 28 B2
Malcata 21 E3
Malhada (Vi) 15 H5
Malhada (Co) 19 H4
Malhada (Po) 29 F2
Malhada do Peres 36 A3
Malhada do Rei 19 H4
Malhada do Velho 30 A5
Malhadal 24 B1
Malhadas 13 G5
Malhada Sorda 21 F1
Malhadinha 30 B5
Malhado do Judeu 35 H3
Malhao 35 E1
Malhao 35 G3
Malho Pao 20 A3
Malhou 23 E4
Maljoga 24 A1
Malpartida 17 E5
Malpensado 30 B4
Malpica de España (Sp) 29 F3
Malpica do Tejo 25 E2
Malpique 32 B2
Malta 16 D5
Malvas (Sp) 10 C1
Malveira (L) 26 A3
Malveira (L) 26 B2
Mamarrosa 18 D2
Mamodeiro 18 D1

Mamouros 15 G5
Manadas 39 G5
Mancelos 15 F1
Mancoca 30 D3
Mandin (Sp) 12 B3
Mangualde 15 H6
Mangualde da Serra 20 B2
Manhoso 26 D4
Manhouce 15 F5
Manigoto 16 D5
Manique do Intendente 22 D5
Ma Noite 31 G6
Mansores 15 E4
Manta Rota 36 B3
Manteigas 20 B2
Manuel Galo 31 G6
Manzalvos (Sp) 12 D2
Manzanal de Arriba (Sp) 13 G2
Manzanal de los Infantes (Sp) 13 G1
Manzano (Sp) 17 F6
Maqueda 22 D4
Mar 10 B5
Maranhao 28 B1
Marateca 27 F4
Marchil 35 G4
Marco 11 G6
Marco 25 F5
Marco de Canaveses 15 F2
Margalha 24 B4
Marialva 16 C4
Marianos 23 G5
Maria Vinagre 34 B1
Marifranca (Sp) 21 H4
Marim 35 H1
Marinha das Ondas 18 C5
Marinha Grande 22 D1
Marinhais 23 E6
Marinhas 10 B5
Mariz 10 C5
Marmelar 31 H1
Marmeleira (Vi) 19 F3
Marmeleira (S) 23 E5
Marmeleiro (G) 20 D2
Marmeleiro (C) 24 A1
Marmelete 34 C2
Marmelos 12 C6
Marofa 17 E4
Maroto 31 E2
Maroufenha 30 B6
Marques 22 D3
Marrancos 10 D4
Marrazes 23 E1
Marteleira 22 B5
Martiago (Sp) 21 H2
Martianas 20 C4
Martillán (Sp) 17 F6
Martim (B) 10 D5
Martim (V) 12 B6
Martim Afonso 30 B1
Martim Longo 35 H1
Martin Branco 20 B5
Martinchel 23 G3
Martin de Yeltes (Sp) 17 H5
Martingança 22 D2
Martinhos da Luz 34 B4
Mártires 28 D2
Marvao 25 E4
Marvao Beira 25 E3
Marvila 19 F6
Marzagao 16 C2
Mascarenhas 12 C5
Masuedo (Sp) 17 G2
Mata (C) 20 C6
Mata (S) 23 F1
Mata (S) 23 F3
Mata (Po) 24 D4
Mata (L) 26 C1
Matacaes 22 C6

Mata da Rainha 20 C4
Mata de Alcántara (Sp) 25 H1
Mata de Lobos 17 E4
Mata Mourisca 18 C5
Matança 16 B6
Matas (Le) 18 C5
Matas (L) 22 B5
Matela (Br) 13 F5
Matela (Vi) 16 B6
Mateus 15 H1
Mato 10 C4
Mato de Miranda 23 F4
Matoeira 22 C4
Matos (S) 23 G2
Matos (Be) 31 F2
Matosinhos 14 C2
Maus de Salas (Sp) 11 G2
Má Velha 20 A3
Maxiais 24 D1
Maxial (C) 19 G6
Maxial (C) 20 A5
Maxial (L) 22 C6
Maxieira 24 B2
Mayorga (Sp) 25 F5
Mazaresfes 10 B4
Mazedo 10 D1
Mazes 15 H3
Mazouco 17 F2
Mea 15 F4
Meada 24 D3
Meadela 10 B4
Mealhada 19 E2
Meas do Campo 18 D4
Meca 22 D6
Mêda 16 C4
Medas 14 D3
Medeiros (Sp) 12 A3
Medelim 20 D5
Medroes 15 H2
Mega Cimeira 19 G5
Mega Fundeira 19 G5
Meia Praia 34 C4
Meimao 20 D3
Meimoa 20 D3
Meinedo 15 E2
Meios 20 C2
Meirinhos 17 E1
Meixedo (Vc) 10 B4
Meixedo (V) 11 H3
Meixedo (Br) 13 E3
Meixide 11 H3
Meixoes de Cima 10 D4
Meixomil 15 E1
Meles 12 C5
Melgaço 11 E1
Mêlhe 12 D4
Meliça 23 H2
Melides 30 B2
Melo 20 B1
Melres 15 E3
Melriça (Le) 19 E6
Melriça (C) 24 A2
Melrico 19 H6
Membrío (Sp) 25 G3
Memória 23 F1
Mendiga 23 E3
Mentiras 32 C1
Mentrestido 10 C3
Merelim 10 D5
Meruge 19 H2
Mesão Frio (B) 11 E6
Mesão Frio (P) 15 G2
Mesquita (Be) 31 H6
Mesquita (F) 34 D2
Mesquitela 16 B6
Mesquitela 17 E6

Messangil 32 B3
Messejana 30 D4
Messines 35 E3
Mestras 35 F1
Mestre Mendo 22 B4
Mexilhoeira Grande 34 C3
Mezio (Vc) 11 E3
Mezio (Vi) 15 G4
Midoes (Co) 19 F3
Midoes (Co) 19 H2
Mieza (Sp) 17 F2
Miguel Anes 36 A3
Milagres (Vc) 10 D2
Milagres (Le) 23 E1
Milano (Sp) 17 G3
Milhao 13 F3
Milharadas 30 C6
Milharado 26 C2
Milhazes 10 C6
Milheiros Lagoa 23 G1
Milreu 23 H2
Milreu 35 G4
Mina da Caveira 30 C2
Mina da Juliana 31 F3
Mina de São Domingos 32 A5
Mina de São João do Deserto 31 E4
Mina do Bugalho 29 E3
Mina do Lousal 30 C3
Minas dos Carris 11 F3
Minde 23 E3
Mindelo 14 C1
Minheo 11 H5
Minhocal 16 C6
Minhotaes 10 C6
Miño Cuevo (Sp) 13 H2
Mioes 35 E3
Mira 18 C2
Mira de Aire 23 E3
Miradezes 12 C5
Miradouro da Boa Vista 15 H2
Miragaia 22 B5
Miramar 14 C3
Miranda 10 D3
Miranda do Corvo 19 F4
Miranda do Douro 13 H5
Mirandela 12 C5
Miro 19 F3
Miuzela 21 E1
Moçarria 23 E5
Modivas 14 C1
Moes 15 G4
Mofreita 12 D2
Mogadouro (Br) 13 E6
Mogadouro (Le) 19 E6
Mogo de Ansiaes 16 C2
Mogofores 19 E2
Moimenta (Br) 12 D2
Moimenta (Vi) 15 F3
Moimenta da Serra 20 B2
Moimenta de Beira 16 A4
Moimenta de Maceira Dao 19 H1
Moinho da Quinta 15 H4
Moinho de Vento 31 E6
Moinhola 27 F4
Moita (A) 19 E2
Moita (Le) 19 F5
Moita (Le) 22 D2
Moita (Se) 26 D4
Moita da Roda 18 C6
Moita da Serra 19 G3
Moita do Boi 18 C5
Moita do Martinho 23 E2
Moita dos Ferreiros 22 C5
Moitas 24 B1
Moitas Venda 23 F3
Moitinha 27 E5
Moitinhas 34 D1
Moldes 15 F4

Moldones (Sp) 13 F3
Moledo (Vi) 15 G5
Moledo (L) 22 B5
Moledo do Minho 10 B3
Molelos 19 G1
Molezuelas de la Carballeda (Sp) 13 H1
Molianos 22 D3
Molinos 32 B2
Mombeja 31 F3
Mombuey (Sp) 13 G1
Monçao 10 D1
Moncarapacho 35 H4
Monchique 34 D2
Monde da Foz 27 E1
Mondim da Beira 15 H3
Mondim de Basto 11 F6
Monfebres 12 B6
Monforte 25 E6
Monforte da Beira 25 E1
Monfortinho 21 F5
Monfurado 27 H4
Moninho 19 H5
Monsanto (C) 20 D5
Monsanto (S) 23 E3
Monsaraz 29 E5
Monsul 11 E5
Montalegre 11 G3
Montalvao 24 D2
Montalvo (S) 23 H3
Montalvo (Be) 31 H4
Monte (B) 11 E5
Monte (A) 14 C5
Monte (M) 40 B5
Monte Alto (Be) 31 E5
Monte Alto (F) 35 E2
Monte Bom 26 B1
Monte Branco da Serra 32 B2
Monte Brasil 39 H2
Monte Carvalho 25 E4
Montechoro 35 E4
Monte Claro 24 C3
Monte Córdova 14 D1
Montecos 30 C4
Monte da Charneca 35 E3
Monte da Estrada 30 C5
Monte da Guia 39 E6
Monte da Légua 31 G5
Monte da Pedra 24 C4
Monte da Perdigova 31 E5
Monte das Flores 28 B4
Monte das Piçarras 27 F4
Monte de Aldeia 29 F6
Monte de Baixo Grande 36 A2
Monte de Goula 20 A6
Monte de Laje 32 A3
Monte de São Gens de Cidaï 14 D1
Monte do Bispo 20 C3
Monte do Outeiro 29 E4
Montedor 10 B4
Monte dos Corvos 31 H5
Monte dos Frades 27 F3
Monte dos Mestres 31 F6
Monte do Trigo 28 C5
Monte Escuro 40 C1
Monte Fernandes 31 H5
Monte Ferro (Sp) 10 B1
Monte Fidalgo 24 D2
Monte Gordo (C) 20 A6
Monte Gordo 26 D1
Monte Gordo (Sp) 36 B2
Monte Gordo (F) 36 B3
Monte Grande (Be) 30 D3
Monte Grande (F) 35 G3
Monteiras 15 G4
Monteiros 11 H5
Monte Juntos 29 E4
Montelavar 26 B2

Monte Margarida 21 E1
Montemor-o-Novo 27 H4
Montemor-o-Velho 18 D4
Montemuro 15 G4
Monte Nobre 31 F4
Monte Novo 27 F5
Monte Real 18 C6
Monte Redondo (Le) 18 C6
Monte Redondo (L) 22 C6
Monterredondo (Sp) 11 E1
Monterrei (Sp) 12 A2
Monte Ruivo 34 C3
Montes (Sp) 12 A2
Montes (G) 16 D6
Montes (S) 23 H2
Monte Sameiro 10 D5
Montes da Senhora 24 C1
Montes de Cima 34 C3
Montes de San Benito (Sp) 32 C5
Montesinho 13 E2
Montes Novos 35 G2
Monte Trigo 39 G5
Monte Velho 32 A2
Monte Viegas 31 G4
Montevil 27 F6
Montijo 26 D3
Montinho (Po) 25 E4
Montinho (Po) 25 E5
Montinho da Dourada 28 B1
Montinhos 31 E4
Montoito 28 D5
Montouto 12 D2
Monumenta (Sp) 13 H6
Mora (Br) 13 F6
Mora (E) 27 H2
Morais 13 E5
Moraleja (Sp) 21 G4
Moralina (Sp) 13 H6
Morcillo (Sp) 21 H5
Moreanes 31 H5
Moreira (Vc) 10 D2
Moreira (P) 14 C2
Moreira de Cima 19 H1
Moreira de Rei 16 C5
Moreira do Castelo 15 F1
Moreira do Lima 10 C3
Moreira do Rei 11 F6
Moreiras (Sp) 11 H2
Moreiras 12 A4
Morelena 26 B2
Morelinho 26 B2
Morgade 11 H4
Morgadinho 35 F1
Moronta (Sp) 17 G3
Morreira 10 D6
Mortágua 19 F2
Mós (Br) 13 E4
Mós (Vi) 15 G4
Mós (G) 16 C3
Mós (Br) 17 E2
Moscavide 26 C3
Mosende (Sp) 10 C1
Mosqueirao 30 C2
Mosteiro (B) 11 F5
Mosteirô 15 G4
Mosteiro (G) 16 B5
Mosteiro (Le) 19 F6
Mosteiro (C) 19 H6
Mosteiro (Be) 31 G4
Mosteiro de Santa Clara 14 C1
Mosteiro de Santa Maria da Vitória 23 E2
Mosteiro de Santa Maria de Alcobaça 22 D3
Mosteiros (Po) 25 E5
Mosteiros (Sm) 40 A1
Motrinos 29 E5
Mouços 15 H1

Mougás (Sp) 10 B1
Mougueira 24 A1
Mougueles 22 B6
Moura 32 A2
Moura Morta 15 G4
Mourao (Br) 16 C2
Mourao (E) 29 E6
Mouraz 19 G2
Moure (B) 10 C5
Moure (B) 10 D4
Mourentán (Sp) 11 E1
Mourilhe 11 G3
Mouriscas 24 A3
Mourisia 19 H3
Mouriz 15 E2
Mouronho 19 G3
Moutedo 15 E6
Moveros (Sp) 13 H4
Moz de Celas 12 D4
Mozelos 15 G6
Muda 30 B3
Mudo 35 F2
Muelas de los caballeros (Sp) 13 G1
Muga de Sayago (Sp) 13 H6
Muge 23 E6
Mugueimes (Munios) (Sp) 11 F2
Muimenta (Sp) 12 B2
Muna 15 F6
Mundao 15 H6
Murça (V) 12 A6
Murça (G) 16 C3
Murganheira 19 G4
Murgeira 26 B1
Múrias 12 C5
Murias (Sp) 13 E1
Muro 14 D1
Murtede 19 E2
Murteira 22 C5
Murteirinha 24 B2
Murtosa 14 C5
Musgos 32 A1
Muxagata 16 D3

Nabais 20 B1
Nabo 16 D1
Nadadouro 22 C4
Nagosa 16 A3
Nagozelo do Douro 16 B2
Namorados 31 G5
Nantes 12 A4
Nariz 18 D5
Navais 10 B6
Navalho 12 B6
Navallo (Sp) 12 B2
Navasfrias (Sp) 21 F3
Nave (G) 21 E2
Nave (Po) 25 F5
Nave (F) 34 C2
Nave de Haver 21 F1
Nave Redonda (G) 17 E4
Nave Redonda (Be) 34 D1
Nazaré 22 C2
Negreiros 10 C6
Negrelos (São Mamede) 15 E1
Negroes 11 G4
Negros 35 F2
Neiva 10 B4
Nelas 19 H1
Nesperal 23 H1
Nespereira (B) 11 E6
Nespereira (P) 15 E2
Netos 18 D5
Nevolgide 10 D4
Nigrán (Sp) 10 B1
Nine 10 C6
Ninho do Açor 20 B5
Nisa 24 C3
Nocedo do Val (Sp) 12 A2

Nogueira (B) 10 D5
Nogueira (Br) 13 E3
Nogueira da Montanha 12 B4
Nogueira do Cravo (A) 14 D4
Nogueira do Cravo (Co) 19 H3
Nogueiró 10 D5
Nora 28 D3
Nora (Sp) 29 H6
Nordeste 40 D1
Nordestinho 40 D1
Norte Grande 39 G5
Norte Pequeno 39 H5
Nossa Senhora da Graça do Divor 28 B4
Nossa Senhora das Neves 31 G3
Nossa Senhora da Torega 28 A5
Nossa Senhora de Boa Fé 28 A4
Nossa Senhora de Machede 28 C4
Nossa Senhora dos Remédios 15 H3
Noura 12 B6
Novelda del Guadiana (Sp) 29 H1
Nozelos (V) 12 B4
Nozelos (Br) 12 C4
Nozelos (Br) 16 D1
Nuez (Sp) 13 F3
Nugeira 11 H4
Numao 16 C3
Nunes 12 D3

Obidos 22 C4
O Canizo (Sp) 12 C1
O Castro (Sp) 12 C1
Odeceixe 34 B1
Odeleite 36 B2
Odelouca 34 D3
Odemira 30 B6
Odiáxere 34 C3
Odivelas (L) 26 C3
Odivelas (Be) 31 E2
Oeiras 26 B3
Oia 18 D1
Oimbra (Sp) 12 A3
Olalhas 23 H2
Olas 16 C3
Oldroes 15 E2
Oledo 20 C5
Oleiros (Vc) 10 D3
Oleiros (B) 10 D5
Oleiros (Br) 13 E3
Oleiros (A) 14 D4
Oleiros (C) 19 H6
Oleiros (Be) 34 C1
Olelas (Sp) 11 E3
Olhalvo 22 D6
Olhao 35 G4
Olhas 31 E3
Olho Marinho 22 C4
Oliva de la Frontera (Sp) 29 G6
Olivais (Le) 23 E1
Olivais (L) 26 C3
Olival (P) 14 D3
Olival (S) 23 F2
Oliveira (Sp) 10 D1
Oliveira 10 D6
Oliveira de Azeméis 14 D5
Oliveira de Barreiros 15 G6
Oliveira de Frades 15 F5
Oliveira do Bairro 19 E1
Oliveira do Conde 19 G2
Oliveira do Douro (P) 14 D3
Oliveira do Douro (Vi) 15 G3
Oliveira do Hospital 19 H2
Oliveira do Mondego 19 F3
Oliveirinha (A) 14 D6
Oliveirinha (Vi) 19 G2
Olivenza (Sp) 29 F3
Olleros de Tera (Sp) 13 H2

Olmedo de Camaces (Sp) 17 F4
Opeia 23 E1
Orada (E) 29 E2
Orada (Be) 31 H2
Orbacém 10 B3
Orca 20 C5
Ordem 31 G2
Orille (Sp) 11 G1
Oriola 28 B6
Oriz 10 D4
Orjais 20 C3
Ormeche 11 G4
Ortiga 24 A3
Ortigosa 18 C6
Orvalho 19 H5
O Seixo (Tomiño) (Sp) 10 B2
Ossela 15 E5
Ota 22 D6
Otero de Bodas (Sp) 13 H2
Otero de Sanabria (Sp) 13 F1
Ouca 18 D1
Ouguela 25 G6
Oura 12 A5
Oural 10 D4
Ourém 23 F2
Ourenta 18 D2
Ourique 31 E5
Ourondo 20 A4
Ourozinho 16 C4
Ousilhao 12 D3
Outao 26 D5
Outeiro (Vc) 10 B4
Outeiro (Vc) 10 C3
Outeiro (B) 10 D6
Outeiro (B) 11 F5
Outeiro (V) 11 G3
Outeiro (Br) 13 F4
Outeiro (Vi) 15 G5
Outeiro (Le) 19 E5
Outeiro (E) 29 E5
Outeiro Alvo 11 E2
Outeiro da Cabeça 22 C5
Outeiro da Cortiçada 23 E4
Outeiro de Gatos 16 C4
Outeiro do Forno 23 H3
Outeiro Seco 12 A4
Outil 18 D3
Outiz 10 C6
Ovadas 15 G3
Ovar 14 D5
Ovoa 19 G2

Paço (Vc) 10 B4
Paçó 12 D3
Paço (A) 14 D5
Paço (Sendim) 16 B3
Paço de Arcos 26 B3
Paço de Sousa 15 E2
Paço dos Negros 23 F6
Paço Ducal 29 E3
Paços (Vc) 10 C2
Paços (Vi) 15 F6
Pacos de Brandao 14 D4
Paços de Ferreira 15 E2
Paços de Gaiolo 15 F3
Paços Novos 23 F6
Padeiro 27 F1
Paderne (Vc) 11 E1
Paderne (F) 35 E3
Padim da Graça 10 D5
Padornelo 10 C2
Padornelo (Sp) 13 E1
Padrao (C) 20 B6
Padrao (Le) 23 E1
Padrao (C) 24 B2
Padroes 11 F4
Padroso 11 G3
Pádua Freixo 12 C4

Paiágua 20 A5
Paialvo 23 G3
Paiao 18 C5
Pailobo 21 E1
Painho 22 D5
Paio Mendes 23 H1
Paio Pires 26 C4
Pai Penela 16 C4
Pai Torto 12 B5
Pala (G) 16 D5
Pala (Vi) 19 F2
Palácios 13 F3
Palacios de Sanabria (Sp) 13 F1
Palaçoulo 13 G6
Palazuelo las Cuevas (Sp) 13 H3
Paleao 18 D5
Palhaça 18 D1
Palhais (G) 16 B5
Palhais (C) 23 H1
Palhais (Se) 26 D4
Palheirinhos 35 H3
Palheiro (V) 12 B6
Palheiros (Co) 19 E3
Palhotas 30 B1
Palma 27 F5
Palmaz 14 D5
Palme 10 C5
Palmeira (B) 10 D5
Palmeira (F) 36 B1
Palmeira de Faro 10 B5
Palmeiros 35 G3
Palmela 26 D4
Palvarinho 20 B6
Pampilhosa 19 E3
Pampilhosa da Serra 19 H5
Panasqueira (C) 20 A4
Panasqueira (Be) 30 D2
Pancas 26 D3
Panoias 30 D4
Panoias do Cima 20 D1
Panque 10 C5
Panxon (Sp) 10 B1
Parada (Vc) 11 E3
Parada (V) 11 G6
Parada (V) 12 D3
Parada (Br) 13 E4
Parada (A) 15 E5
Parada (Br) 17 E1
Parada (G) 21 E1
Parada de Bouro 11 E4
Parada de Cunhos 15 H2
Parada de Ester 15 G4
Parada de Gatim 10 C5
Parada de Gonta 19 G1
Parada de Moteiros 11 H5
Parada de Pinhao 16 A1
Parada do Corgo 11 H6
Paradanca 11 F6
Paradanta 20 B5
Paradela (Vc) 11 E3
Paradela (V) 11 G4
Paradela (V) 12 B3
Paradela (Br) 13 E6
Paradela (Br) 13 H5
Paradela (A) 15 E6
Paradela (Vi) 16 B3
Paradela de Guiaes 16 A2
Paradinha (Br) 13 F4
Paradinha (Vi) 16 A3
Paradinha de Besteiros 13 E5
Paradinha Nova 13 E5
Paraduça 15 H4
Parafita 11 G4
Paraiso 15 E3
Parambos 16 B2
Parâmio 12 D2
Paramos 14 C4
Paranho 15 F6

Parceiros 23 E1
Parceiros de São João 23 F3
Parchal 34 D3
Pardais 29 E3
Pardelhas (A) 14 C5
Pardelhas (V) 15 G1
Pardieiros (Vi) 19 H1
Pardieiros (Be) 32 B4
Pardilhó 14 D5
Pardo 24 C2
Pardornelos 11 H3
Pardoso (Sp) 11 H1
Parede 26 B3
Paredes (B) 10 B5
Paredes (V) 11 H5
Paredes (V) 11 H6
Paredes (Br) 13 E4
Paredes (P) 15 E2
Paredes da Beira 16 B3
Paredes de Coura 10 C3
Paredes de Viadores 15 F2
Paredes de Vitória 22 C2
Paredes do Gravo 15 F6
Parizes 35 G3
Parque da Pena 26 B3
Parque Nacional da Peneda-Gerés 11 F4
Parque Nacional Serra do Xures 11 F2
Parque Natural da Arrábida 26 D5
Parque Natural da Madeira 40 B5
Parque Natural da Ria Formosa 35 G4
Parque Natural da Serra da Estrela 20 B2
Parque Natural da Serra de São Mamede 25 E5
Parque Natural das Serras de Aire e Candeeiros 23 E3
Parque Natural de la Sierra de Aracena (Sp) 32 D2
Parque Natural de Montesinho 12 D2
Parque Natural de Sintra-Cascais 26 A2
Parque Natural do Alvao 11 G6
Parque Natural do Sudoeste Alentejano e Costa Vincentina 30 B5
Parra 25 F5
Partida 20 B5
Pasariegos (Sp) 13 H6
Pascoal 15 G6
Passagem 18 C6
Passô (Br) 13 F4
Passô (Vi) 15 H3
Passos (Br) 12 B6
Passos (Br) 12 C2
Pastores (Sp) 21 H1
Patacao 35 G4
Pataias 22 D2
Pataias Gare 22 D2
Paúl (C) 20 B4
Paúl (L) 22 B6
Paúl (S) 23 H3
Paúl do Mar 40 A5
Pavia 28 B2
Paymogo (Sp) 32 B5
Pazos (Sp) 11 H1
Pechao 35 G4
Pé da Serra 24 D3
Pedernaira 23 F1
Pé de Serra 22 D4
Pedintal 19 H6
Pedome 12 B3
Pedorido 15 E3
Pedrada 11 E2
Pedra Furada 10 C6
Pedraido 11 F5
Pedralba de la Pradería (Sp) 13 E2

Pedralva 11 E5
Pedrario 11 H3
Pedras Blancas 31 E4
Pedras de El Rei 35 H4
Pedras Negras 18 B6
Pedras Salgadas 11 H5
Pedreira (S) 23 G2
Pedreira (Sm) 40 D1
Pedreiras 23 E2
Pedrógao (Le) 18 B6
Pedrógao (C) 20 D4
Pedrogao (S) 23 F3
Pedrógao (E) 27 H3
Pedrógão (Be) 31 H2
Pedrógao Grande 19 G6
Pedrógao Pequeno 19 G6
Pedroso 14 D3
Pedroso de Acim (Sp) 21 H6
Pedroso de la Carballeda (Sp) 13 F2
Pedrotoro (Sp) 17 G6
Pega 20 D2
Pegarinhos 16 B1
Pego (A) 19 E2
Pego (S) 23 H3
Pegoes Estaçao 27 F4
Peireial 25 F1
Peirses 11 H3
Pelados 35 G2
Pelariga 18 D5
Peleias 12 C3
Pelmã 23 G1
Pena 35 F3
Penabeice 12 A6
Penacova 19 F3
Penafiel 15 E2
Penajóia 15 H2
Pena Lobo 20 D2
Penalva 32 B4
Penalva de Alva 19 H3
Penalva do Castelo 15 H6
Penamacor 20 D4
Pena Róia 13 F6
Penascais 10 D4
Pendilhe 15 H4
Peneda 11 E2
Penedo 23 H2
Penedo de Seixo 31 F4
Penedo Gordo 31 F3
Penedono 16 B3
Penela 19 E5
Penela da Beira 16 B3
Penha (B) 11 E6
Penha (Po) 25 E4
Penha de Aguia 16 D4
Penha Garcia 21 E5
Penha Longa 15 F3
Penhascoso 24 A3
Penhas da Saúde 20 B3
Penhas Juntas 12 D4
Peniche 22 B4
Penilhos 31 G5
Penim 10 C3
Penina 35 F2
Península de Tróia 27 E5
Pensalvos 11 H5
Penso (B) 10 D6
Penso (Vi) 16 B4
Penteado 26 D4
Pentes (Sp) 12 C2
Penude 15 H3
Peña Mira (Sp) 13 G2
Peña Nofre (Sp) 12 B1
Peñaparda (Sp) 21 G3
Peña Rubia (Sp) 11 E1
Peñas de Levante (Sp) 21 H4
Pepe 15 H1

Pepim 15 G4
Peque (Sp) 13 H1
Pêra 35 E3
Peraboa 20 C3
Pêra do Moço 16 C6
Perafita 14 C2
Perais 24 D2
Peral (L) 22 C5
Peral (C) 24 C2
Peral (F) 35 G3
Peralejos de Abajo (Sp) 17 H3
Peralejos de Arriba (Sp) 17 H3
Perales del Puerto (Sp) 21 G4
Peralva 35 H2
Peras 19 F5
Peras Ruiu 23 F2
Pêra Velha 16 A
Percira 15 G1
Perdigao 24 C2
Perdigón (Sp) 29 G6
Peredo (Br) 13 E6
Peredo (Br) 17 G1
Peredo dos Castelhanos 16 D3
Pereira (V) 11 G4
Pereira (Br) 12 B6
Pereira (Vi) 16 A5
Pereira (Co) 18 D4
Pereira (F) 34 C3
Pereiras 34 E1
Pereiro (Sp) 12 C1
Pereiro (Vi) 15 F4
Pereiro (G) 16 D5
Pereiro (A) 19 E2
Pereiro (G) 20 A2
Pereiro (S) 23 G1
Pereiro (S) 24 A3
Pereiro (F) 35 H3
Pereiro (F) 36 A1
Pereiro de Palhacana 22 C6
Pereiros (Br) 16 C1
Pereiros (Vi) 16 C3
Pereiros (C) 20 B5
Perelhal 10 C5
Pereña (Sp) 17 G2
Perero (Sp) 32 C3
Pergulho 24 B2
Pema Seca 35 E2
Pemes 23 F4
Peroguarda 31 E2
Pêro Moniz 22 C5
Pêro Negro 34 C2
Pêro Pinheiro 26 B2
Pêro Ponto 35 G2
Pêro Soares 20 C1
Pêro Viseu 20 C4
Perozinho 14 D3
Perraes 19 E1
Perre 10 B4
Perucha 23 G1
Pescueza (Sp) 21 G6
Pés de Pontes 15 F6
Pesinho 20 B4
Peso (Vc) 11 E1
Peso (Br) 13 F6
Peso (P) 15 G2
Peso (C) 20 B4
Peso (Le) 22 C3
Peso (Be) 31 H2
Peso da Régua 15 H2
Pessegueiro (Co) 19 G5
Pessegueiro (S) 24 A4
Pessegueiro (F) 35 G1
Pessegueiro do Vouga 15 E6
Peta 23 G6
Petisqueira 13 F3
Peva (Vi) 15 H4
Peva (G) 17 E6
Pias (Vc) 10 D2

Pías (Sp) 12 D1
Pias (S) 23 G2
Pias (E) 28 D4
Pias (Be) 31 H4
Pias (Be) 32 A3
Picamilho 31 H4
Picanceira 26 B1
Picao 15 G4
Piçarras 31 E5
Picarrel 28 D4
Pico (B) 10 D4
Pico (Pc) 39 F6
Pico Alto 40 B2
Pico da Esperança 39 G5
Pico da Vara 40 D1
Pico de Castelo 40 D3
Pico de Regalados 10 D4
Picoes 17 E2
Picoitos 31 H6
Picones (Sp) 17 G3
Pico Ruivo 40 B5
Picos 34 C2
Pico São Mamede 25 E4
Picote 13 G6
Picoto 14 D3
Piedade (A) 19 E1
Piedade (Pc) 39 G6
Piedras Albas (Sp) 25 G1
Pilado 18 C6
Pindelo 14 D4
Pindelo dos Milagres 15 G5
Pinela 13 E4
Pinelo 13 F4
Pingarelhos 18 D5
Pinhal 35 F3
Pinhal de Leiria 18 B6
Pinhal do Norte 16 C1
Pinhal do Urso 18 C5
Pinhal Novo 26 D4
Pinhanços 20 A2
Pinhão 16 B2
Pinheiro (B) 11 E5
Pinheiro (P) 15 E3
Pinheiro (Vi) 15 F5
Pinheiro (Vi) 15 G4
Pinheiro (G) 16 A5
Pinheiro (A) 19 F3
Pinheiro (Se) 27 E5
Pinheiro da Bemposta 14 D5
Pinheiro de Coja 19 G3
Pinheiro Grande 23 G4
Pinheiro Novo 12 C2
Pinheiros (Vc) 10 D2
Pinheiros (Vi) 16 A3
Pinheiro Velho 12 C2
Pinhel (G) 16 D5
Pinhel (S) 23 F2
Pinho (Vi) 11 H4
Pinho (Vi) 15 G5
Pinhôa 22 C5
Pinilla de Fermoselle (Sp) 13 G6
Pino (Sp) 13 H5
Pino de Valencia (Sp) 25 E4
Pinoucas 15 F6
Pintado 23 G2
Pínzio 16 D6
Piñeira (Sp) 11 G1
Piódao 19 H3
Piornedo (Sp) 12 B2
Pipas 29 E6
Pisão (Av) 19 E3
Pisão (Po) 24 D5
Pisco 16 B5
Pisoes (V) 11 G4
Pisoes (Le) 22 D2
Pisoes (Be) 32 A2
Pisoes-Moura 32 A2
Pitoes das Júnias 11 G3

Pixeiros (Sp) 12 C1
Playa América (Sp) 10 B1
Playa Canela (Sp) 36 C3
Playa de Isla Cristina (Sp) 36 C3
Playa de la Antilla (Sp) 36 C3
Pó 22 C5
Pobladura de Aliste (Sp) 13 G3
Pocariça 18 D2
Poceirao 27 E4
Pocinho (G) 16 D2
Pocinho (F) 36 A3
Poço Barreto 34 D3
Poço do Canto 16 C3
Poço do Inferno 20 B2
Poço dos Câes 19 E5
Poços 31 E4
Podame 10 D2
Poden.ce 12 D5
Podentes 19 E5
Poiares (V) 15 H2
Poiares (Br) 17 E3
Poiso 40 B5
Poldra 34 B3
Pomar 20 A6
Pomares (G) 16 D6
Pomares (Co) 19 H3
Pomar Grande 30 B2
Pomba 35 E1
Pombal (Br) 12 D6
Pombal (Br) 16 C1
Pombal (Le) 18 D6
Pombalinho (Co) 19 E5
Pombalinho (S) 23 F4
Pombeiro da Beira 19 G3
Pombeiro de Riba Vizela 11 E6
Pombeiros 31 F4
Pondras 11 G4
Ponta 40 D3
Ponta da Agulha 40 B1
Ponta da Ajuda 40 C1
Ponta da Atalaia (F) 34 A4
Ponta da Atalaia (F) 34 B2
Ponta da Barca 39 G3
Ponta da Bretanha 40 A1
Ponta da Calheta 40 D4
Ponta da Caveira 39 F3
Ponta da Cruz 37 F5
Ponta da Ferraria 40 A1
Ponta da Galera 40 B2
Ponta da Garça 40 C2
Ponta da Ilha 39 G6
Ponta da Lamporeira 22 B6
Ponta da Madrugada 40 D1
Ponta da Piedade 34 C4
Ponta da Queimada 39 G6
Ponta da Ribeira 40 D1
Ponta das Contendas 39 G6
Ponta da Torre 34 B4
Ponta de Almadena 34 B4
Ponta de Laje 26 B4
Ponta Delgada (Fl) 39 F2
Ponta Delgada (Sm) 40 B2
Ponta Delgada (M) 40 B5
Ponta de Sagres 34 A4
Ponta de São Jorge 40 B5
Ponta de São Lourenço 40 C5
Ponta do Albarnaz 39 E2
Ponta do Arnel 40 D1
Ponta do Castelo (F) 35 E4
Ponta do Castelo (Sm) 40 C3
Ponta do Cintrao 40 B1
Ponta do Clérigo 40 B5
Ponta do Faial 40 D2
Ponta do Garajau 40 B5
Ponta do Mistério 39 G6
Ponta do Pargo 40 A5
Ponta do Queimado 39 G6
Ponta dos Covinhos 22 C3

Ponta dos Ilhéus 39 E3
Ponta do Sol 40 A5
Ponta dos Rosais 39 F5
Ponta do Topo 39 H6
Ponta do Tristao 37 E3
Ponta Garça 40 C2
Pontal 34 A3
Pontao 19 E6
Ponta Torrais 39 F1
Ponte 10 D4
Ponteareas (Sp) 10 D1
Ponte Barxas (Sp) 11 E1
Ponte da Barca 10 D3
Ponte de Lima 10 C4
Ponte de Olo 11 G6
Ponte de Sôr 24 A5
Ponte de Vagos 18 D2
Ponte do Abade 16 B4
Ponte do Rol 22 B6
Ponteira 11 F4
Pontelha 10 B5
Ponte Nova 15 F1
Pontével 23 E6
Ponte Velha 19 F4
Pontido 11 H6
Pontinha 24 B5
Pópulo 12 A6
Porcejal 18 D6
Porrais 13 E6
Porreiras 10 C2
Porriño (Sp) 10 C1
Portagem 25 E4
Portaje (Sp) 21 G6
Portalegre 25 E5
Portas do Capitao Mór 26 D2
Portas do Mardo do Cao 26 D2
Portas do Mouchao da Cabra 26 D2
Porteirinhos 31 F6
Portel 28 C6
Portela (Vc) 10 D2
Portela (Br) 13 E3
Portela (Vi) 15 G6
Portela (Co) 18 D3
Portela (Le) 22 C5
Portela (C) 24 A1
Portela (C) 24 A2
Portela (F) 35 H2
Portela 40 B5
Portela das Corchas 34 D2
Portela de la Canda (Sp) 12 D1
Portela de Leonte 11 E3
Portela de Santa Eluália 11 G5
Portela de Vade 10 D4
Portela do Fojo 19 G5
Portela do Homem 11 F3
Portela do Lagarto 11 E2
Portelas 34 C3
Portelinha (Vc) 11 E1
Portelinha (Se) 30 B4
Portelo 13 E2
Portezuelo (Sp) 21 H6
Portillo del Pardonelo (Sp) 13 E1
Portimao 34 D3
Portinho da Arrábida 26 D5
Porto (Sp) 12 D1
Porto 14 D2
Porto Alto 26 D2
Portocamba (Sp) 12 B1
Porto Carvoeiro 14 D3
Porto Covo 30 A4
Porto da Balça 19 H4
Porto da Calada 22 B6
Porto da Cruz 40 B5
Porto da Espada 25 E4
Porto das Barcas 30 A6
Porto de Barcas 22 B5
Porto de Lagos 34 D3
Porto de Leixoes 14 C2

Porto de Mós 23 E2
Porto de Ovelha 21 E1
Porto do Carro 22 D2
Porto do Codeço 15 H4
Porto Formoso 40 C1
Porto Moniz 37 E3
Porto Mouro 30 D2
Porto Novo 22 B5
Portos 11 F2
Portunhos 18 D3
Portuzelo 10 B4
Possacos 12 B5
Pousada 20 D1
Pousada de Saramagos 10 D6
Pousadas Verdas 18 D5
Pousaflores 19 E6
Pousafoles do Bispo 20 D2
Pousos 23 E1
Poutena 18 D2
Póvoa (V) 11 G5
Póvoa (Br) 13 G5
Póvoa (Vi) 15 H4
Póvoa (V) 16 B2
Póvoa da Atalaia 20 C5
Póvoa das Quartas 19 H2
Póvoa de Lanhoso 11 E5
Póvoa d'El-Rei 16 C5
Póvoa de Midoes 19 G2
Póvoa de Palmeira 19 E2
Póvoa de Penafirme 22 B6
Póvoa de Penela 16 B3
Póvoa de Rio de Moinhos 20 B5
Póvoa de Santa Iria 26 C2
Póvoa de Santarém 23 F5
Póvoa de São Miguel 32 B1
Póvoa de Varzim 10 B6
Póvoa do Concelho 16 C5
Póvoa e Meadas 24 D3
Povolide 15 H6
Pozo del Camino (Sp) 36 C3
Pozos de Hinojo (Sp) 17 H4
Pozuelo de Zarzón (Sp) 21 H4
Pradela 12 A5
Prado 10 D5
Prado (Sp) 12 A1
Pradoalvar (Sp) 12 B1
Pradocabalos (Sp) 12 C1
Prado Gatao 13 G6
Prados (G) 16 C5
Prados (G) 20 C1
Pragança 22 D5
Praia (Gr) 39 H3
Praia (Sm) 40 B3
Praia Azul 22 B6
Praia da Aguda 14 C3
Praia da Alagoa 36 B3
Praia da Areia Branca 22 B5
Praia da Arrifana 34 B2
Praia da Arvore 14 C1
Praia da Bordeira 34 B3
Praia da Caparica 26 B4
Praia da Carreagem 34 B2
Praia da Consolação 22 B4
Praia da Cordama 34 A4
Praia da Culatra 35 H4
Praia da Falesia 35 F4
Praia da Galé 35 E4
Praia da Ilha 30 A4
Praia da Ilha de Faro 35 G4
Praia da Ilha de Tavira 36 A4
Praia da Ingrina 34 B4
Praia da Manta Rota 36 B3
Praia da Mareta 34 A4
Praia da Oura 35 E4
Praia da Penedo 34 B3
Praia da Ponta Ruiva Eiras 34 A4
Praia da Rocha 34 D4
Praia da Salema 34 B4

Praia da Samouqueira 34 B1
Praia das Cabanas 36 A3
Praia das Cascas 36 A4
Praia das Furnas 30 A5
Praia das Maças 26 A2
Praia da Vitoria 39 G6
Praia da Zambujeira 30 A6
Praia de Agudela 14 C2
Praia de Ançao 35 F4
Praia de Ancora 10 B3
Praia de Areinho 14 C5
Praia de Beliche 34 A4
Praia de Boa Nova 14 C2
Praia de Burgau 34 B4
Praia de Cabedelo 10 B4
Praia de Cascais 26 B3
Praia de Comporta 22 C4
Praia de Cortegaça 14 C4
Praia de Dona Ana 34 C4
Praia de Ericeira 26 A1
Praia de Esmoriz 14 C4
Praia de Espinho 14 C4
Praia de Faro 35 G4
Praia de Furadouro 14 C4
Praia de Fuseta 35 H4
Praia de Labruge 14 C1
Praia de Lavadores 14 C3
Praia de Leirosia 18 C5
Praia de Magoito 26 A2
Praia de Maria Luisa 35 F4
Praia de Melides 30 A2
Praia de Mira 18 C2
Praia de Moledo 10 B3
Praia de Monte Branco 14 C5
Praia de Monte Clérigo 34 B2
Praia de Monte Gordo 36 B3
Praia de Morgavel 30 A4
Praia de Murração 34 A3
Praia de Odeceixe 34 B1
Praia de Ofir 10 B5
Praia de Porto Covo 30 A4
Praia de Quarteira 35 F4
Praia de Ribeiro 22 B5
Praia de Samarra 26 A2
Praia de Santo André (P) 10 B6
Praia de Santo André (Se) 30 A2
Praia de São Lourenço 26 A1
Praia de São Sebastiao 26 A1
Praia de São Torpes 30 A3
Praia de Suave Mar 10 B5
Praia de Tonel 34 A4
Praia de Vale de Figueiras 34 B3
Praia do Amado 34 B3
Praia do Baleal 22 B4
Praia do Barranco 34 B4
Praia do Barril 36 A4
Praia do Carvalhal 30 A6
Praia do Carvalho 34 D4
Praia do Castelejo 34 A4
Praia do Farol 35 G5
Praia do Foz do Arelho 22 C4
Praia do Guincho 26 A3
Praia do Martinhal 34 A4
Praia do Norte 39 E5
Praia do Porto Novo 22 B5
Praia do Rei Coriço 22 B4
Praia do Ribatejo 23 G3
Praia do Salgado 22 C3
Praia do São Telheiro 34 A4
Praia dos Mouranitos 34 A3
Praia dos Olhos de Agua 35 F4
Praia dos Tres Irmaos 34 C4
Praia do Vale do Lobo 35 F4
Praia Grande (L) 26 A2
Praia Grande (Be) 30 A5
Praia Nova 22 C3
Praia Velha 22 D1
Praia Verde 36 B3

Prainha (Pc) 39 G6
Prainha (M) 40 C5
Prazeres (E) 29 E1
Prazeres (M) 40 A5
Preguinho 15 F5
Presa (Co) 18 D2
Presa (Co) 18 D5
Préstimo 15 E6
Proença-a-Nova 24 B1
Proença-a-Velha 20 D5
Progo (Sp) 12 B2
Prova 16 C4
Provesende 16 A2
Provoação 40 C2
Puebla de Argeme (Sp) 21 H5
Puebla de Azaba (Sp) 21 F2
Puebla de Guzmán (Sp) 32 B5
Puebla de Sanabria (Sp) 13 F1
Pueblonuevo del Guadiana (Sp) 29 H2
Puente de Sanabria (Sp) 13 F1
Puente Romano (Sp) 25 G1
Puercas (Sp) 13 H3
Puertas (Sp) 17 H3
Puerto de la Zarza (Sp) 32 C4
Puerto de los Brisos (Sp) 25 H5
Puerto de los Castaños (Sp) 21 H6
Puerto de los Conejeros (Sp) 25 G5
Puerto de Outeiro de Augas (Sp) 11 F1
Puerto de Perales (Sp) 21 G3
Puerto Nuevo (Sp) 21 H2
Puerto Seguro (Sp) 17 F5
Puerto Viejo (Sp) 21 H2

Quadrazais 21 E3
Quarteira 35 F4
Quartos 35 G3
Quatrim 35 H4
Quatrim do Sul 35 H4
Quatro Lagoas 19 E5
Quebradas 22 D5
Queguas (Sp) 11 F2
Queijada 10 C4
Queimadela 11 E5
Queira 15 G6
Queiriga 15 H5
Queiriz 16 B5
Queirogás (Sp) 12 B2
Quelfes 35 H4
Queluz 26 B3
Querença 35 G3
Quiaios (Co) 18 C3
Quiaios (Co) 18 C4
Quinta (A) 18 D1
Quinta (Be) 31 G6
Quinta da Cascalheira 16 B2
Quinta da Corona 30 C3
Quinta da Estrada 16 A5
Quinta de Péro Martins 16 D4
Quinta de Santa Maria 28 A6
Quinta de Vale de Peña 13 F4
Quinta do Anjo 26 D4
Quinta do Estácio 31 G3
Quinta do Lago 35 F4
Quinta do Pinheiro 28 B1
Quinta do Ricos 14 C5
Quinta do Rio 20 A2
Quinta dos Bernardos 16 D5
Quinta do Sousa 27 F4
Quintana (Sp) 13 E1
Quintanilha 13 F3
Quinta Nova 16 D5
Quintás (Sp) 11 F2
Quintas (V) 11 H4
Quintas (Av) 14 D6
Quintas da Torre 20 C4
Quintas do Norte 14 C5

Quintela (V) 12 B4
Quintela (Vi) 15 G6
Quintela de Azurara 15 H6
Quintela de Humoso (Sp) 12 C1
Quintela de Lampacas 12 D5
Quintela de Leirada (Sp) 11 F1
Quintos 13 G3
Quirás 12 C2

Ra 27 H4
Rabaça 25 F5
Rabaçal (G) 16 C4
Rabaçal (Co) 19 E5
Rabacinas 24 C1
Rabal (Sp) 11 H2
Rabal (Sp) 12 B3
Rabal (Br) 13 E3
Rabanales (Sp) 13 H3
Rábano de Aliste (Sp) 13 G3
Rábano de Sanabria (Sp) 13 F1
Rabo de Peixe 40 B1
Rabo do Lobo 30 B4
Raimonda 15 E1
Rairiz de Veiga (Sp) 11 G1
Raiva (A) 15 E3
Raiva (Co) 19 F3
Ramalhais 19 E6
Ramalhal 22 C6
Ramalhosa 22 D4
Raminho 39 G1
Ramo Alto 28 D4
Randín (Sp) 11 G2
Ranha de São João 18 D6
Ranhados 16 C3
Raposa 23 F6
Raposeira 34 B4
Rapoula 16 C6
Rapoula do Côa 21 E2
Ras (P) 15 E2
Ras (Vi) 16 A5
Rasca 31 F3
Rates 10 C6
Ratoeira 16 C6
Real 15 E3
Rebolia 18 D5
Rebolosa 21 E2
Rebordainhos 12 D4
Rebordaos 13 E4
Rebordelo (Br) 12 C4
Rebordelo (A) 15 E4
Rebordelo (P) 15 G1
Rebordoes (Vc) 10 C4
Rebordoes (P) 15 E1
Reboreda 10 C2
Recarei 15 E2
Recezinhos 15 F2
Redinha 18 D5
Redondo 28 D4
Redondos 18 D5
Refega 13 F3
Refoios do Lima 10 C3
Refojos de Riba de Ave 14 D1
Regadas (P) 11 F6
Regadas (P) 15 F2
Rego (B) 11 F6
Rego (É) 29 F2
Rego da Barca 16 D2
Rego da Murta 23 G1
Reguengo 25 E4
Reguenga 14 D2
Reguengo 27 H4
Reguengo do Fetal 23 E2
Reguengo Grande 22 C5
Reguengos de Monsaraz 28 D5
Reigada 17 E5
Reigadinho 16 C5
Reigoso 11 G4
Reliquias (E) 28 D3

Relíquias (Be) 30 C5
Relva 40 A2
Relva da Louça 24 B2
Relvas (Co) 19 H4
Relvas (C) 20 B4
Relvas (Le) 22 D4
Relvas Verdes 30 B3
Relva Velha 19 H3
Remal 40 A5
Remédios (Le) 22 B4
Remedios (Sm) 40 A1
Remelhe 10 C6
Remesal (Sp) 13 F1
Remondes 13 E6
Rendo 21 E2
Rendufe (Vc) 10 C3
Rendufé (B) 10 D5
Rendufe (V) 12 B5
Represa 24 D1
Requeixo 14 D6
Requejo (Sp) 13 E1
Requiao 10 D6
Requias (Sp) 11 G3
Reriz 15 G4
Resende 15 G3
Reserva Nacional de Sierra Culebra
   (Sp) 13 G2
Reserva Natural da Berlenga 22 A4
Reserva Natural das Dunas de São
   Jacinto 14 C6
Reserva Natural d'Ilha Berlenga
   22 A4
Reserva Natural do Estuário do Sado
   27 E5
Reserva Natural do Estuário do Tejo
   26 D2
Reserva Natural do Paúl de Arzila
   18 D4
Reserva Natural do Paúl de Boqui-
   lobo 23 F4
Reserva Natural do Sapal de Castro
   Marim e Vila Real de Santo Ant-
   ónio 36 B3
Reserva Natural Serra da Malcata
   21 E3
Retaxo 24 D1
Retiro 29 G1
Retorta (Sp) 12 A2
Retorta 31 H3
Retortillo (Sp) 17 H5
Revel 12 A6
Reveles 18 C4
Rexaldia 23 F3
Riachos 23 F4
Ria da Costa Nova 14 C6
Ria de Aveiro 14 C5
Ria Formosa 35 G4
Riba de Ave 10 D6
Riba de Aves 18 C6
Ribadelago (Sp) 13 E1
Riba de Mouro 11 E2
Ribadouro 15 F3
Ribafeita 15 G5
Ribafria (Le) 22 B5
Ribafria (Le) 22 D4
Ribalonga (V) 12 A6
Ribalonga (Br) 16 B2
Ribamar (L) 22 B5
Ribamar (L) 22 B5
Ribamondego 20 B1
Ribarteme (Sp) 10 D1
Ribas 18 C3
Ribeira (Vc) 10 C4
Ribeira (B) 11 E4
Ribeira (A) 14 C5
Ribeira (Co) 19 F4
Ribeira Branca 23 F3
Ribeira Brava 40 A5

Ribeira Cha 40 B2
Ribeira da Cerca 34 C2
Ribeira da Erra 23 G6
Ribeira da Figueira 31 E2
Ribeira da Foupana 36 A1
Ribeira da Gema 30 C4
Ribeira da Isna (C) 19 H6
Ribeira da Isna (C) 24 A1
Ribeira da Janela 40 A4
Ribeira da Meimoa 20 C4
Ribeira da Murtega 32 D1
Ribeira da Pega 16 D6
Ribeira da Raia 28 B1
Ribeira das Alcáçovas 27 H5
Ribeira das Cabras 16 D6, 21 E1
Ribeira da Serta 19 H6
Ribeira da Sor 23 H6
Ribeira de Abrilongo 25 F6
Ribeira de Aguiar 17 E4
Ribeira de Alcarrache 29 E6
Ribeira de Alenquer 22 C-D6
Ribeira de Alge 19 F5
Ribeira de Algibre 35 F3
Ribeira de Alportel 35 H3
Ribeira de Alpreade 20 C5
Ribeira de Alvacar 31 H5
Ribeira de Arades 21 E5
Ribeira de Ardila 32 A-B1
Ribeira de Asseca 29 E3
Ribeira de Azambuja 28 C5
Ribeira de Azevel 29 E5
Ribeira de Brenhas 32 A-B2
Ribeira de Campilhas 30 C4
Ribeira de Canha 27 F3
Ribeira de Caria 20 C3
Ribeira de Carreiras 31 G6
Ribeira de Chouto 23 G5
Ribeira de Cobres 31 F4
Ribeira de Coja 15 H6
Ribeira de Corona 30 C3
Ribeira de Curral da Velha 31 F5
Ribeira de Divor 27 G2
Ribeira de Figueiró 24 C3
Ribeira de Fraguas 15 E5
Ribeira de Godelim 29 F6
Ribeira de Grândola 30 C2
Ribeira de Lavre 27 G3
Ribeira de Limas 31 H4
Ribeira de Lucefece 28 D3
Ribeira de Marateca 27 G4
Ribeira de Mós 17 E3
Ribeira de Muge 23 F-G6
Ribeira de Nisa 24 D3
Ribeira de Odearce 31 G2
Ribeira de Odeleite 36 A2
Ribeira de Odelouca 34 D2-3
Ribeira de Odivelas 31 E2
Ribeira de Oeiras 31 F6
Ribeira de Ota 22 D6
Ribeira de Pena 11 G5
Ribeira de Peramanca 28 B5
Ribeira de Santa Margarida 24 B6
Ribeira de Santo Estêvão 27 E2
Ribeira de São Cristovao 27 H5
Ribeira de São Domingos 30 C3-4
Ribeira de São João 24 D3
Ribeira de Seda 24 C5
Ribeira de Seixe 34 C2
Ribeira de Serrazola 24 C6
Ribeira de Sor 24 B-C4
Ribeira de Teja 16 C3
Ribeira de Tera 28 B2
Ribeira de Terges 31 F4
Ribeira de Torgal 30 C5
Ribeira de Touroes 17 E6, 21 F1
Ribeira de Toutalga 32 B2
Ribeira de Ulme 23 G4
Ribeira de Vale do Cobrao 27 E2

Ribeira de Valverde 28 A5
Ribeira de Zacarias 17 E1
Ribeiradio 15 E5
Ribeira do Alamo 28 D5
Ribeira do Almadafe 28 B1-2
Ribeira do Almuro 29 E1-2
Ribeira do Aravil 21 E6, 25 F1
Ribeira do Enxoé 32 A3
Ribeira do Fernando 24 A4
Ribeira do Murtigao 32 C2
Ribeira do Roxo 30 D3
Ribeira dos Aivados 31 E4
Ribeira do Salto 30 C5
Ribeira dos Carinhos 16 D6
Ribeira do Seissal 30 C5
Ribeira do Vascao 35 G1
Ribeira do Zebro 29 F6
Ribeira Grande (Po) 24 D6
Ribeira Grande (Sm) 40 B1
Ribeira Nova da Baronia 31 E1
Ribeirao 10 C6
Ribeira Quente 40 C2
Ribeiras 39 G6
Ribeira Seca (Sj) 39 H5
Ribeira Seca (Sm) 40 B1
Ribeirinha (V) 12 A5
Ribeirinha (Br) 12 C6
Ribeirinha (Fa) 39 E5
Ribeirinha (T) 39 G6
Ribeirinha (Sm) 40 B1
Ribeirinho 10 C3
Ribeiro Frio 40 B5
Ribolhos 15 G4
Rincón del Obispo (Sp) 21 H5
Rio 20 A4
Rio Agueda (Sp) 17 F4
Rio Agueda 19 F1
Rio Agueda (Sp) 21 G2
Río Alagón (Sp) 21 G5
Río Alburrel (Sp) 25 E3
Río Alcarrache (Sp) 29 G5
Rio Alfusqueiro 15 E6
Rio Aliste (Sp) 13 G-H3
Rio Almonda 23 F4
Rio Alva 19 G3
Rio Alviela 23 E4
Rio Angueira 13 F5
Rio Arade 34 D3
Rio Arda 15 E4
Río Arnoia (Sp) 12 A1
Río Arrago (Sp) 21 G4
Rio Arunca 18 D4
Rio Asseca 23 E5
Rio Ave 10 C6, 11 E5
Rio Azere 11 E2
Rio Azibo 12 D5, 13 E5
Rio Barosa 15 H3
Rio Beça 11 H4
Rio Beságueda 21 E4
Rio Boco 18 D1
Rio Caia 25 E6, 29 F1
Rio Caima 15 E5
Rio Caldo 11 E4
Rio Calvo 12 B4
Río Camaces (Sp) 17 F3-4
Rio Carnide 18 C5
Rio Cávado 10 C5, 11 F4-G3
Rio Ceira 19 F4
Rio Chança 32 A5
Rio Côa 16 D3, 21 E2
Rioconejos (Sp) 13 G1
Río Confrentes (Sp) 29 G5
Rio Corrus 12 A5
Rio Coura 10 B-C3
Rio Criz 19 G2
Riodades 16 B3
Rio Dao 15 H6, 19 G2
Rio de Carvalhais 12 D5

Rio de Couros 23 F1
Rio de Fomos 12 D3
Rio Degebe 28 D5
Rio de Guide 12 C4
Río de las Uces (Sp) 17 G3
Río de la Vega de Matalobos (Sp)
   21 F4
Río de los Angeles (Sp) 21 H3
Rio de Malagón (Sp) 32 B5
Rio de Mel 16 B5
Rio de Moinhos (P) 15 E3
Rio de Moinhos (Vi) 15 H6
Rio de Moinhos (S) 23 H3
Rio de Moinhos (E) 28 D3
Rio de Moinhos (Se) 30 D1
Rio de Moinhos (Be) 31 E4
Rio de Mouro 26 B3
Rio de Onor 13 F2
Rio de São Matinho 27 G4
Río Deva (Sp) 11 E1
Rio Dom 12 A5
Rio Douro 11 F5
Rio Douro 13 H5, 15 E3, 16 B2, 17 F2
Río Duero (Sp) 13 H5, 17 F2
Río Erges 25 G1
Río Erjas (Sp) 21 F5
Rio Este 10 D6
Rio Ferreira 15 E1
Rio Frio (Vc) 10 D3
Rio Frio (Br) 13 F4
Rio Frio (Se) 27 E4
Riofrio de Aliste (Sp) 13 H3
Río Gavilanes (Sp) 17 H6
Río Gévora (Sp) 25 F5
Río Godolid (Sp) 29 H5
Rio Guadiana 29 E6, 31 H2-6
Río Guadiana (Sp) 36 B2
Rio Homem 11 E4
Río Huebra (Sp) 17 F3
Río Laboreiro 11 E2
Rio Leça 14 D2
Rio Lena 23 E1-2
Rio Lima 10 C4
Rio Lis 18 B6
Rio Louredo 11 G6
Rio Maças 13 F5
Rio Maior 22 D4
Riomanzanas (Sp) 13 F2
Rio Massueime 16 C4-5
Rio Mau (P) 10 C6
Rio Mau (B) 10 D4
Río Mena (Sp) 13 H4
Rio Mente 12 C3
Rio Milheiro 19 G2
Rio Minho 10 C2
Río Miño (Sp) 10 D1
Rio Mira 30 B5, 31 E6
Rio Mondego 18 D4, 19 G2, 20 C2
Rio Mouro 11 E2
Río Murtiga (Sp) 32 D2
Rio Nabao 19 E6, 23 G2
Río Negro (Sp) 13 G1
Rionegro del Puente (Sp) 13 H2
Rio Neiva 10 B5
Rio Noéme 20 D1
Rio Ocreza 20 C5, 24 C2
Río Odiel (Sp) 32 D6
Rio Olo 11 G6
Río Oraque (Sp) 32 D5
Rio Paiva 15 F4-H5, 19 G1
Río Piedras (Sp) 36 C2
Rio Ponsul 20 C6, 21 E5
Rio Rabaçal 12 C3
Riós (Sp) 12 B2
Rio Sabor 13 E2-F5, 16 D2
Rio Sado 27 E5, 30 D2-4
Río Salor (Sp) 25 G3
Rio Samora 26 D2

Rio Seco (G) 17 E5
Rio Seco (F) 35 G4
Rio Seco (F) 36 B3
Rio Seia 19 H2
Rio Sizandro 22 C6
Rio Sorraia 27 E1-G1
Rio Sousa 15 E2
Rio Sul 15 G5
Rio Tâmega 11 G6, 12 A3 15 F2
Río Tâmega (Sp) 12 A1
Rio Távora 16 B3
Río Tea (Sp) 10 D1
Rio Tedo 16 A3
Rio Tejo 23 E6-H3, 24 A3-D2, 26 D3
Río Tera (Sp) 13 G-H2
Rio Tinhela 12 A6
Rio Tinto 18 D1
Río Tormes (Sp) 17 H1
Rio Torto 12 B5
Rio Torto (V) 12 B5, 16 B2
Rio Torto (G) 20 B1
Rio Torto 20 D4
Rio Tripeiro 20 B6
Rio Tua 12 C6
Rio Tuela (Sp) 12 D1
Rio Tuella 12 C5-D3
Río Turones (Sp) 17 E5
Rio Vale de Moinhos 13 E5
Rio Vez 11 E2
Rio Vide 19 F4
Rio Vouga 15 E6
Rio Xarrama 28 A6
Rio Xévora 25 G6
Río Yeltes (Sp) 17 G4
Río Zapatón (Sp) 25 H4, 29 G1
Rio Zêzere 19 H5, 20 C3. 23 G3
Rivera Aurela (Sp) 25 E2
Rivera de Albarragena (Sp) 25 G4
Rivera de Alcorneo (Sp) 25 F5
Rivera de Anlconchel (Sp) 29 F4
Rivera de Azaba (Sp) 17 F6
Rivera de Chanza (Sp) 32 C3
Rivera de Fresnedosa (Sp) 21 G6
Rivera de Gata (Sp) 21 G4
Rivera de la Cobica (Sp) 32 B5
Rivera de la Peña (Sp) 17 G2
Rivera del Fraile (Sp) 25 F4
Rivera de Meca (Sp) 32 C6
Rivera de Peramora (Sp) 32 C3
Roalde 16 A2
Robleda (Sp) 21 G2
Robleda Cervantes (Sp) 13 F1
Robledillo de Gata (Sp) 21 H2
Robledo (Sp) 13 F2
Robledo Hermoso (Sp) 17 G3
Rocamondo 16 C6
Rocas do Vouga 15 E5
Rocha (Vc) 10 B3
Rocha (Vc) 10 B4
Rocha Brava 34 D4
Rochas de Baixo 20 B5
Rochoso 21 E1
Roda (Vi) 15 G5
Roda (S) 24 B2
Roda Grande 23 G3
Rodeios 24 C1
Rodeiro 23 G4
Roge 15 E5
Rogil 34 B2
Rogodeiro 12 C5
Rojao Grande 19 G2
Rolao 31 F5
Roliça 22 C4
Roma 26 B1
Romarigaes 10 C3
Romariz 14 D4
Romas 16 A5
Romeira 23 E5

Romeu 12 C5
Ronçao (Se) 30 B2
Ronçao (Be) 31 G6
Roncao (Be) 31 H6
Ronfe 10 D6
Roriz (B) 10 C5
Roriz (P) 15 E1
Roriz (Vi) 15 H6
Rosais 39 G5
Rosal (Sp) 10 B2
Rosal (Sp) 12 A2
Rosal de la Frontera (Sp) 32 B3
Rosário (E) 29 E4
Rosário (Be) 31 E6
Rosinos da Requejada (Sp) 13 F1
Rosmaninhal (Po) 24 B4
Rosmaninhal (C) 25 F1
Rossão 15 G4
Rossas (B) 11 F5
Rossas (A) 15 E4
Rossio ao Sul do Tejo 23 H4
Rouças 11 E2
Rozas (Sp) 13 F1
Rua 16 A4
Rubiaes 10 C3
Rubiùs (Sp) 10 D1
Ruínas Romanas de Cetóbriga
    26 D5
Ruivaes 11 F4
Ruivo 31 F1
Ruivo do Paúl 40 A5
Runa 22 C6
Ruvina 21 E2

Sá (Vc) 10 D2
Sá (V) 12 B4
Sabacheira 23 G2
Sabóia 30 C6
Sabrosa 16 A2
Sabroso 11 H5
Sabugal 21 E2
Sabugo 26 B2
Sabugosa 19 G1
Sabugueiro (G) 20 B2
Sabugueiro (E) 28 A3
Sacavém 26 C2
Saelices el Chico (Sp) 17 F6
Safara 32 B2
Safira 27 H4
Safurdao 16 D6
Sagallos (Sp) 13 G2
Sago 10 D2
Sagrajas (Sp) 29 H1
Sagres 34 A4
Saiceira 34 B2
Sail 19 G3
Saixo da Beira 19 H2
Salamonde 11 F4
Salavessa 24 D2
Salcidos (Sp) 10 B3
Saldanha 13 F6
Saldeana (Sp) 17 F3
Saldonha 12 D6
Salema 34 B4
Salgueirais 16 B6
Salgueiro (Br) 13 E6
Salgueiro (A) 18 D1
Salgueiro (C) 20 C3
Salgueiro (L) 21 G4
Salgueiro do Campo 20 B6
Salgueiros (V) 12 B6
Salgueiros (Br) 12 C2
Salgueiros (Be) 31 H6
Salir 35 F3
Salir de Matos 22 C4
Salir do Porto 22 C3
Salorino (Sp) 25 G3
Salreu 14 D5

Salsas 13 E4
Salselas 12 D5
Salto (V) 11 G4
Salto (Be) 31 F5
Salto de Cavalo 40 C1
Salto Saucelle (Sp) 17 E3
Salvada 31 G3
Salvador (C) 21 E4
Salvador (S) 23 G5
Salvador do Monte 15 F2
Salvaterra de Magos 27 E1
Salvaterra de Miño (Sp) 10 D1
Salvaterra do Extermo 21 F6
Salzedas 15 H3
Samaioes 12 A4
Samarda 11 H6
Sambade 12 D6
Sambado 19 F6
Sambrana 31 F6
Sameice 20 A2
Sameiro 20 B2
Samel 18 D2
Samil 13 E3
Samir de los Caños (Sp) 13 H4
Samoes 16 C1
Samora Correia 27 E2
Samouco 26 D3
Samouqueira (F) 34 B1
Samouqueira (F) 34 B3
Sampaio (Br) 13 E6
Sampaio (Br) 16 D1
Sampriz 10 D3
Samuel 18 D4
Sanabria Mamed (Sp) 13 G4
San Antón (Sp) 25 F4
San Antonio de Baldio 29 E5
San Bartolomé de la Torre (Sp)
    36 D1
San Benito de la Contienda (Sp)
    29 F4
San Blas (Sp) 13 G3
Sanchón de la Ribera (Sp) 17 G3
San Cibrao (Sp) 12 C1
San Cibrau (Sp) 12 A3
San Ciprián (Sp) 12 D2
San Cristábal de Aliste (Sp) 13 G3
San Cristobo (Sp) 12 B2
Sancti Spíritus (Sp) 17 H5
Sande (B) 10 D5
Sande (P) 15 F3
Sandiaes 10 C5
Sandiás (Sp) 11 H1
Sandim (Br) 12 C3
Sandim (P) 14 D3
Sandim da Ribeira 17 E1
Sandoeira 23 G2
Sandomil 19 H3
San Felices de los Gallegos (Sp)
    17 F4
Sanfins 12 B3
Sanfins do Douro 16 B1
San Francisco de Olivença (Sp)
    29 G3
Sangalhos 19 E2
Sanguedo 14 D3
Sanguinhal 22 C5
Sanguinhedo 15 H1
Sanhoane 13 F6
San Jorge de Alor (Sp) 29 G4
San José (Sp) 29 H6
San Juan (Sp) 21 G3
San Juan de la Cuesta (Sp) 13 F1
San Juan del Rebollar (Sp) 13 G4
Sanjurge 12 A4
San Justo (Sp) 13 F1
San Lourenzo (Sp) 12 C2
Sanlúcar de Guadiana (Sp) 36 B1
San Mamed (Sp) 11 G2

San Martín de Castañeda (Sp) 13 E1
San Martin del Pedroso (Sp) 13 F4
San Martin de Trevejo (Sp) 21 F3
San Martiño (Sp) 12 A2
San Millán (Sp) 11 H3
San Paio (Sp) 11 G2
San Pedro (Sp) 25 E4
San Pedro de las Herrerías (Sp)
    13 G2
San Pedro Fins 14 D2
San Rafael de Olivenza (Sp) 29 G3
San Roque (Padrenda) (Sp) 11 E1
San Silvestre de Guzmán (Sp) 36 C1
Santa Amara 19 H2
Santa Ana (Sp) 13 G4
Santa Bárbara (Be) 34 C1
Santa Bárbara (T) 39 G1
Santa Bárbara (Sa) 40 B2
Santa Bárbara (Sm) 40 B1
Santa Bárbara de Casa (Sp) 32 C4
Santa Bárbara de Nexe 35 G4
Santa Bárbara de Padroes 31 F5
Santa Catarina (Le) 22 D4
Santa Catarina (Se) 27 G5
Santa Catarina da Fonte do Bispo
    35 H3
Santa Catarina da Serra 23 E2
Santa Catarinha 18 D2
Santa Cita 23 G3
Santa Clara-a-Nova 31 E6
Santa Clara-a-Velha 30 C6
Santa Clara do Louredo 31 F3
Santa Comba (Vc) 10 C4
Santa Comba (P) 15 E3
Santa Comba (G) 16 D4
Santa Comba (G) 20 A2
Santa Comba Dao 19 G2
Santa Comba de Rossas 13 E4
Santa Comba de Vilariça 12 D6
Santa Combinha 12 D5
Santa Cristina 19 F2
Santa Cruz (L) 22 B6
Santa Cruz (Se) 30 B2
Santa Cruz (Be) 35 G1
Santa Cruz (M) 40 B5
Santa Cruz da Graciosa 39 H3
Santa Cruz das Flores 39 F2
Santa Cruz da Trapa 15 F5
Santa Cruz de Abranes (Sp) 13 E2
Santa Cruz do Douro 15 G3
Santa Eufémia (G) 16 C5
Santa Eufémia (Le) 23 E1
Santa Eugénia 16 B1
Santa Eulália (B) 10 D6
Santa Eulalia (Sp) 13 H1
Santa Eulália (P) 15 E1
Santa Eulália (G) 19 H2
Santa Eulália (L) 26 B2
Santa Eulalia (Po) 29 F1
Santa Helena 15 H4
Santa Iria 31 H4
Santa Iria da Azója 26 C2
Santa Justa (V) 16 D1
Santa Justa (S) 27 H1
Santa Justa (E) 28 B3
Santa Justa (F) 35 H1
Santa Leocádia (V) 10 C4
Santa Leocádia (P) 15 F3
Santa Leocádia (Vi) 16 A3
Santalha 12 C2
Santa Luzia 10 B4
Santa Luzia (Be) 30 D5
Santa Luzia 32 A5
Santa Luzia (Pc) 39 F6
Santa Margarida da Coutada 23 G4
Santa Margarida da Serra 30 C2
Santa Margarida do Sado 30 D2
Santa Maria 10 C4

Santa Maria (Arnoso) 10 D6
Santa Maria da Montanha 11 H5
Santa Maria de Émeres 12 B5
Santa Maria de Feira 14 D4
Santa Maria de Sardoura 15 E3
Santa Marinha (V) 10 D2
Santa Marinha (G) 20 A2
Santa Marinha do Zézere 15 G2
Santa Marta 31 H6
Santa Marta de Penaguiao 15 H2
Santana (Vc) 10 B3
Santana (Co) 18 C4
Santana (Se) 26 C5
Santana (E) 28 C6
Santana (M) 40 B5
Santana da Serra 30 D6
Santana de Cambas 31 H5
Santana do Campo 28 A3
Santa Olalla de Yeltes (Sp) 17 H5
Santa Quitéria 15 F1
Santar 19 H1
Santarém 23 E5
Santa Sofia 28 A4
Santa Susana (Se) 27 G5
Santa Susana (E) 28 C4
Santa Susana (Be) 35 E2
Santa Valha 12 B4
Santa Vitória 31 F3
Santa Vitória do Ameixial 28 C2
San Telmo (Sp) 32 D4
Santiago (Br) 13 F6
Santiago (Vi) 15 H3
Santiago (G) 20 A2
Santiago (Po) 25 E5
Santiago (Sp) 25 F2
Santiago Cassurraes 15 H6
Santiago de Alcántara (Sp) 25 F2
Santiago de Besteiros 19 G1
Santiago de Guarda 19 E6
Santiago de la Requejada (Sp)
    13 F1
Santiago de Litém 18 D6
Santiago de Piaes 15 F3
Santiago de Riba-Ul 14 D5
Santiago de Ribeira de Alhariz
    12 B5
Santiago do Cacém 30 B3
Santiago do Escoural 27 H4
Santiago dos Velhos 26 C2
Santiago Maior 28 D4
Santiais 18 D6
Santibáñez el Alto (Sp) 21 G4
Santieiras 23 H3
Santo Aleixo 29 E2
Santo Aleixo da Restauração 32 C2
Santo Aleixo de Além Tâmega
    11 G5
Santo Amador 32 B2
Santo Amaro (G) 16 C3
Santo Amaro (Po) 28 D1
Santo Amaro de Bouça 18 C4
Santo André (V) 11 H3
Santo André (Se) 30 B2
Santo André das Tojeiras 24 C1
Santo Antao 39 H6
Santo Antao do Tojal 26 C2
Santo António (M) 40 B5
Santo António (Pc) 39 F6
Santo António (Sj) 39 G5
Santo António (Sm) 40 B1
Santo António das Areias 25 E4
Santo António da Serra 40 B5
Santo António de Alcôrrego 28 B1
Santo António de Monforte 12 B3
Santo António Velho 31 H3
Santo Cruz do Bispo 14 C2
Santo Domingo (Sp) 29 G4
Santo Emiliano 11 E5

Santo Espíritu 40 C3
Santo Estêvao (V) 12 B4
Santo Estêvao (G) 20 D3
Santo Estêvao (S) 27 E2
Santo Estevao (E) 28 D2
Santo Estêvao (F) 35 H3
Santo Estêvao das Gales 26 B2
Santo Ildefonso 29 F2
Santo Isidoro (P) 15 F2
Santo Isidoro (L) 26 B1
Santo Isidro de Pegoes 27 F3
Santo Quintino 26 C1
Santo Tirso 14 D1
Santos (S) 23 E4
Santos (S) 24 B2
Santos Evos 15 H6
Santulhao 13 F5
San Vicente de Alcántara (Sp) 25 F4
San Vincente de la Cabeza (Sp)
    13 H3
San Vitero (Sp) 13 G3
Sanxián (Sp) 10 B2
São Bartolomeu (Po) 24 B4
São Bartolomeu (Be) 31 G6
São Bartolomeu (F) 36 B3
São Bartolomeu da Serra 30 B3
São Bartolomeu de Messines 35 E2
São Bartolomeu do Outeiro 28 B6
São Bartolomeu dos Galegos 22 B5
São Bento (Vc) 10 C2
São Bento (Le) 23 E3
São Bento do Ameixial 28 D2
São Bento do Cortiço 28 D2
São Bernabé 35 F2
São Bernardino 22 B5
São Brás (Be) 31 E6
São Brás (Be) 31 H4
São Brás de Alportel 35 G3
São Bras do Regedouro 28 A5
São Brissos (E) 28 A5
São Brissos (Be) 31 F2
São Cibrao 12 D4
São Cipriano 15 G3
São Cosmado 16 A3
São Cristovao 27 H5
São Cristóvao de Nogueira 15 F3
São Domingos (S) 23 H2
São Domingos (Se) 30 C3
São Domingos da Ordem 28 C4
São Domingos de Ana Loura 28 D2
São Domingos de Rana 26 B3
São Donato 14 D5
São Facundo 24 A4
São Félix 15 G5
São Félix da Marinha 14 D3
São Francisco da Serra 30 B2
São Frutuoso de Montélios 10 D5
São Gemil 19 G1
São Gens (B) 11 F6
São Gens (E) 28 D3
São Geraldo 27 H3
São Gonçalo 40 B5
São Gregorio (Vi) 11 E1
São Gregório (E) 28 B3
São Gregorio da Fanadia 22 C4
São Jacinto 14 C6
São Joanico 13 G4
São Joaninho (Vi) 15 H4
São Joaninho (Vi) 19 G2
São João (Se) 26 B4
São João (Pc) 39 F6
São João da Boa Vista 19 G3
São João da Corveira 12 A5
São João da Madeira 14 D4
São João da Ribeira 23 E5
São João da Serra 15 F5
São João das Lampas 26 B2
São João da Talha 26 C2

São João de Areias 19 G2
São João de Loure 14 D6
São João de Negrilhos 31 E3
São João de Pesqueira 16 B2
São João de Tarouca 15 H4
São João de Ver 14 D4
São João do Campo 19 E3
São João do Monte (Vi) 15 F6
São João do Monte (Vi) 19 H1
São João do Peso 24 A2
São João dos Caldeireiros 31 G6
São João dos Montes 26 D2
São Jornil 12 C3
São Jorge (Vc) 10 D3
São Jorge (A) 14 D4
São Jorge (Le) 23 E2
São Jorge (M) 40 B5
São Jorge da Beira 20 A4
São José da Lamarosa 23 G6
São Jose das Matas 24 B3
São Juliao 25 E4
São Juliao de Montenegro 12 B4
São Juliao de Palácios 13 F3
São Juliao do Tojal 26 C2
São Julilao 10 C2
São Leonardo 29 F6
São Lourenço (V) 12 B4
São Lourenço (Br) 16 B1
São Lourenço (F) 35 G4
São Lourenço de Mamporcao 28 D2
São Lourenço de Ribapinhao 16 A1
São Lourenço do Bairro 19 E2
São Luís 30 B5
São Maciário 15 G4
São Mamede (Le) 22 C4
São Mamede (Le) 23 E2
São Mamede de Ribatua 16 B2
São Mamede do Sado 30 D2
São Manços 28 C5
São Marcos (S) 32 A4
São Marcos (F) 35 H3
São Marcos da Ataboeira 31 F5
São Marcos da Serra 35 E2
São Marcos do Campo 28 D6
São Martinho (A) 14 D5
São Martinho (G) 16 C5
São Martinho (A) 19 E1
São Martinho (C) 20 A4
São Martinho 20 C6
São Martinho (M) 40 B5
São Martinho da Cortiça 19 G3
São Martinho das Amoreiras 30 D5
São Martinho das Chas 16 A3
São Martinho de Angueira 13 G4
São Martinho de Antas 16 A2
São Martinho de Arvore 18 D3
São Martinho de Mouros 15 G3
São Martinho do Bispo 19 E4
São Martinho do Peso 13 F6
São Martinho do Porto 22 C3
São Mateus (Pc) 39 F6
São Mateus (T) 39 G2
São Matias (Po) 24 C3
São Matias (E) 28 B4
São Matias (Be) 31 G2
São Miguel 35 H4
São Miguel de Acha 20 C5
São Miguel de Machede 28 C4
São Miguel de Pinheiro 31 G6
São Miguel de Poiares 19 F4
São Miguel de Vila Boa 15 H6
São Miguel do Mato (A) 15 E4
São Miguel do Mato (Vi) 15 G5
São Miguel do Outeiro 15 G6
São Miguel do Rio Torto 23 H4
São Nicolau 19 F5
São Paio 20 B1
São Paio da Farinha Podre 19 G3

São Paulo de Frades 19 E3
São Pedro (V) 11 G3
São Pedro (Br) 12 C6
São Pedro (Br) 16 B2
São Pedro 28 C6
São Pedro (Be) 31 G2
São Pedro da Cadeira 22 B6
São Pedro da Cova 14 D2
São Pedro da Torre 10 C2
São Pedro de Açor 19 H3
São Pedro de Agostém 12 A4
São Pedro de Alva 19 F3
São Pedro de Estsval 24 B2
São Pedro de France 15 H6
São Pedro de Moel 22 D1
São Pedro de Rio Seco 17 E6
São Pedro de Serracenos 13 E3
São Pedro de Solis 31 F6
São Pedro de Tomar 23 G3
São Pedro de Veiga de Lila 12 B5
São Pedro do Sul 15 F5
São Pedro Santa Luzia 35 H4
São Pedro Velho (V) 12 C4
São Pedro Velho (A) 15 E5
São Romao (G) 20 A2
São Romao (E) 27 H4
São Romao (E) 29 E3
São Romao de Aregos 15 G3
São Romao do Sado 30 D1
São Roque (Sm) 40 B2
São Roque (M) 40 B5
São Roque do Pico 39 F6
São Salvador (Br) 12 C6
São Salvador (L) 22 D5
São Salvador (Po) 25 E4
São Saturnino 24 D6
São Sebastiao (Co) 19 E5
São Sebastiao (T) 39 G6
São Sebastiao de Giesteira 28 A4
São Sebastiao dos Carros 31 G6
São Silvestre 19 E3
São Simao (A) 14 C5
São Simao (S) 23 G2
São Simao de Litém 18 D6
São Teotónio 30 B6
São Tomé do Castelo 15 H1
São Torcato (B) 11 E6
São Torcato (S) 27 F2
São Vicente (V) 12 B3
São Vicente (P) 15 E3
São Vicente (E) 28 B6
São Vicente (Be) 31 E2
São Vicente (M) 40 B5
São Vicente da Beira 20 B5
São Vicente da Cha 11 G3
São Vicente de Ferreira 40 B1
São Vicente de Lafoes 15 F6
São Vicente de Pereira Jusa 14 D5
São Vicente do Paúl 23 F4
São Vicente do Pigeiro 28 D5
São Vicente e Ventosa 29 F1
Sapataria 26 C1
Sapelos 11 H4
Sapiaos 11 H4
Sapos (Be) 31 G5
Sapos (Be) 31 H5
Saravigoes 15 F4
Sardao 17 E1
Sardeiras de Baixo 19 H6
Sardoal 23 H3
Sardón de los Fraíles (Sp) 17 H2
Sarilhos Grandes 26 D3
Samadas 35 F2
Samadas de Baixo 19 G5
Samadas de Ródao 24 D1
Samadas de São Simao 20 A6
Samadela 19 G3
Sarracin de Aliste (Sp) 13 H3

Sarraquinhos 11 H3
Sarreaus (Sp) 11 H1
Sarzeda 16 B4
Sarzedas 20 A6
Sarzedela 19 E6
Sarzedo (Vi) 16 A3
Sarzedo (Co) 19 G3
Sarzedo (C) 20 C2
Sátao 15 H5
Sauceda (Sp) 21 H3
Saucelle (Sp) 17 F3
Sazes da Beira 20 A3
Seara 11 E4
Seara Velha 11 H3
Sebadelhe 16 C3
Sebadelhe da Serra 16 B4
Sebal 19 E4
Sebolido 15 E3
Secarias 19 G3
Seda 24 C5
Sedielos 15 H2
Segirei 12 C3
Segoes 16 A4
Segude 10 D1
Segura 21 E6
Seia 20 A2
Seiça 23 F2
Seiçal 25 E4
Seixa 11 G5
Seixal (L) 22 B5
Seixal (Se) 26 C4
Seixal (M) 40 A5
Seixas (Vc) 10 B3
Seixas (Br) 12 C2
Seixas (G) 16 C3
Seixo (V) 12 A4
Seixo (Co) 18 D2
Seixo (Be) 31 F4
Seixo Amarelo 20 C2
Seixo de Ansiaes 16 C2
Seixo de Gatoes 18 D3
Seixo de Manhoses 16 C2
Seixo do Côa 21 E2
Seixos Alvos 19 G2
Sejas de Aliste (Sp) 13 G4
Sela (Sp) 10 D1
Selho 10 D6
Selmes 31 G2
Selores 16 C2
Semide 19 F4
Semideiro 23 G4
Sendas 13 E5
Sendim (P) 11 E6
Sendim (V) 11 H3
Sendim (Br) 13 G6
Sendim da Serra 16 D1
Senhora 19 H3
Senhora da Estrada 16 B3
Senhora da Graça 20 D6
Senhora da Graça de Padroes
   31 F6
Senhora da Ribeira 16 C2
Senhora da Rocha 34 D3
Senhora de Araceli 31 F5
Senhora de Monte Alto 19 G4
Senhora do Bom Sucesso 21 E4
Senhora do Desterro 20 A2
Senhora do Rosário 25 E6
Senhorim 19 H1
Senouras 17 E6
Sentinela 36 B2
Señora (Sp) 29 G5
Seoane de Arriba (Sp) 12 C1
Sepins 19 E2
Sequeiros (B) 10 D4
Sequeiros (Br) 16 D2
Serapicos (V) 12 B5
Serapicos (Br) 13 E5

Serapicos (Br) 13 G4
Serdedelo 10 C4
Serena 19 E2
Semada 14 D6
Semadas 19 F2
Semades 10 D2
Semadinha (Vi) 15 F5
Semadinha (C) 24 C1
Semancelhe 16 B4
Seroa 15 E2
Serominheiro 34 B2
Serpa 31 H3
Serpins 19 F4
Serra (S) 23 H2
Serra (Po) 24 B6
Serra Amarela 11 E3
Serra da Adiça 32 B3
Serra da Agua 40 B5
Serra da Arada 15 F5
Serra da Arrábida 26 D5
Serra da Brejeira 34 C1
Serra da Cabreira 11 F4-5
Serra da Carapinha 34 D2
Serra da Coroa 12 D2-3
Serra da Estrêla 20 B3-C2
Serra da Gralheira 15 E5
Serra da Lapa 16 A4-B5
Serra da Lousa 19 F5
Serra da Malcata 21 E-F3
Serra da Padrela 12 A5
Serra da Peneda 11 E2
Serra das Neves 30 C5
Serra da Vila 22 B6
Serra de Açor 19 H3
Serra de Aire 23 F3
Serra de Alvao 11 H6
Serra de Alvelos 19 H6
Serra de Arga 10 B3
Serra de Bigorne 15 G4
Serra de Bornes 12 D6
Serra de Dentro 40 D3
Serra de Grândola 30 C2
Serra de Leomil 15 H4
Serra d'El Rei 22 B4
Serra de Malcata 21 E3
Serra de Mangues 22 C3
Serra de Mendro 28 C6
Serra de Mértola 31 H5
Serra de Monchique 34 C-D2
Serra de Monfurado 27 H4
Serra de Monjunto 22 C-D5
Serra de Montemuro 15 F-G4
Serra de Montesinho 13 E2
Serra de Mouro 19 E6
Serra de Nogueira 12 D4
Serra de Ossa 28 C-D3
Serra de Santo António 23 E3
Serra de São Mamede 25 E4-5
Serra de Serpa 31 H4
Serra de Sicó 18 D6
Serra de Sintra 26 A-B3
Serra de Vilarelho 12 A6
Serradilla del Arroyo (Sp) 21 H1
Serradilla del Llano (Sp) 21 H1
Serra do Barroso 11 G4-5
Serra do Bouro 22 C4
Serra do Caldeirao 35 E-F2
Serra do Canizo (Sp) 12 C-D1
Serra do Caramulo 15 F6
Serra do Cercal 30 B4
Serra do Cume 39 F-G6
Serra do Espinhaço de Cao 34 B3
Serra do Gerês 11 F3
Serra do Larouco 11 H3
Serra do Leiranco 11 H4
Serra do Malhao 35 F2
Serra do Marao 15 G2
Serra do Muradal 19 H5

Serra do Porto de Urso 18 C6
Serra do Reboredo 17 E2
Serra dos Candeeiros 22 D3-4
Serra do Soajo 11 E3
Serra do Topo 39 H5
Serra Gorda 40 B1
Serranillo (Sp) 17 F5
Serrasqueira 24 D2
Serrazes 15 F5
Serreleis 10 B4
Serreta 39 G1
Serrinha 25 G6
Serro Ventoso 23 E3
Serta 24 A1
Serves 26 C2
Servoi (Sp) 12 B2
Serzedelo 11 E5
Serzedo 14 C3
Sesimbra 26 C5
Sesmarias 30 C2
Sete 31 F5
Sete Cidades 40 A1
Setil 23 E6
Setúbal 26 D5
Sever do Vouga 15 E5
Sevilha 19 G2
Sexmiro (Sp) 17 F6
Sezelhe 11 G3
Sezulfe 12 D5
Sezures 16 A6
Sidrós 11 F4
Sierra de Coria (Sp) 21 G5
Sierra de la Canchera (Sp) 21 H2
Sierra de la Culebra (Sp) 13 G-H2
Sierra de la Garrapata (Sp) 21 F5
Sierra de la Malvana (Sp) 21 E-F3
Sierra de las Contiendas (Sp) 32 D2
Sierra del Centinela (Sp) 25 G5
Sierra del Naranjal (Sp) 25 F5
Sierra de los Angeles (Sp) 21 H3
Sierra del Pendón (Sp) 29 G5-6
Sierra del Puerto (Sp) 25 F-G5
Sierra del Zarzoso (Sp) 29 H5
Sierra de Peñeas Libres (Sp) 12 B2
Sierra de Santa Olalla (Sp) 21 F4
Sierra de Santiago (Sp) 25 H5
Sierra de Xurés (Sp) 11 F3
Sierra El Vescar (Sp) 32 C1
Sierra Grande (Sp) 21 H6
Sierra Grijona (Sp) 32 D6
Sierra Madroñera (Sp) 32 B6
Sierra Pelada (Sp) 32 D4
Sigarrosa 15 H1
Silleta (Sp) 21 H6
Silos (Sp) 21 G4
Silva (Vc) 10 C2
Silva (B) 10 C5
Silva (V) 12 B5
Silva (Br) 13 G5
Silva Escura 15 E5
Silvalde 14 C4
Silvares (B) 11 E6
Silvares (P) 15 E2
Silvares (Vi) 15 H5
Silvares (C) 20 A4
Silveira 22 B6
Silveirona 28 D2
Silveiros 10 C6
Silverinho 19 F3
Silves 34 D3
Sines 30 A3
Sintra 26 B3
Sipote 28 B1
Sistelo 10 D2
Sítio das Eguas 35 F2
Soajo 11 E3
Soalhaes 15 F2
Soalheia 20 B5

Soalheiras 25 F2
Sobradelo do Goma 11 E5
Sobradillo (Sp) 17 F4
Sobradinho 35 F2
Sobrado 14 D2
Sobral (A) 14 D4
Sobral (Co) 18 C5
Sobral (Co) 19 G4
Sobral (C) 19 G5
Sobral da Abelheira 26 B1
Sobral da Adiça 32 B3
Sobral da Lagoa 22 C4
Sobral da Serra 16 C6
Sobral de Baixo 18 D5
Sobral de Casegas 20 A3
Sobral de Monte Agraço 26 C1
Sobral do Campo 20 B5
Sobral Fernando 24 C1
Sobralinho 26 D2
Sobral Pichorro 16 B6
Sobral Valado 19 H5
Sobreda 19 H2
Sobreira (P) 15 E2
Sobreira (G) 20 D2
Sobreira Formosa 24 B1
Sobreiro (A) 14 D6
Sobreiro (L) 26 B1
Sobreiro de Cima 12 C3
Sobrena 22 D5
Sobreposta 10 D5
Sobrosa (P) 15 E2
Sobrosa (Be) 32 C2
Soeima 12 D6
Soeira 12 D3
Solbeira (Sp) 12 C1
Sol Posto 30 B4
Solveira 11 H3
Sonim 12 C4
Sopo 10 B3
Sortelha 20 D3
Sortelhao 20 D2
Sortes 13 E4
Sosa 18 D1
Sotillo de Sanabria (Sp) 13 E1
Soudes 36 A2
Sourao 18 D6
Soure 18 D5
Souro Pires 16 D5
Sousel 28 C1
Souselas 19 E3
Souselo 15 F3
Soutana 23 F2
Soutelinho 11 H6
Soutelinho da Raia 11 H3
Soutelo (B) 10 D5
Soutelo (B) 11 E5
Soutelo (V) 12 A4
Soutelo (Br) 13 E6
Soutelo (A) 15 E6
Soutelo (Vi) 15 G5
Soutelo (V) 15 H2
Soutelo de Aguiar 11 H6
Soutelo do Douro 16 B2
Soutelo Mourisco 12 D4
Soutelo Verde (Sp) 12 A1
Soutilha 12 C4
Souto (Vc) 10 D3
Souto (B) 11 E4
Souto (A) 14 D4
Souto (Vi) 16 C3
Souto (Le) 18 D6
Souto (C) 20 B4
Souto (G) 21 E2
Souto (S) 23 H3
Soutochao (Sp) 12 C2
Soutocico 23 E2
Souto da Carpalhosa 18 C6
Souto da Velha 17 E2

Souto de Aguiar da Beira 16 B5
Souto de Escaro 11 H6
Souto Maior 16 A1
Soutosa 16 A4
Subportela 10 B4
Suçaes 12 B5
Sul 15 G5
Sume 24 B4

Tabagón (Sp) 10 B2
Taberna Seca 20 B6
Taboeira 14 D6
Taboeiras 18 D3
Tábua 19 G2
Tabuaças 11 E4
Tabuaço 16 A3
Tabuadelo 11 E6
Tabuado 15 F2
Tacoes 36 A1
Tadim 10 D5
Tagarro 22 D5
Tagilde 11 E6
Taiao 10 C2
Taide 11 E5
Taipadas 27 F3
Talabita 31 H2
Talavera la Real (Sp) 29 H2
Talefe 22 B6
Talhadas 15 E6
Talhas 13 E5
Taliga (Sp) 29 G4
Taliscas 20 B3
Talurdo 34 D2
Tamaguelos (Sp) 12 B3
Tameirón (Sp) 12 C2
Tamengos 19 E2
Tancos 23 G3
Tanganhal 30 C2
Tanganheira 30 B4
Tangil 10 D2
Tapada (P) 15 G2
Tapada (S) 23 F5
Tapéus 18 D5
Tariquejo (Sp) 36 D1
Tarouca 15 H3
Tarouquela 15 F3
Tavarede 18 C4
Taveiro 19 E4
Tavila 24 C2
Tavira 36 A3
Távora (Vc) 10 D3
Távora (Vi) 16 B3
Tazem 12 A5
Tebra (Sp) 10 B2
Teira 22 D4
Teixeira (Br) 13 F6
Teixeira (P) 15 G2
Teixeira (Co) 19 H4
Teixeira (G) 20 A3
Teixelo 15 H4
Teixoso 20 C3
Tejarejo (Sp) 25 H4
Telhada (Co) 18 C5
Telhada (Co) 19 G5
Telhadela 14 D5
Telhado (Co) 19 F3
Telhado (C) 20 B4
Telheiro (E) 29 E5
Telheiro (Be) 30 B6
Teloes 11 H6
Tendais 15 G3
Tenebrón (Sp) 17 H6
Tenencia 36 B2
Tentúgal 18 D3
Terça 27 F5
Terena 29 E4
Termas 15 F5
Termas de Alcafache 15 H6

Termas de Monfortinho 21 F5
Terrachán (Entrimo) (Sp) 11 F2
Terras de Bouro 11 E4
Terreiro das Bruxas 20 D3
Terroso 10 B6
Terroso (Sp) 13 E1
Terrugem (L) 26 B2
Terrugem (Po) 29 E2
Tesó 10 B6
Tesoureira 26 C2
Texós (Sp) 11 H2
Tharsis (Sp) 32 C6
The Sanctuary 23 F2
Tinalhas 20 B5
Tinhela 12 B4
Tinhela de Baixo 12 A5
Tó 17 G1
Tocha 18 C3
Tojal 27 H5
Tola (Sp) 13 G3
Toledo 22 B5
Tolilla (Sp) 13 H4
Toloes 15 G2
Tolosa 24 C4
Tomadias 16 D3
Tomar 23 G2
Tomina 32 C2
Tonda 19 G1
Tondela 19 G1
Topo 39 H6
Tórgueda 15 H2
Tornada 22 C4
Torneiro 11 G5
Torneiros (Sp) 11 F3
Toro (Sp) 12 A1
Torrados 15 F1
Torrao (Po) 24 B4
Torrao (Se) 27 H6
Torrao do Lameiro 14 C5
Torre (Vc) 10 B4
Torre (Co) 19 G2
Torre (G) 20 B3
Torre (G) 21 E2
Torre (C) 21 E5
Torre (Le) 23 E2
Torre (Se) 27 E6
Torre (F) 35 G4
Torrecilla de los Angeles (Sp) 21 H3
Torre da Gadanha 27 H4
Torre das Vargens 24 B4
Torre de Aspa 34 A4
Torre de Bolsa 29 F2
Torre de Coelheiros 28 C5
Torre de Dona Chama 12 C4
Torre de Don Miguel (Sp) 21 G3
Torredeita 15 G6
Torre de Miguel Sesmero (Sp) 29 H4
Torre de Moncorvo 16 D2
Torre de Pinhao 11 H6
Torre de Vale de Todos 19 E5
Torre do Couto 12 A3
Torre do Torrenho 16 C4
Torregamones (Sp) 13 H6
Torreira 14 C5
Torrejón (Sp) 25 F4
Torrejoncillo (Sp) 21 H6
Torrenho 16 C4
Torres 16 C5
Torres Novas 23 F3
Torres Vedras 22 B6
Torrico de San Pedro (Sp) 25 G4
Torrinheiras 11 F5
Torroal 27 H6
Torroña (Sp) 10 B2
Torrozelas 19 G4
Torrozelo 19 H2
Tortosende 20 B3
Tosende (Sp) 11 G2

Totenique 30 C6
Touça 16 C3
Touca 20 C4
Toucinhos 23 F2
Touguinha 10 C6
Touloes 21 E6
Tourem 11 G3
Tourigo 19 F2
Touril 30 B6
Touro 15 H4
Toutosa 15 F2
Touvedo 10 D3
Trabanca (Sp) 17 H2
Trabazos (Sp) 13 F3
Trafaria 26 B4
Trafeiras 31 G5
Traguntía (Sp) 17 H4
Tramaga 24 A5
Tramagal 23 H4
Trancoso 16 C5
Tras de Outerio 22 C4
Trasmiras (Sp) 11 H2
Travaços (B) 11 E5
Travaços (B) 11 E6
Travanca (Br) 12 D3
Travanca (Br) 13 F6
Travanca (A) 14 D5
Travanca (P) 15 F2
Travanca de Lagos 19 H2
Travanca de Tavares 16 A6
Travanca do Mondego 19 F3
Travancas 12 B3
Travancinha 19 H2
Travasso (B) 11 F5
Travasso (A) 14 D6
Travassos 11 G3
Travessa 32 C2
Trefacio (Sp) 13 F1
Treixedo 19 G2
Tremés 23 E4
Tres Arroyos (Sp) 29 G2
Tresminas 12 A6
Tresouras 15 G2
Trevejo (Sp) 21 F4
Trevoes 16 B3
Trez (Sp) 12 B1
Trezoi 19 F2
Trigaches 31 F2
Trigais 20 A3
Trindade (Br) 12 D6
Trindade (B) 31 F4
Trinta 20 C1
Triufé (Sp) 13 F1
Trofa (P) 11 E6
Trofa (Br) 14 D1
Trofa (A) 14 D6
Tróia 26 D5
Tronco 12 B3
Troporiz 10 C2
Troviscais 30 B5
Troviscal (A) 18 D1
Troviscal (C) 19 G6
Trutas 22 D1
Trutos 23 H2
Tua 16 B2
Tubaral 24 A4
Tudera (Sp) 13 H6
Tui (Sp) 10 C1
Tuias 15 F2
Tuizelo 12 C3
Tulhas 19 G5
Tunes 35 E3
Turcifal 22 B6
Turquel 22 D3

Ucanha 15 H3
Ucha 10 D5
Ulme 23 G4

Ulmo 31 F3
Umbrias de Camacho 35 H2
Uña de Quintana (Sp) 13 H1
Ungilde (Sp) 13 F2
Unhais da Serra 20 B3
Unhais-o-Velho 19 H4
Unhos 26 C2
Unhos 26 C2
Urgal 16 D3
Urgeses (Co) 11 E6
Urgueira (S) 19 G3
Urqueira 23 F1
Urra 25 E5
Urrós 13 G6
Urros 16 D3
Urza 31 E5
Urzelina 39 G5
Uva 13 F5

Vacariça 19 E2
Vade 10 D3
Vagos 18 D1
Vagueira 18 C1
Vaiamonte 24 D6
Vairao 14 C1
Valada 23 E6
Vala da Azambuja 23 E6
Valadares (Vc) 10 D1
Valadares (P) 14 C3
Valadares (Vi) 15 F5
Valadas (C) 23 H2
Valadas (Be) 32 A3
Valado dos Frades 22 D3
Valbom (P) 14 D3
Valbom (G) 16 D5
Valbom (C) 20 B5
Valbom (Le) 23 H1
Val de Algoso 13 F5
Valdebótoa (Sp) 29 G1
Valdecarpinteros (Sp) 17 G6
Valdelamusa (Sp) 32 D4
Valdemerilla (Sp) 13 G1
Valdenoguera (Sp) 17 E4
Valderrodrigo (Sp) 17 G3
Val de Santa Maria (Sp) 13 H2
Valdespino (Sp) 13 F1
Valdeterrazo del Marqués (Sp) 29 F5
Valdigem 15 H3
Valdreu 11 E4
Valdrez 13 E5
Valdujo 16 C5
Vale 10 D3
Vale Alto 23 F3
Vale Beijinha 30 B5
Vale Bemfeito 12 D5
Vale Covo (Le) 22 C5
Vale Covo (Be) 32 A4
Vale da Couda 19 E6
Vale da Feiteira 24 C4
Vale da Gavioes 24 B4
Vale da Grade 31 E6
Vale da Madre 13 E6
Vale da Mó 19 E2
Vale da Mua 24 B2
Vale da Pinta 23 E6
Vale da Rosa 35 G2
Vale da Seda 24 C6
Vale da Senhora da Póvoa 20 D3
Vale das Fontes 12 C4
Vale das Mós 24 A4
Vale das Onegas 24 A3
Vale da Telha 34 B2
Vale da Torre 20 C5
Vale da Ursa 24 B1
Vale da Vinha 24 B4
Vale de Açor (S) 23 H4
Vale de Açor (Po) 24 B5
Vale de Açor (Be) 31 G4

Vale de Afonsinho 16 D4
Vale de Agua 24 A4
Vale de Agua (Se) 30 B4
Vale de Agua (Be) 30 D4
Vale de Aguia 13 H5
Vale de Anta 12 A4
Vale de Asnes 12 D6
Vale de Azares 16 C6
Vale de Bajouca 18 C6
Vale de Cambra 15 E5
Vale de Carneiro 19 F2
Vale de Cavalos (S) 23 F5
Vale de Cavalos (Po) 25 E5
Vale de Coelha 17 E5
Vale de Couço 12 C5
Vale de Cunho 12 A6
Vale de Ebros 36 A3
Vale de Égua 12 B5
Vale de Espinho 21 E3
Vale de Esterla 20 C1
Vale de Ferro 30 C5
Vale de Figueira (Vi) 16 C2
Vale de Figueira (S) 23 F5
Vale de Figueiras 24 A6
Vale de Frades 13 F4
Vale de Gouvinhas 12 C5
Vale de Guiso 27 G6
Vale de Ilhavo 14 C6
Vale de Janeiro 12 C3
Vale de Lagoa 12 C5
Vale de Lobos 30 C5
Vale de Maceiras 28 D1
Vale de Madeira 16 D5
Vale de Mendiz 16 B2
Vale de Mira 13 G5
Vale de Mula 17 E6
Vale de Nogueira 13 E4
Vale de Ossos 30 C1
Vale de Pereiros 16 C3
Vale de Pinheiro 36 B2
Vale de Porco 17 F1
Vale de Pradinhos 12 D5
Vale de Prados (Br) 12 C5
Vale de Prados (Br) 12 D5
Vale de Prazeres 20 C4
Vale de Remígio 19 F2
Vale de Rocins 31 G4
Vale de Salgueiro 12 C5
Vale de Sancha 12 C6
Vale de Santarém 23 E5
Vale de Santiago 30 D5
Vale de Telhas 12 C5
Vale de Torno 16 C2
Vale de Urso 20 B4
Vale de Vaide 19 F4
Vale de Vargo 32 A3
Vale de Vilao 24 A6
Vale de Vinagre 31 H3
Vale de Zebrinho 24 A4
Vale de Zebro 30 D3
Vale do Arco 24 B4
Vale do Coelheiro 24 C1
Vale do Homem 24 C1
Vale do Horto 23 E2
Vale do Judeu 35 F3
Vale do Lobo 35 F4
Vale do Paraíso 22 D6
Vale do Pereiro 28 C3
Vale do Peso 24 C4
Vale do Rio 19 F6
Vale do Seixo 16 C5
Vale dos Reis 27 G5
Valefanado 31 F4
Vale Feitoso 21 E4
Vale Figueira 35 E2
Vale Flor 16 C4
Vale Florido 19 E5
Vale Formoso 20 C2

Vale Formoso 34 C2
Vale Frechoso 12 C6
Válega 14 D5
Vale Glaciário do Zêzere 20 B2
Vale Grande 19 H4
Valeixe (Sp) 11 E1
Vale Longo 30 D4
Valença do Douro 16 A2
Valença do Minho 10 C2
Valencia de Alcántara (Sp) 25 F4
Valepaço 12 C3
Vale Pereiro 12 D6
Valer (Sp) 13 H3
Vales (Br) 12 D6
Vales (C) 20 A6
Vales (C) 20 B4
Vales (Be) 30 C4
Vales (F) 34 B2
Vales (F) 35 G2
Vale Salgueiro 22 D2
Vale (São Cosme) 10 D6
Vales de Pêro Viseu 20 C4
Vales Mortos 32 A4
Vale Verde (Br) 12 C6
Vale Verde (G) 17 E5
Vale Vinagre 30 C3
Valezim 20 A2
Valhascos 23 H3
Valhelas 20 C2
Valinho 10 C3
Valle de la Venta (Sp) 21 E4
Valle de Matamoros (Sp) 29 H5
Valle de Sanabria (Sp) 13 E-F1
Valle de Santa Ana (Sp) 29 H5
Valleluengo (Sp) 13 H1
Valmaior 14 D6
Valongo (P) 14 D2
Valongo (Po) 24 B5
Valongo das Meadas 12 C5
Valongo de Milhais 12 B6
Valongo dos Azeites 16 B3
Valongo do Vouga 14 D6
Valoura 12 A5
Valpaços 12 B5
Valparaíso (Sp) 13 G2
Valrió (Sp) 21 H5
Valsalabroso (Sp) 17 G2
Valugas 12 A5
Valverde (G) 16 B5
Valverde (Br) 17 E1
Valverde (C) 20 C4
Valverde (S) 23 E3
Valverde (E) 28 A5
Valverde de Leganés (Sp) 29 G3
Valverde del Frenso (Sp) 21 F3
Vaqueiro 15 H1
Vaqueiros (S) 23 F4
Vaqueiros (F) 35 H2
Varadouro 39 E5
Varge 13 E3
Vargem 25 E4
Vargens 31 G6
Variz 13 F6
Várzea (Vc) 11 E3
Várzea (P) 15 F1
Várzea (P) 15 G1
Várzea (Co) 19 G2
Várzea (Co) 19 G5
Várzea (S) 23 E5
Várzea (Sm) 40 A1
Várzea Cova 11 F6
Várzea da Ovelha 15 F2
Várzea de Serra 15 H4
Várzea de Trevoes 16 B3
Várzea dos Cavaleiros 24 A1
Várzeas 18 D6
Varziela (P) 15 F1
Varziela (Co) 18 D2

Varzielas 15 F6
Vasco Esteves de Baixo 20 A3
Vasco Esteves de Cima 20 A3
Vasconha 15 F6
Vascoveiro 16 D5
Vassal 12 B5
Vau 22 C4
Vega del Castillo (Sp) 13 G1
Vega de Tera (Sp) 13 H2
Vega de Terron (Sp) 17 E3
Vegalatrave (Sp) 13 H4
Vegas de Domingo Rey (Sp) 21 H2
Vegaviana (Sp) 21 G5
Veiga de Lila 12 B5
Veigas 13 F3
Veiros (A) 14 D5
Veiros (E) 28 D1
Vela 20 C2
Velada 24 C3
Velas 39 G5
Velosa 16 C6
Venade (Vc) 10 B3
Venade (Vc) 10 C2
Vences (Sp) 12 A2
Venda 29 E4
Vendada 16 D6
Venda da Esperança 19 H3
Venda da Serra 19 G3
Venda do Cepo 16 B5
Venda do Pinheiro 26 C2
Venda do Preto 23 G1
Venda Nova (V) 11 F4
Venda Nova (Le) 18 D5
Venda Nova (S) 23 G2
Venda Nova (S) 24 B2
Venda Seca 26 B3
Vendas Novas 27 G3
Ventas da Barreira (Sp) 12 B2
Ventosa (B) 11 E4
Ventosa (L) 22 B5
Ventosa (L) 22 B6
Ventosa (L) 22 C5
Ventosa (L) 22 D6
Ventosa do Bairro 19 E2
Vera Cruz 31 G1
Verba 18 D1
Verdelhos 20 C2
Vergas 18 D1
Vergeira 30 B3
Verigo 18 D6
Verim 11 E5
Verín (Sp) 12 B2
Vermelha 22 C5
Vermelhos 35 G2
Vermil 10 D6
Vermiosa 17 E5
Vermoil 18 D6
Vermoin 10 D6
Verride 18 D4
Viade de Baixo 11 G4
Vialonga (S) 23 H2
Vialonga (L) 26 C2
Viana do Alentejo 28 B6
Viana do Castelo 10 B4
Viatodos 10 C6
Vicentes 35 F3
Vidago 11 H4
Vidais 22 D4
Vide 20 A3
Vide de Alba (Sp) 13 H4
Vide entre Vinhas 16 B6
Videferre (Sp) 12 A3
Videmonte 20 C1
Vidigal (C) 20 A6
Vidigal (Le) 23 E1
Vidigal (E) 27 G3
Vidigueira 31 G1
Vidual 19 H4

Viduedo 13 E6
Viegas 32 A4
Vieira 18 B6
Vieira de Leiria 18 B6
Vieira do Minho 11 E4
Vieirinhos 18 C5
Vigia 30 D5
Vigo (Sp) 13 E1
Vila Alva 31 F1
Vila Azeda 31 G3
Vila Baleira 40 D3
Vila Boa 15 G4
Vila Boa de Ousilhao 12 D3
Vila Boa do Bispo 15 F3
Vila Boim 29 E2
Vilaça 10 D5
Vila Caiz 15 F2
Vila Cha (B) 10 B5
Vila Cha (Vc) 10 D3
Vila Cha (V) 11 G6
Vila Cha (Br) 13 F5
Vila Cha (P) 14 C1
Vila Cha (Vi) 15 G6
Vila-Cha (V) 16 B1
Vila Cha (G) 16 B6
Vila Cha (Le) 18 D6
Vila Cha de Braciosa 13 G6
Vila Cha de Ourique 23 E5
Vila Chao 15 G1
Vilacoba (Sp) 10 D1
Vila Cortês da Serra 20 B1
Vila Cortês do Mondego 16 C6
Vila Cova (V) 15 H1
Vila Cova a Coelheira 15 H4
Vila Cova de Alva 19 H3
Vila Cova do Covelo 16 A6
Vila da Ponte (V) 11 G4
Vila da Ponte (Vi) 16 B4
Vila de Ala 17 F1
Vila de Cucujaes 14 D4
Vila de Frades 31 G1
Vila de Punhe 10 B4
Vila de Rei 23 H2
Vila do Bispo 34 B4
Vila do Conde (P) 10 B6
Vila do Conde (V) 12 A5
Vila do Porto 40 B3
Vila do Ruivo 23 H1
Vila dos Sinos 17 F1
Vila do Touro 20 D2
Vila Facaia 19 F6
Vila Fernando (G) 20 D1
Vila Fernando (Po) 29 E2
Vila Flor (Br) 16 D1
Vila Flor (Po) 24 C3
Vila Formosa 24 C5
Vila Franca (Vc) 10 B4
Vila Franca (Br) 13 E5
Vila Franca (Co) 19 H2
Vila Franca da Serra 16 B6
Vila Franca das Naves 16 C5
Vila Franca de Xira 26 D1
Vila Franca do Campo 40 C2
Vila Franca do Rosário 26 B1
Vila Fresca de Azeitao 26 D5
Vila Frescainha 10 C5
Vila Garcia (G) 16 C5
Vila Garcia (G) 20 D1
Vila (Lobeira) (Sp) 11 F2
Vila Longa 16 A5
Vilamaior (Sp) 11 H2
Vila Maior 15 G5
Vila Marim 15 H1
Vilameá (Sp) 11 F3
Vila Mea (Br) 13 F3
Vila Mea (P) 15 F2
Vila Mea (Vi) 19 F2

Vilameán (Sp) 10 B2
Vila Mendo de Tavares 20 B1
Vila Moinhos (Sobral) 19 F2
Vila Moreira 23 E3
Vilamoura 35 F4
Vila Nogueira de Azeitao 26 D5
Vila Nova (Br) 12 C4
Vila Nova (Br) 12 C5
Vila Nova (Br) 13 E3
Vila Nova (Co) 19 F5
Vila Nova (S) 23 H3
Vila Nova (F) 36 B3
Vila Nova da Anços 18 D4
Vila Nova da Barca 18 D4
Vila Nova da Baronia 28 A6
Vila Nova da Rainha 22 D6
Vila Nova de Barquinha 23 G3
Vila Nova de Cacela 36 A3
Vila Nova de Cerveira 10 B2
Vila Nova de Corvo 39 F1
Vila Nova de Famalicao 10 C6
Vila Nova de Foz Côa 16 D3
Vila Nova de Gaia 14 D3
Vila Nova de Milfontes 30 A5
Vila Nova de Monsarros 19 E2
Vila Nova de Muiá 10 D3
Vila Nova de Ourém 23 F2
Vila Nova de Paiva 15 H5
Vila Nova de Poiares 19 F4
Vila Nova de São Bento 32 A3
Vila Nova de São Pedro 23 E5
Vila Nova de Tazem 20 A1
Vila Nova do Ceira 19 G4
Vila Novinha 16 B5
Vila Nune 11 F6
Vila Pouca 19 G2
Vila Pouca da Beira 19 H3
Vila Pouca de Aguiar 11 H5
Vila Praia de Ancora 10 B3
Vilar (Sp) 11 E1
Vilar (B) 11 E4
Vilar (Sp) 11 G3
Vilar (V) 11 H4
Vilar (Vi) 15 G4
Vilar (Vi) 16 B4
Vilar (Le) 19 F5
Vilar (L) 22 C5
Vilarandelo 12 B4
Vilar Barroco 19 H5
Vilar Chao 13 E6
Vilar da Lomba 12 C3
Vilar da Veiga 11 E4
Vilar de Amargo 16 D4
Vilar de Arca 15 F3
Vilar de Boi 24 C2
Vilar de Cervos (Sp) 12 B3
Vilar de Cunhas 11 G5
Vilar de Ferreiros 11 G6
Vilar de Ledra 12 C5
Vilar de Maçada 16 A1
Vilardemilo (Sp) 12 C1
Vilar de Mouros 10 B3
Vilar de Murteda 10 B4
Vilar de Ossos 12 D3
Vilar de Paraiso 14 D3
Vilar de Perdizas 11 H3
Vilar de Peregrinos 12 D3
Vilar de Pinheiro 14 C2
Vilar de Rei (Sp) 11 H2
Vilar de Rei 17 F1
Vilar de Santos (Sp) 11 G1
Vilar de Soente 11 E3
Vilardevós (Sp) 12 B2
Vilar do Monte 12 D5
Vilar dos Prazeres 23 F2
Vila Real 15 H1
Vila Real de Santo António
   36 B3

Vilarelho 12 A5
Vilarelho da Raia 12 A3
Vilarelhos 12 D6
Vilares (V) 12 A6
Vilares (Br) 12 C4
Vilares (G) 16 C5
Vilar Fermoso 17 E6
Vilariça 13 F6
Vilarinha 34 B3
Vilarinho (Vc) 10 B3
Vilarinho (B) 10 D4
Vilarinho (V) 11 G4
Vilarinho (Br) 13 E2
Vilarinho (P) 14 C1
Vilarinho (Vi) 15 F5
Vilarinho (Co) 19 F4
Vilarinho (Be) 31 F2
Vilarinho da Castanheira 16 C2
Vilarinho das Azenhas 12 C6
Vilarinho das Cambas 10 C6
Vilarinho de Agrochao 12 D4
Vilarinho de Cotas 16 B2
Vilarinho de Samarda 11 H6
Vilarinho de São Luís 15 E5
Vilarinho de São Romao 16 A2
Vilarinho do Bairro 19 E2
Vilarinho do Monte 12 C4
Vilarinho dos Galegos 17 F1
Vilariño das Poldras (Sp) 11 G1
Vilariño de Conso (Sp) 12 C1
Vilar Maior 21 E1
Vilarouco 16 B3
Vilar Seco 13 G5
Vilar Seco de Lomba 12 C3
Vilar Torpim 17 E5
Vila Ruiva (Vi) 19 H1
Vila Ruiva (Be) 31 F1
Vilas Boas 16 C1
Vilas do Pedro 19 F5
Vilaseco (Sp) 12 D1
Vila Seca (B) 10 C5
Vila Seca (Vi) 16 A3
Vila Seca (Co) 19 E4
Vilas Ruivas 24 C2
Vila Velha de Ródao 24 C2
Vilavella (Sp) 12 D1
Vila Verde (B) 10 D4
Vila Verde (V) 12 A4
Vila Verde (V) 12 A6
Vila Verde (Br) 12 C6
Vila Verde (Br) 12 D3
Vila Verde (Co) 18 C4
Vila Verde (L) 26 B2
Vila Verde da Raia 12 B3
Vila Verde de Ficalho 32 B3
Vila Verde dos Francos 22 C6
Vila Verdinho 12 C5
Vila Viçosa 29 E3
Vileila 10 D3
Vilela (V) 11 H5
Vilela (V) 16 A2
Vilela do Tâmega 12 A4
Vilela Seca 12 A3
Vilharinhos 35 G3
Villablanca (Sp) 36 C2
Villa del Campo (Sp) 21 H4
Villa del Rey (Sp) 25 H2
Villadepera (Sp) 13 H5
Villadesuso (Sp) 10 B1
Villafranco del Guadiana (Sp)
   29 H2
Villalverde (Sp) 13 H1
Villamiel (Sp) 21 F4
Villamor de la Ladre (Sp) 13 H6
Villanueva de las Cruces (Sp) 32 D5
Villanueva de la Sierra (Sp) 12 D1
Villanueva de la Sierra (Sp) 21 H4
Villanueva del Fresno (Sp) 29 F6

Villanueva de los Castillejos (Sp)
   32 B6
Villanueva de Valrojo (Sp) 13 H2
Villar da Farfón (Sp) 13 H2
Villar de Argañan (Sp) 17 F6
Villar de Ciervo (Sp) 17 F5
Villardeciervos (Sp) 13 G2
Villar de la Yegua (Sp) 17 F5
Villar del Buey (Sp) 13 H6
Villar del Rey (Sp) 25 H6
Villar de Samaniego (Sp) 17 G2
Villardiegua de la Ribera (Sp) 13 H5
Villareal (Sp) 29 F3
Villares de Yeltes (Sp) 17 G4
Villargordo (Sp) 17 H3
Villarino (Sp) 17 G1
Villarino de Cebal (Sp) 13 G3
Villarino de Manzanas (Sp) 13 F3
Villarino Tras la Sierra (Sp) 13 G4
Villarmuerto (Sp) 17 H3
Villasbuenas (Sp) 17 F3
Villasbuenas de Gata (Sp) 21 G4
Villasbuenas (Sp) 21 G2
Villavieja de Yeltes (Sp) 17 G4
Villaza (Sp) 12 A2
Villoria de Buenamadre (Sp) 17 H4
Vilvestre (Sp) 17 F3
Vimeiro (L) 22 B5
Vimeiro (Le) 22 D3
Vimieiro 28 C2
Vimioso 13 F5
Vincios (Sp) 10 B1
Vinha da Rainha 18 C5
Vinhais 12 D3
Vinhas 13 E5
Viñas (Sp) 13 G3
Violeiro 20 B5
Virgilios 35 G4
Virtudes 23 E6
Viseu 15 G6
Viseus 31 F5
Vista Alegre 14 C6
Vitigudino (Sp) 17 G3
Vitorino dos Piaes 10 C4
Viuvas 31 F6
Viveiro 11 G4
Vivinena (Sp) 13 G4
Volta do Vale 27 G1
Vouguinha 15 H5
Vouzela 15 F5
Vreia de Bornes 12 A5
Vreia de Jales 11 H6

Xartinho 23 E4
Xendive (Sp) 11 F2
Xerez de Baixo 29 E5
Xinzo de Limia (Sp) 11 H1
Xironda (Sp) 11 H3

Yecla de Yeltes (Sp) 17 G4

Zafara (Sp) 13 H6
Zahinos (Sp) 29 G6
Zamarra (Sp) 21 H1
Zambuja 19 E5
Zambuja de Cima 26 C5
Zambujal (Le) 22 C4
Zambujal (Le) 23 G1
Zambujal (Se) 27 E4
Zambujal (F) 35 H2
Zambujeira do Mar 30 A6
Zambujeiras 30 B5
Zambujeiro 28 D4
Zarza la Mayor (Sp) 21 F6
Zava 17 F1
Zavial 34 B4
Zebreira 21 E6
Zedes 16 C1

Zeive 12 D2
Zibreira 23 F3
Zimao 11 H6
Zimbral 36 A3
Zoio 12 D4

BEACHES
Adraga 26 A3
Agua de Madeiros 22 D1
Algar Seco 34 D4
Costa de Prata 22 C2
Costa do Estoril 26 A-B4
Costa do Sol 26 B4
Foz do Lisandro 26 A2
Gralha 22 C3
Meia Praia 34 C4
Paredes de Vitória 22 C2
Pedras Negras 18 B6
Playa Canela (Sp) 36 C3
Playa de Isla Cristina (Sp) 36 C3
Playa de la Antilla (Sp) 36 C3
Porto de Calada 22 B6
Porto de Barcas 22 B5
Porto de Leixoes 14 C2
Praia Azul 22 B6
Praia da Alagoa 36 B3
Praia da Arrifana 34 B2
Praia da Arvore 14 C1
Praia da Bordeira 34 B3
Praia da Caparica 26 B4
Praia da Carreagem 34 B2
Praia da Consolaçao 22 B4
Praia da Cordama 34 A4
Praia da Culatra 35 H4
Praia da Falesia 35 F4
Praia da Galé 35 E4
Praia da Ilha 30 A4
Praia da Ilha de Faro 35 G4
Praia da Ilha de Tavira 36 A4
Praia da Ingrina 34 B4
Praia da Manta Rota 36 B3
Praia da Mareta 34 A4
Praia da Oura 35 E4
Praia da Penedo 34 B3
Praia da Ponta Ruiva Eiras 34 A4
Praia da Rocha 34 D4
Praia da Salema 34 B4
Praia da Samouqueira 34 B1
Praia das Cabanas 36 A3
Praia das Cascas 36 A4
Praia das Furnas 30 A5
Praia da Zambujeira 30 A6
Praia de Agudela 14 C2
Praia de Ançao 35 F4
Praia de Ancora 10 B3
Praia de Areinho 14 C5
Praia de Beliche 34 A4
Praia de Boa Nova 14 C2
Praia de Burgau 34 B4
Praia de Cabedelo 10 B4
Praia de Cascais 26 B3
Praia de Comporta 27 E6
Praia de Dona Ana 34 C4
Praia de Ericeira 26 A1
Praia de Espinho 14 C4
Praia de Faro 35 G4
Praia de Furadouro 14 C4
Praia de Fuseta 35 H4
Praia de Labruge 14 C1
Praia de Leirosa 18 C5
Praia de Magoito 26 A2
Praia de Maria Luisa 35 F4
Praia de Melides 30 A2
Praia de Moledo 10 B3
Praia de Monte Branco 14 C5
Praia de Monte Clérigo 34 B2
Praia de Monte Gordo 36 B3
Praia de Morgavel 30 A4

Praia de Murraçao 34 A3
Praia de Odeceixe 34 B1
Praia de Porto Covo 30 A4
Praia de Quarteira 35 F4
Praia de Ribeiro 22 B5
Praia de Samarra 26 A2
Praia de Santo André (P) 10 B6
Praia de Santo André (Se) 30 A2
Praia de São Lourenço 26 A1
Praia de São Sebastiao 26 A1
Praia de São Torpes 30 A3
Praia de Suave Mar 10 B5
Praia de Tonel 34 A4
Praia de Vale de Figueiras 34 B3
Praia do Amado 34 B3
Praia do Baleal 22 B4
Praia do Barranco 34 B4
Praia do Barril 36 A4
Praia do Carvalhal 30 A6
Praia do Carvalho 34 D4
Praia do Castelejo 34 A4
Praia do Farol 35 G5
Praia do Foz do Arelho 22 C4
Praia do Martinhal 34 A4
Praia do Porto Novo 22 B5
Praia do Salgado 22 C3
Praia do São Telheiro 34 A4
Praia dos Mouranitos 34 A3
Praia dos Olhos de Agua 35 F4
Praia dos Tres Irmaos 34 A4
Praia do Vale do Lobo 35 F4
Praia Grande (C) 26 A2
Praia Grande (Be) 30 A5
Praia Nova 22 C3
Praia Velha 22 D1
Praia Verde 36 B3
Prainha 40 C5

CAPES & HEADLANDS
Boca do Inferno 26 A3
Cabo Carvoeiro (Le) 22 B4
Cabo Carvoeiro (F) 34 D4
Cabo da Roca 26 A3
Cabo de Santa Maria 35 G5
Cabo de São Vicente 34 A4
Cabo de Sines 30 A3
Cabo Espichel 26 C5
Cabo Girao 40 B5
Cabo Mondego 18 C4
Cabo Raso 26 A3
Cabo Sardao 30 A6
Cabo Silleiro (Sp) 10 B1
Faja do Ouvidor 39 G5
Faja dos Cubres 39 H5
Península de Tróia 27 E5
Ponta da Agulha 40 B1
Ponta da Ajuda 40 C1
Ponta da Atalaia (F) 34 A4
Ponta da Atalaia (F) 34 B2
Ponta da Barca 39 G3
Ponta da Bretanha 40 A1   .
Ponta da Calheta 40 D4
Ponta da Caveira 39 F3
Ponta da Cruz 37 F5
Ponta da Ferraria 40 A1
Ponta da Galera 40 B2
Ponta da Garça 40 C2
Ponta da Ilha 39 G6
Ponta da Lamporeira 22 B6
Ponta da Madrugada 40 D1
Ponta da Piedade 34 C4
Ponta da Queimada 39 G6
Ponta da Ribeira 40 D1
Ponta das Contendas 39 G6
Ponta da Torre 34 B4
Ponta de Almadena 34 B4
Ponta da Laje 26 B4
Ponta de Sagres 34 A4

Ponta de São Jorge 40 B4
Ponta de São Lourenço 40 C5
Ponta do Albarnaz 39 E2
Ponta do Arnel 40 D1
Ponta do Castelo (F) 35 E4
Ponta do Castelo (Sa) 40 C3
Ponta do Cintrao 40 B1
Ponta do Clérigo 40 B5
Ponta do Faial 40 D2
Ponta do Garajau 40 B5
Ponta do Mistério 39 G6
Ponta do Pargo 40 A5
Ponta do Queimado 39 G1
Ponta dos Covinhos 22 C3
Ponta dos Ilhéus 39 A3
Ponta dos Rosais 39 F5
Ponta do Topo 39 H6
Ponta do Tristao 37 E3
Pontal 34 A3
Ponta Torrais 39 F1

CASTLES & FORTS
Ansiaes 16 C2
Azagala (Sp) 25 H5
Castelo Branco 20 C6
Fortaleza da Santa Catarina 34 D4
Forte de Nossa Senhora da Graça 29 F2
Forte de Santa Luzia 29 F2
Paço Ducal 29 E3

CAVES
Furna do Enxorfe 39 H3
Furnas do Enxofre 39 H1
Grutas de Alvados 23 E3
Grutas de Santo António 23 E3
Mira de Aire 23 E3

CHURCHES
Antigo Convento de Santa Maria de Aguiar 17 E4
Bom Jesus do Monte 10 D5
Convento de Cristo 23 G3
Convento de Tomina 32 C2
Mosteiro de Santa Clara 14 C1
Mosteiro de Santa Maria da Vitória 23 E2
Mosteiro de Santa Maria de Alco baça 22 D3
Nossa Senhora da Penha 24 D4
Nossa Senhora dos Remédios 15 H3
Santa Luzia 10 B4
São Frutuoso de Montélios 10 D5
Senhora de Monte Alto 19 G4
Senhora do Bom Sucesso 21 E4
The Sanctuary 23 F2
Trigais 20 A3

DUNES
Dunas de Cantanhede 18 C2-3
Dunas de Ovar 14 C4
Dunas de Quiaios 18 C3
Pinhal do Urso 18 C5

ISLANDS
Berlenga 22 A4
Bugio 26 B4
Estelas 22 A4
Farilhoes 22 A3
Ilha da Armona 35 H4
Ilha da Barreta 35 G5
Ilha da Culatra 35 H4
Ilha de Faro 35 G5
Ilha das Flores 39 E-F 2-3
Ilha de Santa Maria 40 B-C 2-3
Ilha de São Jorge 39 F5-G6
Ilha de São Miguel 40 A-D 1-2

Ilha de Tavira 35 H4
Ilha do Corvo 39 F1
Ilha do Faial 39 E5-6
Ilha do Pico 39 F-G6
Ilha do Porto Santo 40 D3
Ilha Graciosa 39 G3
Ilhas Desertas 40 C-D6
Ilha Terceira 39 F-65
Ilhéu de Baixo ou da Cal 40 D4
Ilhéu de Cima 40 D3
Ilhéu de Ferro 40 D3
Islas As Estelas (Sp) 10 B1

MOUNTAINS & PASSES
Aboboreira 31 G4
Achada da Mina 31 H6
Agua Negra 32 A4
Aire 23 F3
Alagoa da Forca 31 E4
Alcaria do Cume 35 H3
Almeirim 23 F6
Alor (Sp) 32 A2
Alto das Cabeças 28 D3
Alto de Estivadas (Sp) 12 A2
Alto de Forriolo (Sp) 11 G1
Alto de Furnaces (Sp) 12 B2
Alto de Nevosa 11 F3
Alto de São Martinho 22 D3
Alto de Velao 15 G1
Alto de Vieiro (Sp) 11 F1
Alto do Canizo (Sp) 12 C1
Alto do Espinho 15 G1
Alto do Trevim 19 F4
Altura do Monte Novo 31 F2
Arieiro 40 B5
Armada 11 G4
Aroche (Sp) 32 D2
Arrifana 34 B2
Atalaia (Se) 30 B2
Atalaia (F) 34 C4
Atalaia da Contenda 25 F6
Azelha 23 E3
Balurcos 36 B1
Bando dos Santos 24 B2
Barbas de Gaio 31 G4
Barranco do Milho 34 C3
Barrosa 40 B2
Basteiros 30 D5
Bispo 35 G3
Boavista 35 F1
Boca de Encumeada 40 B5
Bolla (Sp) 21 H2
Bombel 27 F3
Borrachina (Sp) 29 G4
Bramadero (Sp) 32 B5
Bravo 19 G6
Brenha 35 E1
Buarcos 18 C4
Bujardo (Sp) 29 G5
Caballo (Sp) 21 F5
Cabeça Alta 20 C1
Cabeça da Velha 20 A2
Cabeça Gorda 30 B6
Cabeço Alto (V) 11 G3
Cabeço Alto (C) 25 G1
Cabeço da Neve 19 F1
Cabeça do Velho 20 B2
Cabeço Rainha 19 H6
Cabezo Gordo (Sp) 32 C4
Cabreiro (Sp) 11 G2
Cabreiro 11 H6
Cachaza (Sp) 21 F4
Caixeiro 28 D2
Caldeira (Fa) 39 E5
Caldeira (T) 39 G1
Caldeira das Sete Cidades 40 A1
Caldeirao 39 F1
Cansado 24 A5

Capela 24 D6
Caramulinho 19 F1
Carrascais 30 D1
Carvalhoso 17 E2
Carvao 40 A1
Casa Branca 25 F6
Cascalho 27 E2
Cebollar (Sp) 36 D2
Cerro da Mina 31 F2
Cerro Grande 31 F6
Cevada 31 F1
Chas 15 F5
Chorlo (Sp) 25 H4
Cid Almeida 32 A1
Colos 24 A4
Corona 12 D2
Courelas 28 D6
Cruz 31 H6
Cruzes 15 E6
Cumeada do Malhao 35 G2
Dos Hermanas (Sp) 25 G6
Durao 17 E3
Eira do Serrado 40 B5
El Buitrón (Sp) 32 B4
Espinheira 28 C5
Estacas 30 C6
Ferro 40 C1
Figueiras 23 G4
Fóia 34 C2
Fontes 31 G2
Fonte Santa 34 C2
Fornalha 36 A1
Fraga Negra 11 E4
Galiñeiro (Sp) 10 C1
Gaviao 30 C5
Gia 15 F3
Gibraltar (Sp) 32 B5
Giestoso 11 F2
Godeal 27 H3
Golilla (Sp) 25 H4
Granado (Sp) 32 A6
Groba (Sp) 10 B1
Isidro (Sp) 29 G6
Jabarrieja (Sp) 25 H6
Jalama (Sp) 21 F3
Junceda 11 E4
l.adaino 12 D6
Lagoa 35 H2
Lamparona (Sp) 25 F5
Lançadoiras 31 F6
Lapa 31 F4
La Pedreira 40 D3
Lapones (Sp) 25 F3
Las Mesas (Sp) 21 F3
Las Navas (Sp) 21 F5
Legua 31 G4
Los Cristales (Sp) 32 D6
Los Perales (Sp) 25 G2
Lousado (Sp) 10 B2
Luz 13 G4
Luzim 15 E2
Mairos (Sp) 12 B3
Malhada do Velho 30 A5
Malhao 35 E1
Malpique 32 B2
Ma Noite 31 G6
Marco 11 G6
Marifranca (Sp) 21 H4
Marofa 17 E4
Meliça 23 H2
Mentiras 32 C1
Mesquita 34 D2
Miguel Anes 36 A3
Minheo 11 H5
Miño Cuevo (Sp) 13 H2
Moinho da Quinta 31 E4
Molinos 32 B2
Monfurado 27 H4

Monsanto 20 D5
Monte Brasil 39 H2
Monte da Guia 39 E6
Monte Escuro 40 C1
Monte Ferro (Sp) 10 B1
Monte Gordo 26 D1
Monte Gordo (Sp) 36 B2
Montemuro 15 G4
Monte Ruivo 34 C3
Monte Sameiro 10 D5
Monte Trigo 39 G5
Mudo 35 F2
Negros 35 F2
Nora (Sp) 29 H6
Oural 10 D4
Outeiro Alvo 11 E2
Pardieiros 32 B4
Pedrada 11 E2
Pelados 35 G2
Peña Mira (Sp) 13 G2
Peña Nofre (Sp) 12 B1
Peña Rubia (Sp) 11 E1
Peñas de Levante (Sp) 21 H4
Peneda 11 E2
Penedo de Seixo 31 F4
Penha (B) 11 E6
Penha (Po) 25 E4
Perdigón (Sp) 29 G6
Perero (Sp) 32 C3
Pico 39 F6
Pico Alto 40 B2
Pico da Esperança 39 G5
Pico da Vara 40 D1
Pico de Castelo 40 D3
Pico Ruivo 40 B5
Picos 34 C2
Pico São Mamede 25 E4
Pinoucas 15 F6
Pipas 29 E6
Pisco 16 B5
Pisoes-Moura 32 A2
Poiso 40 B5
Poldra 34 B3
Pomba 35 E1
Portela 40 B5
Portela das Corchas 34 D2
Portela de la Canda (Sp) 12 D1
Portela de Leonte 11 E3
Portela do Homem 11 F3
Portela do Lagarto 11 E2
Portillo del Pardonelo (Sp) 13 E1
Puerto de la Zarza (Sp) 32 C4
Puerto de los Brisos (Sp) 25 H5
Puerto de los Castaños (Sp) 21 H6
Puerto de los Conejeros (Sp) 25 G5
Puerto de Outeiro de Augas (Sp)
    11 F1
Puerto de Perales (Sp) 21 G3
Puerto Nuevo (Sp) 21 H2
Puerto Viejo (Sp) 21 H2
Ramo Alto 28 D4
Rasca 31 F3
Rego 29 F2
Remal 40 A5
Rodeiro 23 G4
Roma 26 B1
Ruivo do Paúl 40 A5
Salto de Cavalo 40 C1
San José (Sp) 29 H6
Santa Helena 15 H4
Santa Luzia (Vc) 10 B4
Santa Luzia (Be) 32 A5
Santa Quitéria 15 F1
Santiago 25 F2
São Gens 28 D3
São Maciário 15 G4
São Martinho 20 C6
São Miguel 35 H4

São Pedro 28 C6
São Pedro de Açor 19 H3
São Pedro Velho 15 E5
São Vicente 28 B6
Seixa 11 G5
Senhora de Araceli 31 F5
Señora (Sp) 29 G5
Serra 24 B6
Serra Amarela 11 E3
Serra da Adiça 32 B3
Serra da Arada 15 F5
Serra da Arrábida 26 D5
Serra da Brejeira 34 C1
Serra da Cabreira 11 F4-5
Serra da Carapinha 34 D2
Serra da Coroa 12 D2-3
Serra da Estrêla 20 B3-C2
Serra da Gralheira 15 E5
Serra da Lapa 16 A4-B5
Serra da Lousa 19 F5
Serra da Malcata 21 E-F3
Serra da Padrela 12 A5
Serra da Peneda 11 E2
Serra das Neves 30 C5
Serra de Açor 19 H3
Serra de Aire 23 F3
Serra de Alvao 11 H6
Serra de Alvelos 19 H6
Serra de Arga 10 B3
Serra de Bigorne 15 G4
Serra de Bornes 12 D6
Serra de Grândola 30 C2
Serra de Leomil 15 H4
Serra de Malcata 21 E3
Serra de Mendro 28 C6
Serra de Mértola 31 H5
Serra de Monchique 34 C-D2
Serra de Monfurado 27 H4
Serra de Montejunto 22 C-D5
Serra de Montemuro 15 F-G4
Serra de Montesinho 13 E2
Serra de Nogueira 12 D4
Serra de Ossa 28 C-D3
Serra de São Mamede 25 E4-5
Serra de Serpa 31 H4
Serra de Sicó 18 D6
Serra de Sintra 26 A-B3
Serra de Vilarelho 12 A6
Serra do Barroso 11 G4-5
Serra do Caldeirao 35 E-F2
Serra do Canizo (Sp) 12 C-D1
Serra do Caramulo 15 F6
Serra do Cercal 30 B4
Serra do Cume 39 F-G6
Serra do Espinhaço de Cao
    34 B3
Serra do Gerês 11 F3
Serra do Larouco 11 H3
Serra do Leiranco 11 H4
Serra do Malhao 35 F2
Serra do Marao 15 G2
Serra do Muradal 19 H5
Serra do Reboredo 17 E2
Serra dos Candeeiros 22 D3-4
Serra do Soajo 11 E3
Serra do Topo 39 H5
Serra Gorda 40 B1
Serves 26 C2
Sierra de Coria (Sp) 21 G5
Sierra de la Canchera (Sp) 21 H2
Sierra de la Culebra (Sp) 13 G-H2
Sierra de la Garrapata (Sp) 21 F5
Sierra de la Malvana (Sp) 21 E-F3
Sierra de las Contiendas (Sp)
    32 D2
Sierra del Centinela (Sp) 25 G5
Sierra del Naranjal (Sp) 25 F5
Sierra de los Angeles (Sp) 21 H3

Sierra del Pendón (Sp) 29 G5-6
Sierra del Puerto (Sp) 25 F-G5
Sierra del Zarzoso (Sp) 29 H5
Sierra de Peñeas Libres (Sp) 12 B2
Sierra de Santa Olalla (Sp) 21 F4
Sierra de Santiago (Sp) 25 H5
Sierra de Xurés (Sp) 11 F3
Sierra El Vescar (Sp) 32 C1
Sierra Grande (Sp) 21 H6
Sierra Grijona (Sp) 32 D6
Sierra Madroñera (Sp) 32 B6
Sierra Pelada (Sp) 32 D4
Silleta (Sp) 21 H6
Sobrosa 32 C2
Torre 20 B3
Torre de Aspa 34 A4
Torrejón (Sp) 25 F4
Torrico de San Pedro (Sp) 25 G4
Torrinheiras 11 F5
Travessa 32 C2
Urza 31 E5
Vale da Grade 31 E6
Vale de Agua 24 A4
Vale de Figueiras 24 A6
Vale de Lobos 30 C5
Vale Formoso 34 C2
Vaqueiro 15 H1
Viegas 32 A4
Vigia 30 D5

**NATIONAL PARKS &
FORESTS**
Parque da Pena 26 B3
Parque Nacional da Peneda-Gerés
    11 F4
Parque Nacional Serra do Xures
    11 F2
Parque Natural da Arrábida 26 D5
Parque Natural da Madeira 40 B5
Parque Natural da Ria Formosa
    35 G4
Parque Natural da Serra da Estrela
    20 B2
Parque Natural da Serra de São
    Mamede 24 D4, 25 E5
Parque Natural das Serras de Aire
    e Candeeiros 23 E3
Parque Natural de la Sierra de
    Ara-cena (Sp) 32 D2
Parque Natural de Montesinho
    12 D2
Parque Natural de Sintra-Cascais
    26 A2
Parque Natural do Alvao 11 G6
Parque Natural do Sudoeste
    Aletejano e Costa Vincentina
    30 A-B3-6, 34 B1-A4
Pinhal de Leiria 18 B6
Reserva Nacional do Sierra Cule-
    bra (Sp) 13 G2
Reserva Natural da Berlenga 22 A4
Reserva Natural das Dunas de São
    Jacinto 14 C6
Reserva Natural d'Ilha Berlenga
    22 A4
Reserva Natural do Estuário do Sado
    27 E5
Reserva Natural do Estuário do Tejo
    26 D2
Reserva Natural do Paúl de Arzila
    18 D4
Reserva Natural do Paúl de
    Boquilobo 23 F4
Reserva Natural do Sapal de Castro
    Marim e Vila Real de Santo
    António 36 B3
Reserva Natural Serra da Malcata
    21 E3

RIVERS, BAYS & LAKES
Albufeira de Mourao 29 E5
Arroyo de Albanacar (Sp) 32 B4
Arroyo de Cuncos (Sp) 29 F5
Arroyo de Jumadiel (Sp) 25 G-H3
Arroyo Freigamuñoz (Sp) 29 F5
Arroyo Zaos (Sp) 29 G6
Azud de Matacavas (Sp) 36 B-C1
Baía de Lagos 34 C4
Baia de Setúbal 26 D6, 30 A1
Baia do São Lourenço 40 C2
Barra de El Rompido (Sp) 36 D3
Barragem da Aguieira 19 F2
Barragem da Bravura 34 C3
Barragem da Idanha 20 D5
Barragem da Penida 10 C5
Barragem das Mercês 32 C-D2
Barragem da Vigia 28 D4
Barragem de Alto Cávado 11 G3
Barragem de Arade 34 D3
Barragem de Beliche 36 A-B2
Barragem de Belver 24 B3
Barragem de Campilhas 30 B4
Barragem de Fagilde 15 H6
Barragem de Fronhas 19 G3
Barragem de Magos 27 E-F1
Barragem de Maranhao 24 B6
Barragem de Meimoa 20 D3
Barragem de Montargil 24 A6
Barragem de Monte da Rocha
    30 D5
Barragem de Monte Novo 28 C4-5
Barragem de Morgavel 30 B3-4
Barragem de Odivelas 31 E1
Barragem de Paradela 11 F3
Barragem de Peramanca 28 A5
Barragem de Póvoa 24 D3
Barragem de Pracana 24 C3
Barragem de Santa Clara 30 D6
Barragem de Santa Luzia 19 H4
Barragem de Santa Maria 17 E4
Barragem de Tapada Grande 32 A5
Barragem de Vale de Gaio 27 H6,
    30 D1
Barragem de Venda Nova 11 G4
Barragem de Vilar 16 B4
Barragem do Alto Lindoso 11 E3
Barragem do Alto Rabagao 11 G4
Barragem do Alvito 28 B3
Barragem do Cabril 19 G6
Barragem do Caia 25 F6
Barragem do Castelo de Bode
    23 H3
Barragem do Divor 28 B3
Barragem do Funcho 35 E2
Barragem do Pego do Altar 27 G-H5
Barragem do Poio 24 D3
Barragem do Roxo 31 E-F3
Barragem Fonte Serne 30 C4
Barragem Penha Garcia 21 E5
Barragem Toulica 21 E6
Barragem Vilarinho das Furnas
    11 E3
Canal de El Granado (Sp) 32 A6
Canal del Piedras (Sp) 36 C2
Canal de São Jorge 39 B-C5
Canal do Faial 39 E6
Canal do Sado Morgavel 30 C-D3
Embalse de Alcántara (Sp) 21 F6,
    25 H1
Embalse de Almendra (Sp) 17 H1-2
Embalse de Bao (Sp) 12 C1
Embalse de Borbollón (Sp) 21 G4
Embalse de Castro (Sp) 13 H5
Embalse de Cernadilla (Sp) 13 F1-2
Embalse del Agueda (Sp) 21 H1
Embalse de Lagunazo (Sp) 32 C6
Embalse de la Hoja (Sp) 32 D5

Embalse de las Conchas (Sp) 11 F2
Embalse de las Portas (Sp) 12 C1
Embalse del Calabazar (Sp) 32 D5
Embalse del Chanza (Sp) 32 A6
Embalse de los Machos (Sp) 36 C2
Embalse del Risco (Sp) 32 B6
Embalse de Pías (Sp) 12 D1
Embalse de Piedra Aguda (Sp)
  29 G3-4
Embalse de Piedras (Sp) 36 C1
Embalse de Portaje (Sp) 21 H6
Embalse de Puente Porto (Sp) 13 E1
Embalse de Rivera de Gata (Sp)
  21 G4
Embalse de Salas (Sp) 11 F2
Embalse de Sancho (Sp) 32 C6
Embalse de San Sebastián (Sp)
  12 D1
Embalse de Tres Picos (Sp) 32 B6
Embalse de Valparaíso (Sp) 13 G2
Embalse de Villar del Rey (Sp) 25 H5
Embalse de Zamores (Sp) 25 F3
Embalse Grande (Sp) 32 C-D6
Lagoa Azul 40 A1
Lagoa Comprida 20 B2
Lagoa das Furnas 40 C2
Lagoa da Vela 18 C3
Lagoa de Albufeira 26 C5
Lagoa de Obidos 22 C4
Lagoa do Fogo 40 B-C2
Lagoa Funda 39 E3
Lagoa Verde 40 A1
Lago de Sanabria (Sp) 13 E1
Lago de Santo André 30 A2
Largo da Coroa 14 C5
Ria da Costa Nova 14 C6
Ria de Aveiro 14 C5
Ria Formosa 35 G4
Ribeira da Cerca 34 C2
Ribeira da Erra 23 G6
Ribeira da Figueira 31 E2
Ribeira da Foupana 36 A1
Ribeira da Gema 30 C4
Ribeira da Isna 24 A1
Ribeira da Meimoa 20 C4
Ribeira da Murtega 32 D1
Ribeira da Pega 16 D6
Ribeira da Raia 28 B1
Ribeira das Alcáçovas 27 H5
Ribeira das Cabras 16 D6, 21 E1
Ribeira da Serta 19 H6
Ribeira da Sor 23 H6
Ribeira de Abrilongo 25 F6
Ribeira de Aguiar 17 E4
Ribeira de Alcarrache 29 E6
Ribeira de Alenquer 22 C-D6
Ribeira de Alge 19 F5
Ribeira de Algibre 35 F3
Ribeira de Alportel 35 H3
Ribeira de Alpreade 20 C5
Ribeira de Alvacar 31 F5
Ribeira de Arades 21 E5
Ribeira de Ardila 32 A-B1
Ribeira de Asseca 29 E3
Ribeira de Azambuja 28 C5
Ribeira de Azevel 29 E5
Ribeira de Brenhas 32 A-B2
Ribeira de Campilhas 30 C4
Ribeira de Canha 27 F3
Ribeira de Caria 20 C3

Ribeira de Carreiras 31 G6
Ribeira de Chouto 23 G5
Ribeira de Cobres 31 F4
Ribeira de Coja 15 H6
Ribeira de Corona 30 C3
Ribeira de Curral da Velha 31 F5
Ribeira de Divor 27 G2
Ribeira de Figueiró 24 C3
Ribeira de Godelim 29 F6
Ribeira de Grândola 30 C2
Ribeira de Lavre 27 G3
Ribeira de Limas 31 H4
Ribeira de Lucefece 28 D3
Ribeira de Marateca 27 G4
Ribeira de Mós 17 E3
Ribeira de Muge 23 F-G6
Ribeira de Nisa 24 D3
Ribeira de Odearce 31 G2
Ribeira de Odeleite 36 A2
Ribeira de Odelouca 34 D2-3
Ribeira de Odivelas 31 E2
Ribeira de Oeiras 31 F6
Ribeira de Ota 22 D6
Ribeira de Peramanca 28 B5
Ribeira de Santa Margarida 24 B6
Ribeira de Santo Estêvao 27 E2
Ribeira de São Cristovao 27 H5
Ribeira de São Domingos 30 C3-4
Ribeira de São João 24 D3
Ribeira de Seda 24 C5
Ribeira de Seixe 34 C2
Ribeira de Serrazola 24 C6
Ribeira de Sor 24 B-C4
Ribeira de Teja 16 C3
Ribeira de Tera 28 B2
Ribeira de Terges 31 F4
Ribeira de Torgal 30 C5
Ribeira de Touroes 17 E6, 21 F1
Ribeira de Toutalga 32 B2
Ribeira de Ulme 23 G4
Ribeira de Vale do Cobrao 27 E2
Ribeira de Valverde 28 A5
Ribeira de Zacarias 17 E1
Ribeira do Alamo 28 D5
Ribeira do Almadafe 28 B1-2
Ribeira do Almuro 29 E1-2
Ribeira do Aravil 21 E6, 25 F1
Ribeira do Enxoé 32 A3
Ribeira do Murtigao 32 C2
Ribeira do Roxo 30 D3
Ribeira dos Aivados 31 E4
Ribeira do Vascao 35 G1
Ribeira do Zebro 29 F6
Ribeira Grande 24 D6
Ribeira Nova da Baronia 31 E1
Río Agueda (Sp) 17 F4
Río Agueda 19 F1
Río Agueda (Sp) 21 G2
Río Alagón (Sp) 21 G5
Río Alburrel (Sp) 25 E3
Río Alcarrache (Sp) 29 G5
Río Alfusqueiro 15 E6
Río Aliste (Sp) 13 G-H3
Río Almonda 23 F4
Río Alva 19 G3
Río Alviela 23 E4
Río Angueira 13 F5
Río Arade 34 D3
Río Arda 15 E4
Río Arnoia (Sp) 12 A1

Río Arrago (Sp) 21 G4
Río Arunca 18 D4
Río Asseca 23 E5
Río Ave 10 C6, 11 E5
Río Azere 11 E2
Río Azibo 12 D5, 13 E5
Río Barosa 15 H3
Río Beça 11 G5
Río Beságueda 21 E4
Río Boco 18 D1
Río Caia 25 E6, 29 F1
Río Caima 15 E5
Río Calvo 12 B4
Río Camaces (Sp) 17 F3-4
Río Carnide 18 C5
Río Cávado 10 C5, 11 F4-G3
Río Ceira 19 F4
Río Chança 32 A5
Río Côa 16 D3, 21 E2
Río Confrentes (Sp) 29 G5
Río Corrus 12 A5
Río Coura 10 B-C3
Río Criz 19 G2
Río Dao 15 H6, 19 G2
Río de Carvalhais 12 D5
Río Degebe 28 D5
Río de Guide 12 C4
Río de las Uces (Sp) 17 G3
Río de la Vega de Matalobos (Sp)
  21 F4
Río de los Angeles (Sp) 21 H3
Río de Malagón (Sp) 32 B5
Río de Onor 13 F2
Río de São Matinho 27 G4
Río Deva (Sp) 11 E1
Río Douro 13 H5, 15 E3, 16 B2,
  17 F2
Río Duero (Sp) 13 H5, 17 F2
Río Erges 25 G1
Río Erjas (Sp) 21 F5
Río Este 10 D6
Río Ferreira 15 E1
Río Gavilanes (Sp) 17 H6
Río Gévora (Sp) 25 F5
Río Godolid (Sp) 29 H5
Río Guadiana 29 E6, 31 H2-6
Río Guadiana (Sp) 36 B2
Río Homem 11 E4
Río Huebra (Sp) 17 F3
Río Laboreiro 11 E2
Río Leça 14 D2
Río Lena 23 E1-2
Río Lima 10 C4
Río Lis 18 B6
Río Louredo 11 G6
Río Maças 13 F5
Río Massueime 16 C4-5
Río Mena (Sp) 13 H4
Río Mente 12 C3
Río Minho 10 C2
Río Miño (Sp) 10 D1
Río Mira 30 B5, 31 E6
Río Mondego 18 D4, 19 G2, 20 C2
Río Mouro 11 E2
Río Murtiga (Sp) 32 D2
Río Nabao 19 E6, 23 G2
Río Negro (Sp) 13 G1
Río Neiva 10 B5
Río Noéme 20 D1
Río Ocreza 20 C5, 24 C2

Río Odiel (Sp) 32 D6
Río Olo 11 G6
Río Oraque (Sp) 32 D5
Río Paiva (Av) 15 F4-H5
Río Pavia (Vi) 19 G1
Río Piedras (Sp) 36 C2
Río Ponsul 20 C6, 21 E5
Río Rabaçal 12 C3
Río Sabor 13 E2-F5, 16 D2
Río Sado 27 E5, 30 D2-4
Río Salor (Sp) 25 G3
Río Samora 26 D2
Río Seco 17 E5
Río Seia 19 H2
Río Sizandro 22 C6
Río Sorraia 27 E1-G1
Río Sousa 15 E2
Río Sul 15 G5
Río Támega 11 G6, 12 A3, 15 F2
Río Támega (Sp) 12 A1
Río Távora 16 B3
Río Tea (Sp) 10 D1
Río Tedo 16 A3
Río Tejo 23 E6-H3, 24 A3-D2, 26 D3
Río Tera (Sp) 13 G-H2
Río Tinhela 12 A6
Río Tormes (Sp) 17 H1
Río Torto 12 B5, 16 B2, 20 D4
Río Tripeiro 20 B6
Río Tua 12 C6
Río Tuela (Sp) 12 D1
Río Tuella 12 C5-D3
Río Turones (Sp) 17 E5
Río Vale de Moinhos 13 E5
Río Vez 11 E2
Río Vouga 15 E6
Río Xarrama 28 A6
Río Xévora 25 G6
Río Yeltes (Sp) 17 G4
Río Zapatón (Sp) 25 H4, 29 G1
Río Zêzere 19 H5, 20 C3, 23 G3
Rivera Aurela (Sp) 25 E2
Rivera de Albarragena (Sp) 25 G4
Rivera de Alcorneo (Sp) 25 F5
Rivera de Anlconchel (Sp) 29 F4
Rivera de Azaba (Sp) 17 F6
Rivera de Chanza (Sp) 32 C3
Rivera de Fresnedosa (Sp) 21 G6
Rivera de Gata (Sp) 21 G4
Rivera de la Cobica (Sp) 32 B5
Rivera de la Peña (Sp) 17 G2
Rivera del Fraile (Sp) 25 F4
Rivera de Meca (Sp) 32 C6
Rivera de Peramora (Sp) 32 C3
Vala da Azambuja 23 E6

RUINS
Centum Cellas 20 C2
Citania de Briteiros 11 E5
Conimbriga 19 E4
La Atalaya (Sp) 21 G3
Milreu 35 G4
Puente Romano (Sp) 25 G1
Ruínas Romanas de Cetóbriga 26 D5

VALLEYS
Vale Glaciário do Zêzere 20 B2
Valle de Sanabria (Sp) 13 E-F1

PLANET TALK

Lonely Planet's FREE quarterly newsletter

We love hearing from you and think you'd like to hear from us.

When...is the right time to see reindeer in Finland?
Where...can you hear the best palm-wine music in Ghana?
How...do you get from Asunción to Areguá by steam train?
What...is the best way to see India?

For the answer to these and many other questions read PLANET TALK.

Every issue is packed with up-to-date travel news and advice including:

- a letter from Lonely Planet co-founders Tony and Maureen Wheeler
- go behind the scenes on the road with a Lonely Planet author
- feature article on an important and topical travel issue
- a selection of recent letters from travellers
- details on forthcoming Lonely Planet promotions
- complete list of Lonely Planet products

To join our mailing list contact any Lonely Planet office.

Also available: Lonely Planet T-shirts. 100% heavyweight cotton.

LONELY PLANET ONLINE

Get the latest travel information before you leave or while you're on the road

Whether you've just begun planning your next trip, or you're chasing down specific info on currency regulations or visa requirements, check out the Lonely Planet World Wide Web site for up-to-the-minute travel information.

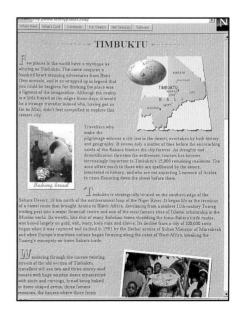

As well as travel profiles of your favourite destinations (including interactive maps and full-colour photos), you'll find current reports from our army of researchers and other travellers, updates on health and visas, travel advisories, and the ecological and political issues you need to be aware of as you travel.

There's an online travellers' forum (the Thorn Tree) where you can share your experiences of life on the road, meet travel companions and ask other travellers for their recommendations and advice. We also have plenty of links to other Web sites useful to independent travellers.

With tens of thousands of visitors a month, the Lonely Planet Web site is one of the most popular on the Internet and has won a number of awards including GNN's Best of the Net travel award.

http://www.lonelyplanet.com

SELECTED LONELY PLANET GUIDES TO EUROPE

Portugal
This lively guide takes you to all corners of Portugal, from the bustling cities of Lisbon and Porto to the back-of-beyond villages of Trás-os-Montes. All you'll need to discover this bewitching country is right here, whether you're looking for empty beaches, medieval castles, colourful markets and festivals, or the anguished songs of *fado*. A companion guide to *Portugal travel atlas*.

France
From the megaliths of Carnac to the pyramid of the Louvre, from Piaf to Les Négresses Vertes, and from Bonifacio to Calais, this guide will prove invaluable.

Italy
The surprises of this vibrant country are limitless and range from festivals to fashion. Discover the best Italy has to offer with this thorough and practical guide.

Spain
From a bullring in the hot afternoon sun to a cool water garden in Alhambra, from the *rías* to the *costas* and from the Prado to the Picos – wherever in Spain your imagination leads, this new guide will take you there.

Mediterranean Europe
Detailed information for travel in Albania, Andorra, Bosnia-Hercegovina, Croatia, Cyprus, France, Greece, Italy, Macedonia, Malta, Morocco, Portugal, Slovenia, Spain, Tunisia, Turkey and Yugoslavia (Montenegro and Serbia).

Western Europe
Practical advice and travel information for Andorra, Austria, Belgium, Britain, France, Germany, Greece, Ireland, Italy, Liechtenstein, Luxembourg, the Netherlands, Portugal, Spain and Switzerland.

Western Europe phrasebook
Words and phrases for Basque, Catalan, Dutch, French, German, Greek, Irish, Italian, Portuguese, Scottish Gaelic, Spanish (Castilian) and Welsh.

Other Lonely Planet guides to Europe:
Amsterdam, Austria, Baltic States & Kaliningrad, Britain, Central Europe, Czech & Slovak Republics, Denmark, Dublin, Eastern Europe, Finland, Greece, Hungary, Iceland, Greenland & the Faroe Islands, Ireland, Italy, Paris, Poland, Prague, Russia, Ukraine & Belarus, Scandinavian & Baltic Europe, Slovenia, St Petersburg, Switzerland, Trekking in Greece, Trekking in Spain, Vienna, Walking in Britain, Walking in Switzerland

Phrasebooks
Baltic States, Central Europe, Eastern Europe, French, Greek, Mediterranean Europe, Russian, Scandinavian Europe, Spanish, Ukrainian

LONELY PLANET PRODUCTS

AFRICA
Africa on a shoestring • Arabic (Moroccan) phrasebook • Cape Town city guide • Central Africa • East Africa • Egypt • Egypt travel atlas • Ethiopian (Amharic) phrasebook • Kenya • Kenya travel atlas • Morocco • North Africa • South Africa, Lesotho & Swaziland • South Africa, Lesotho & Swaziland travel atlas •Swahili phrasebook • Trekking in East Africa• West Africa • Zimbabwe, Botswana & Namibia • Zimbabwe, Botswana & Namibia travel atlas

Travel Literature: The Rainbird: A Central African Journey • Songs to an African Sunset: A Zimbabwean Story

ANTARCTICA
Antarctica

AUSTRALIA & THE PACIFIC
Australia • Australian phrasebook • Bushwalking in Australia • Bushwalking in Papua New Guinea • Fiji • Fijian phrasebook • Islands of Australia's Great Barrier Reef • Melbourne city guide • Micronesia • New Caledonia • New South Wales & the ACT • New Zealand • Northern Territory • Outback Australia • Papua New Guinea • Papua New Guinea phrasebook • Queensland • Rarotonga & the Cook Islands • Samoa ∈ Solomon Islands • South Australia • Sydney city guide • Tahiti & French Polynesia • Tasmania • Tonga • Tramping in New Zealand • Vanuatu • Victoria • Western Australia

Travel Literature: Islands in the Clouds • Sean & David's Long Drive

CENTRAL AMERICA & THE CARIBBEAN
Bermuda • Central America on a shoestring • Costa Rica • Cuba • Eastern Caribbean • Guatemala, Belize & Yucatán: La Ruta Maya • Jamaica

EUROPE
Austria • Baltic States & Kaliningrad • Baltics States phrasebook • Britain • Central Europe on a shoestring • Central Europe phrasebook • Czech & Slovak Republics • Denmark • Dublin city guide • Eastern Europe on a shoestring • Eastern Europe phrasebook • Finland • France • Greece • Greek phrasebook • Hungary • Iceland, Greenland & the Faroe Islands • Ireland • Italy • Mediterranean Europe on a shoestring • Mediterranean Europe phrasebook • Paris city guide • Poland • Portugal travel atlas • Prague city guide • Russia, Ukraine & Belarus • Russian phrasebook • Scandinavian & Baltic Europe on a shoestring • Scandinavian Europe phrasebook • Slovenia • Spain • St Petersburg city guide • Switzerland • Trekking in Greece • Trekking in Spain • Ukrainian phrasebook • Vienna city guide • Walking in Britain • Walking in Switzerland • Western Europe on a shoestring • Western Europe phrasebook

INDIAN SUBCONTINENT
Bangladesh • Bengali phrasebook • Delhi city guide • Hindi/Urdu phrasebook • India • India & Bangladesh travel atlas • Indian Himalaya • Karakoram Highway • Nepal • Nepali phrasebook • Pakistan • Sri Lanka • Sri Lanka phrasebook • Trekking in the Indian Himalaya • Trekking in the Karakoram & Hindukush • Trekking in the Nepal Himalaya

Travel Literature: In Rajasthan • Shopping for Buddhas

ISLANDS OF THE INDIAN OCEAN
Madagascar & Comoros • Maldives & Islands of the East Indian Ocean • Mauritius, Réunion & Seychelles

MIDDLE EAST & CENTRAL ASIA
Arab Gulf States • Arabic (Egyptian) phrasebook • Central Asia • Iran • Israel & the Palestinian Territories • Israel & the Palestinian Territories travel atlas • Jordan & Syria • Jordan, Syria & Lebanon travel atlas • Middle East • Turkey • Turkish phrasebook • Yemen

Travel Literature: The Gates of Damascus • Kingdom of the Film Stars: Journey into Jordan

NORTH AMERICA
Alaska • Backpacking in Alaska • Baja California • California & Nevada • Canada • Florida • Hawaii • Honolulu city guide • Los Angeles city guide • Mexico • Miami city guide • New England • New Orleans city guide • Pacific Northwest USA • Rocky Mountain States • San Francisco city guide • Southwest USA • USA phrasebook

NORTH-EAST ASIA
Beijing city guide • Cantonese phrasebook • China • Hong Kong city guide • Hong Kong, Macau & Guangzhou • Japan • Japanese phrasebook • Japanese audio pack • Korea • Korean phrasebook • Mandarin phrasebook • Mongolia • Mongolian phrasebook • North-East Asia on a shoestring • Seoul city guide • Taiwan • Tibet • Tibet phrasebook • Tokyo city guide

Travel Literature: Lost Japan

SOUTH AMERICA
Argentina, Uruguay & Paraguay • Bolivia • Brazil • Brazilian phrasebook • Buenos Aires city guide • Chile & Easter Island • Chile & Easter Island travel atlas • Colombia • Ecuador & the Galápagos Islands • Latin American Spanish phrasebook • Peru • Quechua phrasebook • Rio de Janeiro city guide • South America on a shoestring • Trekking in the Patagonian Andes • Venezuela

Travel Literature: Full Circle: A South American Journey

SOUTH-EAST ASIA
Bali & Lombok • Bangkok city guide • Burmese phrasebook• Cambodia • Ho Chi Minh city guide • Indonesia • Indonesian phrasebook • Indonesian audio pack • Jakarta city guide • Java • Laos • Laos travel atlas • Lao phrasebook • Malaysia, Singapore & Brunei • Myanmar (Burma) • Philippines • Pilipino phrasebook • Singapore city guide • South-East Asia on a shoestring • South-East Asia phrasebook • Thailand • Thailand travel atlas • Thai phrasebook • Thai Hill Tribes phrasebook • Thai audio pack • Vietnam • Vietnamese phrasebook • Vietnam travel atlas

LONELY PLANET TRAVEL ATLASES

Conventional fold-out maps work just fine when you're planning your trip on the kitchen table, but have you ever tried to use one – or the half-dozen you sometimes need to cover a country – while you're actually on the road? Even if you have the origami skills necessary to unfold the sucker, you know that flimsy bit of paper is not going to last the distance.

"Lonely Planet travel atlases are designed to make it through your journey in one piece – the sturdy book format is based on the assumption that since all travellers want to make it home without punctures, tears or wrinkles, the maps they use should too."

The travel atlases contain detailed, colour maps that are checked on the road by our travel authors to ensure their accuracy. Place name spellings are consistent with our associated guidebooks, so you can use the atlas and the guidebook hand in hand as you travel and find what you are looking for. Unlike conventional maps, each atlas has a comprehensive index, as well as a detailed legend and helpful 'getting around' sections translated into five languages. Sorry, no free steak knives...

Features of this series include:

- full-colour maps, plus colour photos
- maps researched and checked by Lonely Planet authors
- place names correspond with Lonely Planet guidebooks, so there are no confusing spelling differences
- complete index of features and place names
- atlas legend and travelling information presented in five languages: English, French, German, Spanish and Japanese

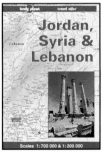

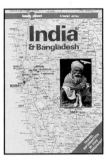

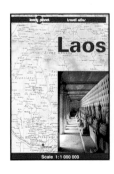

THE LONELY PLANET STORY

Lonely Planet published its first book in 1973 in response to the numerous 'How did you do it?' questions Maureen and Tony Wheeler were asked after driving, bussing, hitching, sailing and railing their way from England to Australia.

Written at a kitchen table and hand collated, trimmed and stapled, *Across Asia on the Cheap* became an instant local bestseller, inspiring thoughts of another book.

Eighteen months in South-East Asia resulted in their second guide, *South-East Asia on a shoestring*, which they put together in a backstreet Chinese hotel in Singapore in 1975. The 'yellow bible', as it quickly became known to backpackers around the world, soon became *the* guide to the region. It has sold well over half a million copies and is now in its 9th edition, still retaining its familiar yellow cover.

Today there are over 240 titles, including travel guides, walking guides, language kits & phrasebooks, travel atlases and travel literature. The company is the largest indepenent travel publisher in the world. Although Lonely Planet initially specialised in guides to Asia, today there are few corners of the globe that have not been covered.

The emphasis continues to be on travel for independent travellers. Tony and Maureen still travel for several months of each year and play an active part in the writing, updating and quality control of Lonely Planet's guides.

They have been joined by over 70 authors and 170 staff at our offices in Melbourne (Australia), Oakland (USA), London (UK) and Paris (France). Travellers themselves also make a valuable contribution to the guides through the feedback we receive in thousands of letters each year and on the web site.

The people at Lonely Planet strongly believe that travellers can make a positive contribution to the countries they visit, both through their appreciation of the countries' culture, wildlife and natural features, and through the money they spend. In addition, the company makes a direct contribution to the countries and regions it covers. Since 1986 a percentage of the income from each book has been donated to ventures such as famine relief in Africa; aid projects in India; agricultural projects in Central America; Greenpeace's efforts to halt French nuclear testing in the Pacific; and Amnesty International.

'I hope we send people out with the right attitude about travel. You realise when you travel that there are so many different perspectives about the world, so we hope these books will make people more interested in what they see.'

– Tony Wheeler

LONELY PLANET PUBLICATIONS

AUSTRALIA (HEAD OFFICE)
PO Box 617, Hawthorn 3122, Victoria
tel: (03) 9819 1877   fax: (03) 9819 6459
e-mail: talk2us@lonelyplanet.com.au

UK
10 Barley Mow Passage,
Chiswick, London W4 4PH
tel: (0181) 742 3161 fax: (0181) 742 2772
e-mail: 100413.3551@compuserve.com

USA
Embarcadero West,155 Filbert St, Suite 251,
Oakland, CA 94607
tel: (510) 893 8555   TOLL FREE: 800 275-8555
fax: (510) 893 8563
e-mail: info@lonelyplanet.com

FRANCE
71 bis rue du Cardinal Lemoine, 75005 Paris
tel: 1 44 32 06 20   fax: 1 46 34 72 55
e-mail: 100560.415@compuserve.com

World Wide Web: http://www.lonelyplanet.com/

Notes

Notes

Notes

PORTUGAL TRAVEL ATLAS

Dear Traveller,

We would appreciate it if you would take the time to write your thoughts on this page and return it to a Lonely Planet office. Only with your help can we continue to make sure this atlas is as accurate and travel-friendly as possible.

Where did you acquire this atlas?

Bookstore ☐   In which section of the store did you find it, i.e. maps or travel guidebooks? ....

Map shop ☐   Direct mail ☐   Other ....

How are you using this travel atlas?

On the road ☐   For home reference ☐   For business reference ☐

Other ....

When travelling with this atlas, did you find any inaccuracies?

....

....

....

How does the atlas fare on the road in terms of ease of use and durability?

....

Are you using the atlas in conjunction with an LP guidebook/s?   Yes ☐   No ☐

Which one/s?...

Have you bought any other LP products for your trip?...

Do you think the information on the travel atlas maps is presented clearly?   Yes ☐   No ☐

If English is not your main language, do you find the language sections useful?   Yes ☐   No ☐

Please list any features you think should be added to the travel atlas.

....

....

....

Would you consider purchasing another atlas in this series?   Yes ☐   No ☐

Please indicate your age group.

15-25 ☐   26-35 ☐   36-45 ☐   46-55 ☐   56-65 ☐   66+ ☐

Do you have any other general comments you'd like to make?

....

....

....

....

....

P.S. Thank you very much for this information. The best contributions will be rewarded with a free copy of a Lonely Planet book. We give away lots of books, but, unfortunately, not every contributor receives one.